W____ _____iagram
C_____ction

PIE BOOKS

2-32-4, Minami-Otsuka, Toshima-ku, Tokyo 170-0005 Japan
Tel: +81-3-5395-4811 Fax: +81-3-5395-4812
e-mail: editor@piebooks.com
        sales@piebooks.com
http://www.piebooks.com
ISBN 4-89444-572-7 C3070

Printed in Japan

本書は好評につき完売した「ベスト インフォメーショナル ダイアグラム」の改訂版です。
序文は上記タイトルのために書かれたものをそのまま使用しています。
This book was previously published in a popular hardcover edition entitled
"The Best Informational Diagrams".
References to the title in the foreword of hence reflect the original title.

Contents ⅲⅲ➡

Grundy
& Northedge

Profile Ⅲ➡

Grundy and Northedge is a small studio which specializes in providing creative solutions to information design problems.
Much of our work involves developing diagrams, maps and charts to communicate complicated statistical and technical information.
We like being small because we value the freedom and flexibility this gives us to develop a distinctive and individual style.

グランディ・アンド・ノースエッジは、インフォメーション・デザインについてクリエイティブな提案を行う、小規模なデザイン・スタジオである。
複雑な統計的、専門的な情報をダイアグラム、地図、チャートに表現するという仕事が多い。
小規模なスタジオにこだわるのは、自由や柔軟性があり、独自のスタイルを発展させることができるためである。

Designing diagrams or maps or charts poses rather different problems for designers than other areas of graphic design. In particular, there is often a tension between the aesthetic demands of a design and the need to communicate complicated information accurately and effectively.

*The first challenge is to understand the information which is to be communicated and see how it relates to its context. Many projects involve specialized technical information and this can be difficult to interpret correctly. For instance, before designing the *?* booklet, I spent some time ensuring that I fully understood all the processes involved, and checking details with their technical experts. Without a full understanding of complicated data, it is very easy to produce diagrams which look good but which fail to communicate accurately.*

The next issue relates to statistical validity. Often it can be tempting to manipulate the presentation of data so that it fits the design. However, this means that the information no longer means anything statistically. We attempt to apply our knowledge of statistical techniques to ensure that this does not happen, but this can impose difficult limitations on the finished chart or diagram. A solution which is statistically valid risks being visually boring.

Finally, a design has to be lively and appealing. It needs to draw the viewer in, to catch their eye and then communicate clearly. Any diagram or chart not only needs to work in its own right but also needs to work in the context of an overall design. In a successful design the use of color, shapes, and the balance of all the items will work to create a harmonious whole.

The conflicts and tension involved in information design can never be finally resolved but we continue to find the challenges posed stimulating and exciting.

ダイアグラム、地図、チャートなどのデザインは、他のグラフィック・デザインの分野とは異なった問題をデザイナーに突きつける。とくに、複雑な情報を正確に効果的に伝える必要と、美的要求との間でしばしば葛藤が起こるものである。

最初の課題は、伝えるべき情報を理解し、本文の内容との関係を知ることである。多くのプロジェクトは専門情報を扱うものであり、これを正確に解釈することは困難な場合もある。例えば本書にも収録されている「?」の小冊子をデザインするにあたって、私はすべてのプロセスを十分に理解するため、専門家と詳細について話し合う時間を持った。複雑なデータは十分に理解していないと、見た目は良くても、正確さに欠けるようなダイアグラムを作成することになるからである。

次の課題は、統計的な有効性の問題である。しばしば、デザインに合わせてデータのプレゼンテーションを操作しようという気持ちになるものである。しかしこれでは、情報はもはや統計的に何の意味も持たない。私たちは統計の知識を活用することで、このようなことが起きないようにしているが、仕上がったチャートやダイアグラムが困難なデザインとしての限界を露呈することもある。統計的に有効なデザインとは、ビジュアルとしては退屈なものである。

最後に、デザインとは活力があって、心に訴えるものでなくてはならない。見る者を引き込み、興味をとらえ、明確にコミュニケートする必要がある。どんなダイアグラムもチャートも、それ自身の目的のみでなく、全体のデザインの脈絡の中で作用するものでなくてはならない。優れたデザインとは、色づかい、形、そしてすべての要素が、全体として調和のとれたものをつくり上げているものである。

インフォメーション・デザインにおける葛藤と緊張は、決して解決されることはない。しかし、私たちは刺激的でエキサイティングなチャレンジを今後も続けていくであろう。

Foreword Ⅲ➡

Nigel Holmes

Profile ➡

Nigel Holmes studied at the Royal College of Art, England. From 1966 to 1978 he was a graphic designer in London,
then went to Time Magazine in New York, where he was the Graphics Director until 1994.
Now he does Explanation Graphics for companies like Apple, GE, IBM, Nike, Sony and Visa, as well as charts, diagrams and maps for publications
such as Esquire, Golf Digest, Fortune, Modern Maturity, Sports Illustrated, The New Yorker, The New York Times, Time, and Wired.
He has written six books about information design, and he has lectured in India, Japan, Brazil and all over Europe and the United States.

イギリスのロイヤル・カレッジ・オブ・アート卒業。1966年より1978年までロンドンでグラフィック・デザイナーとして活動。
その後、ニューヨークのタイム誌に移り、1994年までグラフィック・ディレクターを務める。
現在は、アップル、GE、IBM、ナイキ、ソニー、VISAなどのクライアントのためにエクスプラネーション・グラフィックスを手がけており、
Esquire、Golf Digest、Fortune、Modern Maturity、Sports Illustrated、The New Yorker、The New York Times、TimeおよびWiredの各誌に、
チャート、ダイアグラム、地図などを制作している。インフォメーション・デザインについて6冊の著書があり、インド、日本、ブラジル、ヨーロッパ諸国およびアメリカ合衆国で講義をしている。

Diagram graphics are something like cars: they get us from one place to another. While cars transport us from city to city, diagram graphics take us on another kind of journey — from data to understanding.

And like diagram graphics, some cars are fast, some go at a more leisurely pace. Some cars are old workhorses, some are careful and loving recreations of classic styles. Some draw more attention to their shape than to the fact that they are, after all, merely vehicles for getting us from A to B. Some owners spend a lot of time polishing the chrome on cars that seldom leave their home base.

The roads in the land of information are crowded. At times it seems that there are too many crazy drivers out there.

But when they are made well and driven well, both the car and the diagram graphic are beautiful things, because they are examples of form that is joined to function in some sort of inevitable marriage. In such examples, style does not overwhelm information, shape does not obstruct the clear line between data and understanding. There are no roadblocks on these journeys. Yet the vehicles do have style, and they are good to look at.

The maker of anything whose purpose is at base to fulfil a function must be prepared to balance the aesthetics of the form with the requirements of the content.

So, as you look at the examples in this book, first ask the question: What is the content, the information, the data? Then ask: What form does this data take so that readers can efficiently and enjoyably understand it, as though they were drivers getting efficiently and stylishly from A to B?

ダイアグラム・グラフィックスとは車のようなものである。ひとつの地点から他の地点へ私たちを運んでいく。車は町から町へと運んでくれるのに対し、ダイアグラム・グラフィックスは私たちに異なった種類の旅をさせてくれる —— 単なるデータの羅列から理解への旅である。

車のなかには、速いものもあれば、ゆっくり楽しく走るものもある。昔の馬車のような車もあれば、注意深くリメイクされた愛すべきクラシックカーもある。車とは結局のところ、A地点からB地点へ運んでくれる乗り物であるという事実よりも、その外見の方により注意を向けさせるような車もある。めったに外を走らせないにもかかわらず、クロム磨きに余念がない所有者も多い。ダイアグラム・グラフィックスも同じである。

情報ランドの道路は渋滞している。ときにはクレイジーなドライバーが多すぎると思えることもある。

しかし、車もダイアグラムもともにうまくつくってやり、うまく運転してやれば、美しいものになる。なぜならそれらは、互いになくてはならない夫婦関係のように、機能とフォルムとがジョイントしているからである。このような例においては、スタイルが情報を圧倒してしまうことはない。フォルムが、データの羅列と理解とをつなぐ明解なラインを妨害してしまうことはない。このような旅であれば路上に障害物はない。しかし乗り物にはスタイルがあり、眺めても楽しいものである。

つくり手は、その基本的な目的が機能を満たすことであれば、フォルムの美と内容の要求するところとの間でバランスを取らなければならない。

だから、この本の作品を見るときには、まず次のようなことを自問してほしい。「どんな内容、情報、データなのか」そして次に「読者はA地点からB地点まで効率的にスタイリッシュに移動するドライバーであるとする。さて、このデータは、効率的に、また楽しく理解できるようにどのような形をとっているのか」と。

Kenzo Nakagawa

Profile ➡

Graphic designer. Design director. Born in 1947, Osaka.
Graduated in 1966 from the Osaka City High School of Arts and Crafts Drawing Program,
and joined Takashimaya Department Store's Advertising Department.
Left in 1973 to start Bolt Et Nuts Studio. In 1975, joined the Nippon Design Center, and currently serves as Executive Director.
He is also a president of NDC Graphics, Inc. Reconstructing identity and information design, promotion and product graphics,
and environmental design, to unify the graphic design field. Work encompasses everything "from chocolate to airplanes."

グラフィック・デザイナー。デザイン・ディレクター。1947年大阪生まれ。1966年大阪市立工芸高校図案科卒業後、高島屋宣伝部を経て、
1973年ボルト・ナッツスタジオ設立。1975年日本デザインセンター入社、現在同社取締役。株式会社NDCグラフィックス代表。
グラフィック・デザインのフィールドをアイデンティティ、インフォメーション、プロモーション、プロダクト・グラフィックス、環境デザインに再編して統合。
「チョコレートからヒコーキまで」その仕事は多岐にわたる。

The base of Mt. Fuji is wide. This beautiful, high mountain, that tops any other mountain nationwide, is supported by this wide base. Our work is something similar. Instead of a base, a "process" is needed to reach a higher level. In the case of diagram design, however, the wider the base, the more difficulties arise in the journey to the top.

Designing diagrams requires overall ability. To create a beautiful map, not only is it necessary to trace the map accurately for a rough sketch, but ideas are also required to put the various elements together. Overall harmony must be considered by making the best use of the aesthetics of individual forms. "Easy-to-understand" graphs and charts can be designed by first analyzing and understanding the numerical data, which sometimes requires personal scientific examination.

Designing diagrams is tough work; creative leaps of logic are required, utilizing new ideas and expressive power, and much time must be spent on painstaking basics. This explains the high demand for designers who have the overall ability, the force, to realize a unity of science and art. Diagram designers have had a tendency to spend too much time and effort on the wide base (basics), but only a few challengers have received the benefits of successfully reaching the top by incorporating truly creative ideas.

The production environment has been completely changed by the appearance of desktop computers, and the availability of outstanding graphic software and graphic databases. For example, placement of information on a map used to begin with a blank map outline. Very precise and careful drawing skills were required, for such tasks as simplification of the outline if necessary. If the scale of a presentation changed, lines had to be redrawn from scratch. With computers, however, one can start by using maps created by other designers, readily available in databases. You can change line width at will, and retrieve pictograms and text data from various networks. It is as if you were to start climbing Mt. Fuji from halfway up. You can borrow what you need from mountain huts, and even enlist the aid of a helicopter.

Graphic design in Japan has been too trapped in "virtual poster design." Now the time has come for the aesthetics and practicality of diagram design, which help to promote richer communication among people, helping them to more fully understand. I want young designers to know how interesting and challenging it can be to climb up to the top of the "diagram mountain," a relatively new destination in the world of graphic design.

富士の裾野は広い。他峰を制してそびえるその美しい高峰は、広大な裾野に支えられている。私たちの仕事もこれに似て、高いレベルへ到達するための裾野という「過程」を必要としている。しかし裾野が広がれば、それだけ頂上への道が遠くなるという矛盾を抱えることになる。

ダイアグラムのデザインには総合力が求められる。1枚の魅力的な地図をつくるためには、正確な下図をトレースするだけだなく、多様なエレメントを組み合わせられるアイデアが必要だし、ひとつひとつの個別のカタチの美しさを活かしながら、全体の調和も考えなければならない。「物分かりのいい」グラフやチャートをつくるためには、デザインする以前の数値情報を分析して理解する能力もいるし、ときには自身も科学的なアプローチで検証することもあるだろう。

地をはうようなフィールドワークと同時に、新しいアイデアと表現力を駆使した、創造のための飛躍もしなければならないダイアグラムのデザイン。「科学と芸術が一体化」するための、統合力（フォース）を持ったデザイナーが必要とされるゆえんだ。というわけで、これまでのダイアグラム・デザインは、広い裾野（基礎的分野）への対応に時間と労力を取られ、少数のチャレンジャーだけがその登頂の成果を享受してきた。

デザイナーの机上にコンピューターが現れ、優れたグラフィック・ソフトの支援と、過去に蓄積された画像データベースの利用によって、ダイアグラムの制作環境は一変した。例えば情報を地図に置き換えるとき、これまではまず白地図を用意することから始まり、アウトラインを目的に合わせて簡略化し、精密な描画作業が求められた。縮尺比が変われば線幅は初めから書き換えなければならなかった。コンピューターを利用すれば、別のデザイナーがつくった白地図データベースを利用して立ち上がることができる。ライン幅は自在に変化させられるし、ピクトグラムも文章データもネットワークで取り込める。いわば富士登山をいきなり五合目からスタートするようなもの。さらにヘリコプターの助けを借りたり、山小屋の物資を拝借できる仕組みといえる。

日本のグラフィック・デザインは「虚像のポスターデザイン」に目を奪われ過ぎていた。人と人のコミュニケーションを豊かにし、その理解を深めるダイアグラム・デザインの「美と実用性」に注目される時代がきた。グラフィック・デザイナーの挑戦する分野として、いちばん遅れてやってきた「ダイアグラム連峰」への登頂をめざす面白さを、多くの若いデザイナーに知ってほしい。

Tetsuya Ohta

Profile ➡

Born in 1941, Nobeoka City, Miyazaki Prefecture. After graduating from Kuwasawa Design Laboratory in 1963, joined the Ikko Tanaka Design Office. In 1975, opened the Tetsuya Ohta Design Office. In 1991, won the National Book Design Concours' "MITI Prize," the Tokyo Typedirectors Club Exhibition's "Member's Bronze" prize, Japan Typography Association's "Best Work" prize. In 1992, won the Tokyo Art Directors Club's "ADC" and "Hiroshi Hara" prizes. Author of "C·I = Changes in Logos & Trademarks in Japan," published by Rikuyo-sha in 1989. Current projects include editorial, book design, graphic design, and CI design.

1941年宮崎県延岡市生まれ。1963年桑沢デザイン研究所卒業後、田中一光デザイン室に入社。1975年太田徹也デザイン室設立。
1991年全国装丁コンクール「通産大臣賞」、東京TDC展「会員・銅賞」、日本タイポグラフィ協会「ベストワーク賞」、1992年東京アート・ディレクターズクラブ「ADC賞」「原弘賞」などを受賞。
1989年『C・I＝マーク・ロゴの変遷』を六耀社より出版。現在、エディトリアル、ブック・デザイン、グラフィック・デザイン、C・Iを中心に幅広く手がけている。

Every day, many things fall within our field of vision that we are not aware of actually seeing, or that we do not really understand. Some are diagrams. Dictionary definitions of "diagram" include drawing, graph, figure, chart, and construction figure. In elementary school and junior high school, we learned about bar and pie charts, line graphs and maps, coming to know them collectively as "diagrams." Diagrams present hard-to-understand numerical data, which can appear disorderly or conflicting, in a design-supported format organized for first-glance comprehension. More effective than explanations using only words, the roles of diagrams in iconography and design are increasing, as well as the areas of their application.

Living as we are in a flood of information, we tend to depend on the creativity of others. We have become unable to express images, or use our own imaginations. The era in which text information led our culture and society has ended; the time has arrived where diagrams have more importance, and the visualization of data and information is more respected. To live effortlessly in our multi-layered TV- and Information-Age society, we need easy-to-understand methods of presenting information.

Diagrams can be broken down into 6 general categories:
1) Tables: Graphically arranged, ordered textual and numerical data.
2) Graphs: Comparison and coordination of changes in quantitative statistics.
3) Charts: Illustrate and systemize relationships and flows.
4) Scores: Symbolize and illustrate qualitative chronological changes.
5) Illustrations: Intellectual visualization of information and images, free of artistic interpretation.
6) Maps: Visualization of time and distance; systematic location.

The possibilities of diagram design continue to expand without limitation.

Using diagram techniques, strong and energetic designs can be produced from simple materials. Not just for visualization of numerical data, diagrams have power in the multilingual international society in which we live. Diagrams, a new genre of design, are effective communication tools that can cross language barriers to become useful in the development of mutual recognition among humans and countries.

日常、目に触れているものでも案外知られていないものは多い。「ダイアグラム」もそのひとつ。辞書には図、図表、図形、図式、作図と出ています。小・中学校時に教わった棒グラフ、折線グラフ、円グラフそれに地図などをひっくるめて、ダイアグラムと呼んでいます。ダイアグラムとは、一見バラバラで対立するように見えるモノやコトなど、数値情報だけでは伝えにくい内容を、デザイン処理の力を加えてわかりやすくした「図形」のことを指します。このように言葉で説明するより、視覚的に「図像化」「デザイン化」するところに、ダイアグラムの役割と領域が広がっています。

また、現代の情報洪水の中で暮らしていると、私たちはどうしても他人の想像力に依存し、自分のイメージやイマジネーションを発揮できないようになります。文字情報が文化や社会をリードしてきた時代から、近年ではダイアグラムにより大きな比重がおかれ、データ情報を視覚化する時代になってきました。テレビ時代、情報時代というマルチプル社会の中で生きる私たちには、日常生活をスムーズに行うために、わかりやすい情報指示が必要になっているものと思われます。

ダイアグラムは大別して6つに分類することができます。
■言葉、数字を配列でグラフィックに整理し、資料化する（表組……Table）
■情報量の変化を比較、座標化し、統計的に見せる（図表……Graph）
■ものごとの関係や流れを図的にまとめ、系統化してみせる（図式……Chart）
■質的な時間の経過による変化を記号化し、図的に表現する（図譜……Score）
■絵画的な情感を排し、知的なイメージ情報を図像化する（図解……Illustration）
■時間や距離を空間的に視覚図化し、体系的に場所化する（地図……Map）

このようにダイアグラムのデザイン的な可能性は無限に広がっているといえるでしょう。

ダイアグラムの技法によれば、単純な素材からでも迫力のある強いデザインが生まれます。さらに数字やデータを視覚化するだけではなく、私たちが多種言語の国際社会の中で生きるとき、大きな力を発揮します。図像化された効果的なコミュニケーション手段としてのダイアグラムは、コトバの壁を超えて、人間同士、民族や国家同士の共通認識を育てるために役立っていく、新しいジャンルのデザイン領域でもあるのです。

Tor
Pettersen

Profile ⟩⟩⟩➡

Analysis is the basis for most ideas — breaking the task into simple parts. From comparing, examining, deducting and abstracting come discoveries that form ideas. Diagrams by nature must be closely related to the information objectives. Yet, it is worth remembering that images with wit, humour and metaphor — arrived at through intelligence and visual perception — heightens the interest. Through creativity, a diagram can convey information from new angles and provoke fresh responses. In this respect we find that a diagram's message potential can be as challenging and rewarding as any graphic problem.

多くのアイデアの基本は分析である。課せられたタスクを単純なパーツにまで分解し、比較、検証、縮小と抽象化によってアイデアの発見に導く。
ダイアグラムは本来、情報の持つ目的と緊密な関係がなければならない。しかし、ウイットとユーモア、そしてメタファーを兼ねそなえたイメージ ——知識と視覚的な認知をとおして到達しうる—— は、
見る者の興味をより高めるものであることを忘れないでほしい。ダイアグラムは創造性をとおして、情報を新しい角度から伝えることが可能であり、
新鮮な反応を刺激することができる。この点から、われわれは1点のダイアグラムの持つ潜在的なメッセージは、
他のどんなグラフィックの課題にも劣らずチャレンジがあり、また見返りも大きいと思っている。

A message for a dairy client of ours was the building of a central depot to facilitate the best possible scenario for supplying fresh cheese efficiently. We designed a three-dimensional map of England, made up of a cheese, with a tester-knife having removed a sample right in the middle of the cheese leaving a circular hole to mark the location of the depot. The caption read, "Centre of excellence." The map was approved in the yellow cheese colour minus the cheese and the tester. The message was considered too important for childish flippancy, and perhaps it was.

This demonstrates that the line between the puerile and the brilliant visual idea can be very fine in the same way as an over-sophisticated diagram easily inhibits communication. Diagrams succeed because of the clarity of their storytelling and in most instances that means simple two-dimensional bars, segmented circles, or curves.

But when the opportunity arises to successfully elaborate with creative ideas, the medium can be elevated to visual poetry, injecting the message with wit and meaning that will tell a richer story and reflect an image of intelligence upon the organisation concerned.

われわれのクライアントである乳製品メーカーは、新鮮なチーズを効果的に供給するための最善策として、貯蔵センターを建設するというメッセージを消費者に伝えようとしていた。われわれは、チーズでできたイギリスの3-D地図をデザインし、テスターのナイフがチーズのちょうど真ん中からサンプルをくり抜いているように見せた。あとにポッカリと空いた穴が貯蔵センターの位置を示すようにしたのである。キャプションは、「センター・オブ・エクセレンス（イギリスの中心という意と優れたサービス・センターという意をかけている）」。だが結局、チーズとテスターのアイデアは承認されず、地図にチーズの黄色を使用するということで決まった。われわれの提案は、子供だましで軽薄すぎると受け止められたのである。おそらくそのとおりであろう。

このことは、子供だましであることと、際立ったビジュアルのアイデアとは紙ひとえであることを立証している。それは、デザインにこりすぎたダイアグラムが容易にコミュニケーションを遮断するのと同じである。ダイアグラムは伝えようとする内容の明快さが勝負であり、多くの場合それは、シンプルな二次元の棒グラフや円グラフや折線グラフを意味するのである。

しかし、クリエイティブなアイデアを巧みに練り上げて作品を完成させたとき、そのメディアは視覚的な一篇の詩にまで高められる。より豊かなストーリーを伝え、関係者の知識をイメージに反映させた、ウイットと意味に富んだメッセージを吹き込んでくれるのだ。

Editorial Notes

Credit Format
クレジットフォーマット

....

Country from which submitted/
Year of completion
製作国/製作年

....

Creative staff
製作スタッフ

CD: Creative Director
AD: Art Director
D: Designer
P: Photographer
I: Illustrator
CW: Copywriter
DF: Design Firm
CL: Client

....

Explanatory Caption
作品説明文

System Diagrams & Scores

Flow Charts, Organization Charts, Function Diagrams

過程図、系統図、組織図、機能図

Nuclear power made easy **AGR**

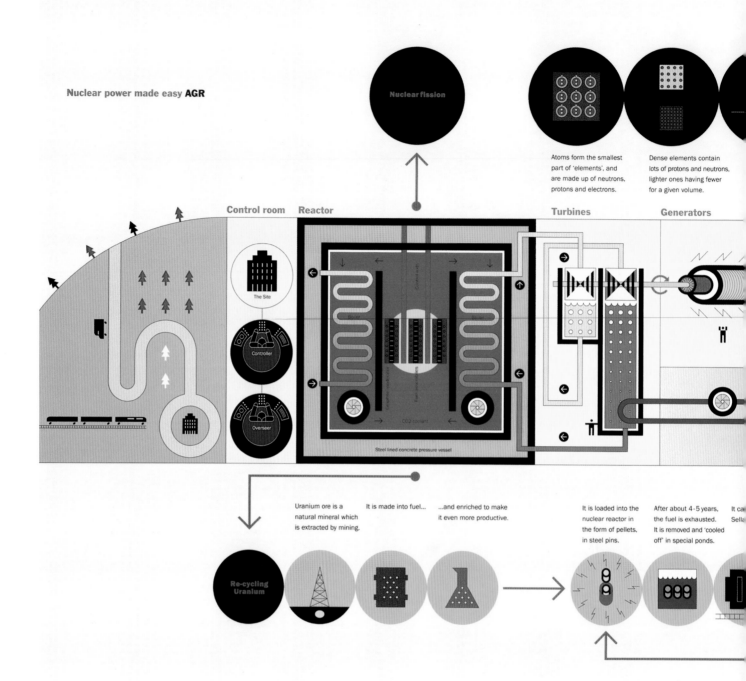

Nuclear fission

Atoms form the smallest part of 'elements', and are made up of neutrons, protons and electrons.

Dense elements contain lots of protons and neutrons, lighter ones having fewer for a given volume.

Control room **Reactor** **Turbines** **Generators**

The Site

Controller

Overseer

Steel lined concrete pressure vessel

Uranium ore is a natural mineral which is extracted by mining.

It is made into fuel...

...and enriched to make it even more productive.

It is loaded into the nuclear reactor in the form of pellets, in steel pins.

After about 4-5 years, the fuel is exhausted. It is removed and 'cooled off' in special ponds.

It ca Sella

Re-cycling Uranium

U.K. 1998
CD, AD, D, I: Peter Grundy
DF: Grundy & Northedge
CL: British Energy

A diagram that easily conveys the workings of the complex production process of nuclear power.
複雑な原子エネルギーの製造過程をわかりやすく説明したダイアグラム。

Atoms have a 'nucleus' (or centre) of neutrons and protons, with electrons orbiting around.

Neutrons can hurtle around at speeds up to 20,000 km/s if released from the nucleus.

Nuclear fission occurs when a neutron collides with, and splits, an atom.

When an atom is split, it releases a tremendous amount of energy and throws out more neutrons.

One of these neutrons may go on to split another atom which throws out more neutrons. The heat from this 'chain reaction' is transferred from the fuel to the coolant, carbon dioxide gas,

which circulates through the reactor. The coolant is then passed over the boiling tubes heating the water to create steam, which drives the turbines, which rotate the

electromagnets, which generate the electricity, which powers your home...

To the grid, and to you

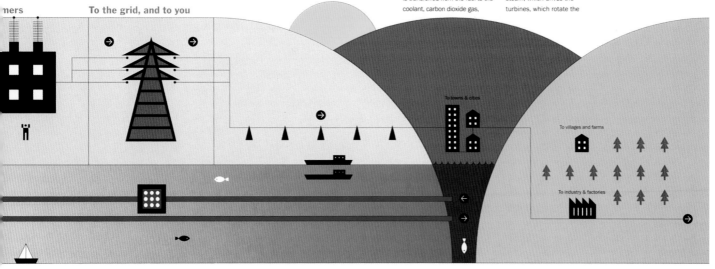

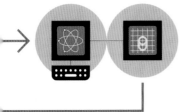

At Sellafield, fuel is chemically separated...

...allowing 98% of it to be recycled as new nuclear fuel and used again.

Control room
This is the nerve centre of the generation process, where our engineers pilot the nuclear reactor. They are assisted by a battery of sensors and monitors, and wholly separate safety systems which are designed to 'fail safe'.

Reactor
At the heart of an AGR is a graphite core known as the 'moderator'. This slows down the neutrons to a speed where they can collide with, and split, other atoms.

Turbines
The tremendous heat energy from the reactor is converted into superheated steam. This is blasted onto the blades of the turbines, rotating them at 3000 rpm.

Generators
Each turbine drives a large electromagnet called a 'rotor'. Each rotor revolves inside the electrical windings of a 'stator' to produce electricity.

Transformers
The electrical output of the power station is then raised by the generator transformer, to anything up to 400,000 volts.

To the grid, and to you
High voltage power is then sent across power lines to the National Grid, for onward transmission to Britain's homes, offices, factories, schools and streets.

British Energy plc   Technology to the core   **AGR Advanced Gas-cooled Reactors**

About North West Water

The North West Water Group is an international company with practical experience in all that is needed to supply pure water and treat wastewater.

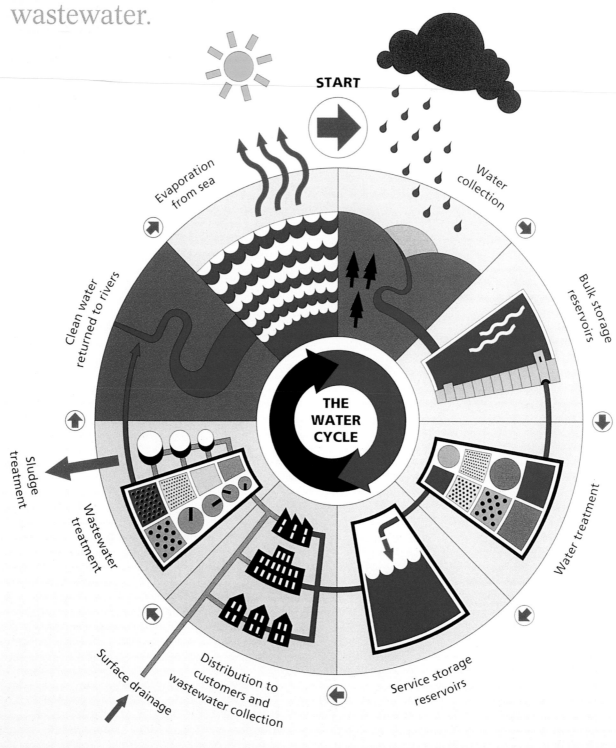

START

Evaporation from sea

Water collection

Clean water returned to rivers

Bulk storage reservoirs

THE WATER CYCLE

Sludge treatment

Wastewater treatment

Water treatment

Distribution to customers and wastewater collection

Surface drainage

Service storage reservoirs

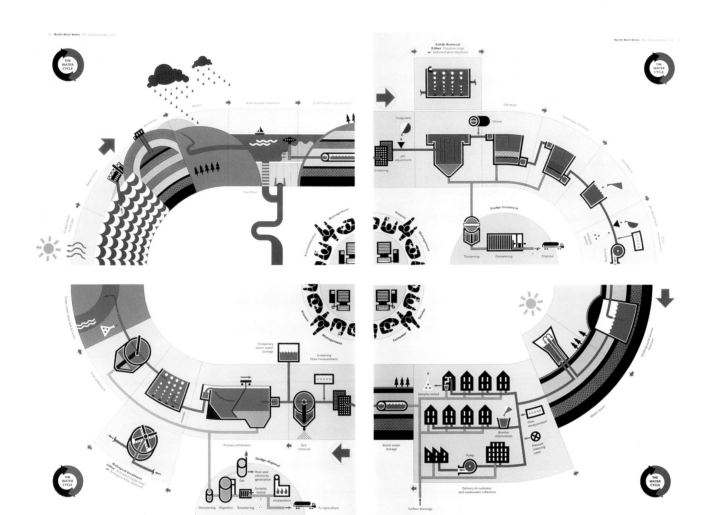

U.K.   1996
AD, D: Ian Lanksbury
I: Tilly Northedge
DF: Addison Design Co.
CL: North West Water

Diagrams in a promotional booklet that explain water purification, delivery to the customer, and treatment of waste water.
浄水システム、顧客への供給および廃水処理について説明している。営業用小冊子より。

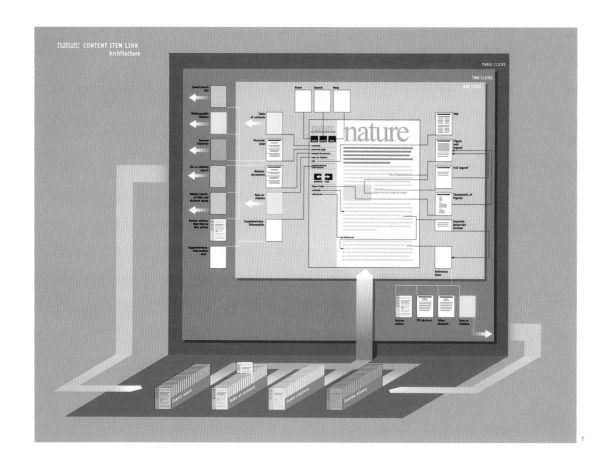

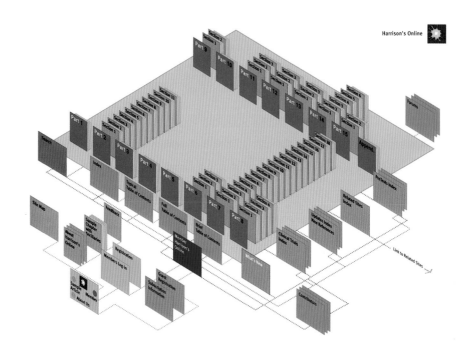

U.S.A. 1998
CD, AD, D: Krzysztof Lenk (2)
CD: Paul Kahn (1)
AD: Krzysztof Lenk (1)
D: Chihiro Hosoe (1)
DF: Dynamic Diagrams
CL: Macmillan Publishers, Ltd. (1)/
        The McGraw-Hill Professional Publishing Group (2)

Diagram showing the article structure of the Nature web site,
identifying incoming and outgoing links on a typical article page. (1)
『ネイチャー』誌のwebサイトにおけるコンテンツの構造を示したダイアグラム。代表的なページで画面の前後のリンクを説明したもの。(1)

This diagram defines the hierarchical organization of the Nature web site.
It illustrates the relationship between the core textbook content and new online-only material; shows the various
access points for the online content; and identifies the free and subscription-based sections of the site. (2)
企業のwebサイトの構造を階層的に表したダイアグラム。基本となる出版物の内容とオンラインのみで扱う新しい素材との相関関係を示し、
オンライン専用コンテンツへのアクセス・ポイントがたくさんあることと、無料または会員専用のセクションの位置を示した。(2)

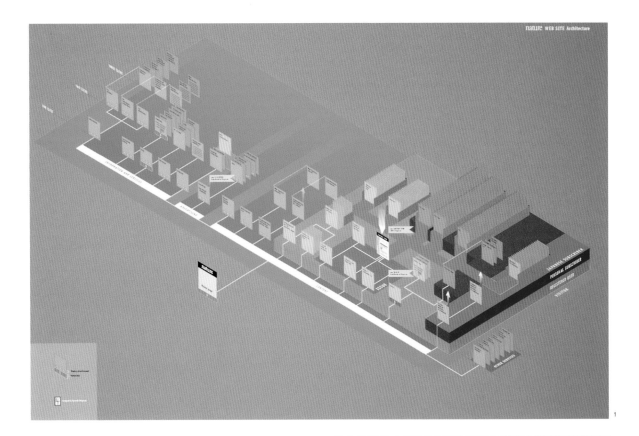

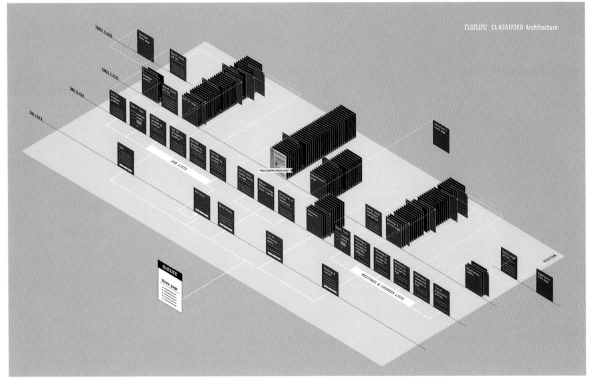

U.S.A. 1998 (2) /1999 (1)
CD: Paul Kahn
AD: Krzysztof Lenk
D: Chihiro Hosoe
DF: Dynamic Diagrams
CL: Macmillan Publishers, Ltd.

Diagram showing the information architecture of the Nature web site.
The diagram was used to analyze and revise the web site's design. (1)

『ネイチャー』誌のwebサイトの情報構造。サイトのデザインを分析し、刷新するために使用された。(1)

Diagram showing the structure of the Classified section of the Nature web site. (2)

『ネイチャー』誌のwebサイトにおけるクラシファイド（分類広告）とセクションの構造を示したダイアグラム。(2)

Holtzbrinck Web Map

Version 1, May 1999

Prepared for Verlagsgruppentagung /
Annual Meeting 1999 in Stuttgart

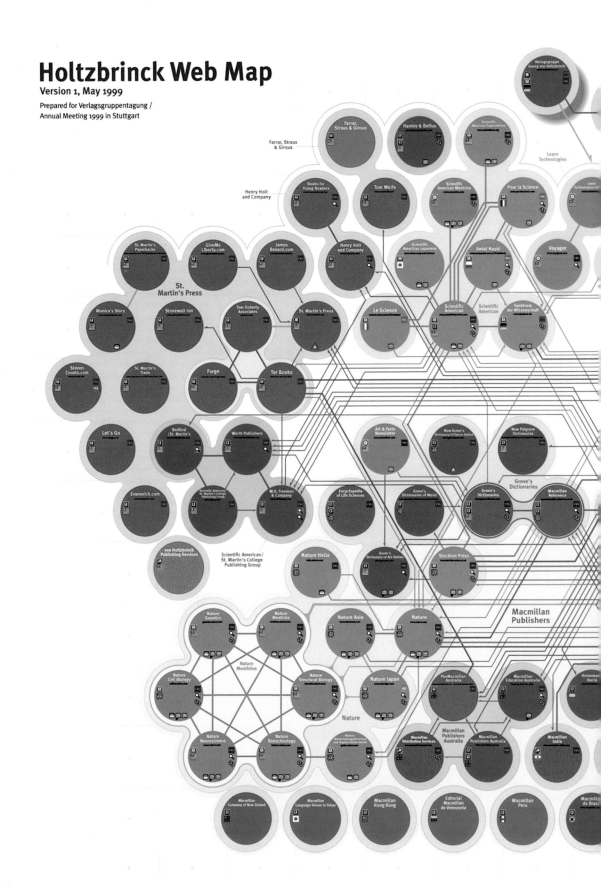

U.S.A.   1999
CD: Paul Kahn
AD: Krzysztof Lenk
D: Piotr Kaczmarek
DF: Dynamic Diagrams
CL: Activ-Consult Multimedia und Training, GmbH

This diagram provides information on over 150 public web sites run by the companies in the Holtzbrinck Group.
It shows all web sites; the businesses, services, and products that these sites represent; and links between the sites.

Holtzbrinck社の運営する150個以上のサイトについての図。
これらのサイトが行うビジネス、サービス、製品と、各サイト間の相互のリンクを示している。

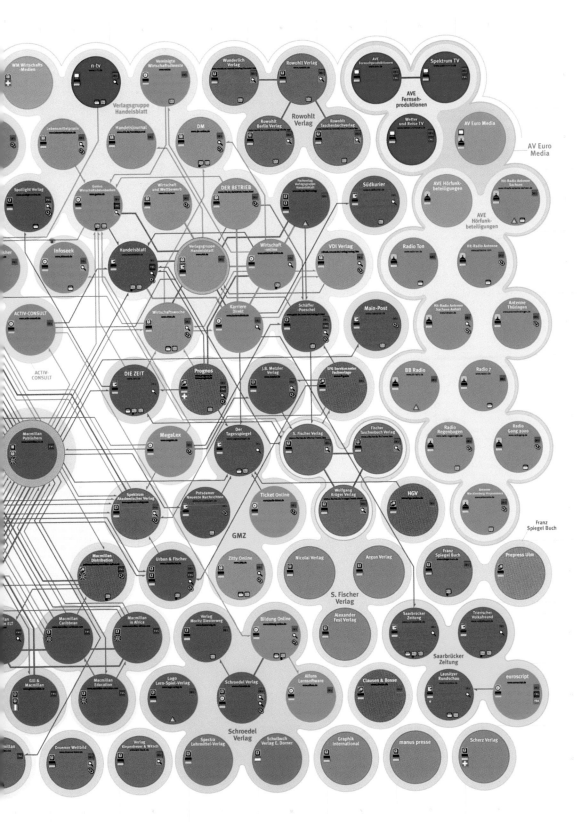

Beyond.com

Software Product Selection and Purchase, January 1999

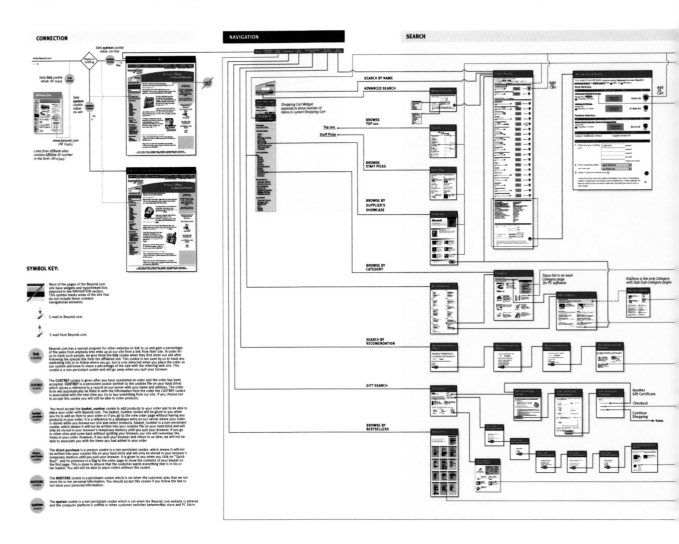

CONNECTION

NAVIGATION

SEARCH

SEARCH BY NAME

ADVANCED SEARCH

BROWSE TOP 100

BROWSE STAFF PICKS

BROWSE BY SUPPLIER'S SHOWCASE

BROWSE BY CATEGORY

SEARCH BY RECOMENDATION

GIFT SEARCH

BROWSE BY BESTSELLERS

SYMBOL KEY:

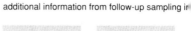

---

true population (number in each housing unit initially unknown)

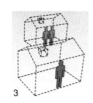
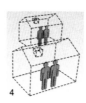
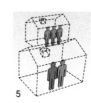

additional information from follow-up sampling in

1   2   3   4   5

information about population following conventional counting methods applied everywhere

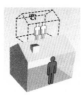

U.S.A.   1999
CD: Paul Kahn
AD: Krzysztof Lenk
D: Piotr Kaczmarek
DF: Dynamic Diagrams
CL: Netscape Communications Corporation

Diagram analyzing the e-commerce transactions and processes of the Beyond.com web site. (1)
Beyond.comのwebサイトにおける電子商取引のプロセスを図解したもの。(1)

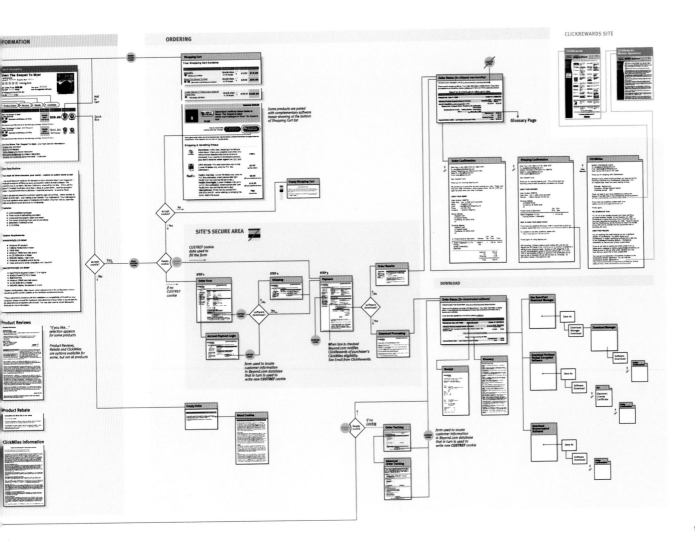

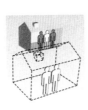

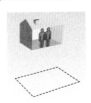

additional information provided from statistical estimation based on follow-up interviews

■ white, non-Hispanic   ■ white, Hispanic   □ missed

count = 7 + 2

measure = 7 + 2 + 1

U.S.A. 1998
AD: Linda K. Huff
D: Aaron Cox/David Schoonmaker
I: Aaron Cox
DF: American Scientist Magazine Art and Design Department
CL: Sigma Xi

Illustration shows how the accuracy of conventional census taking (panel 2) can be improved by random sampling of households (panel 3) and estimating missed individuals (panel 4). (2)
世帯の無作為抽出（パネル3）と不在世帯の数を推定する（パネル4）ことによって、
伝統的な国勢調査法（パネル2）をより正確なものにすることができることを示した図。(2)

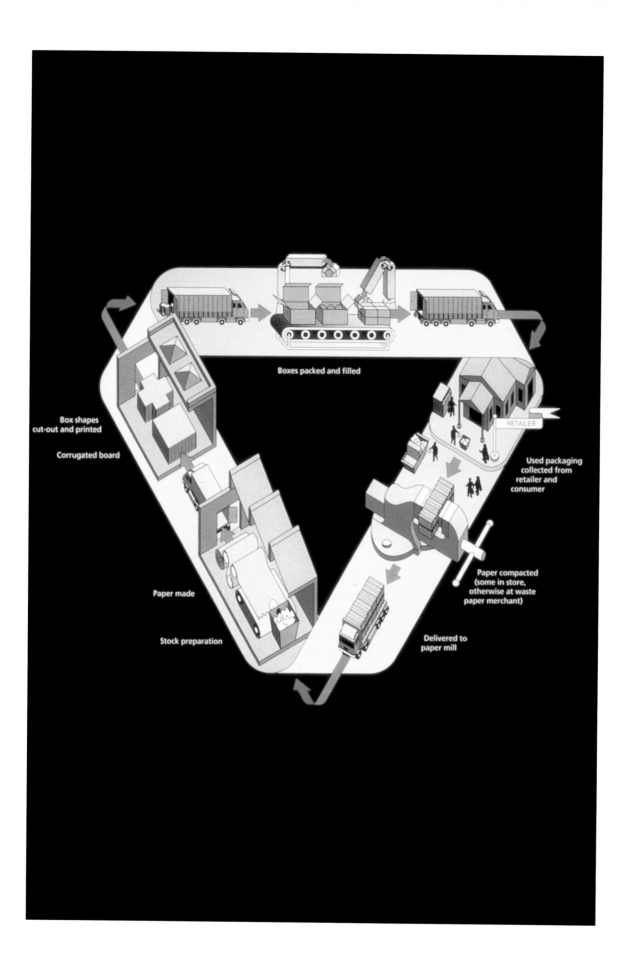

Boxes packed and filled

Box shapes
cut-out and printed

Corrugated board

RETAILER

Used packaging
collected from
retailer and
consumer

Paper compacted
(some in store,
otherwise at waste
paper merchant)

Paper made

Stock preparation

Delivered to
paper mill

U.K.   1995
I: Tilly Northedge
DF: Addison Design Co.
CL: David S. Smith (Holdings) Plc

Diagram showing the cycle of waste paper collection, pulp-making, new paper and corrugated board manufacture and usage.
古紙の回収、パルプ製造、新しい紙と段ボール製造のサイクルおよび利用法を示した図。

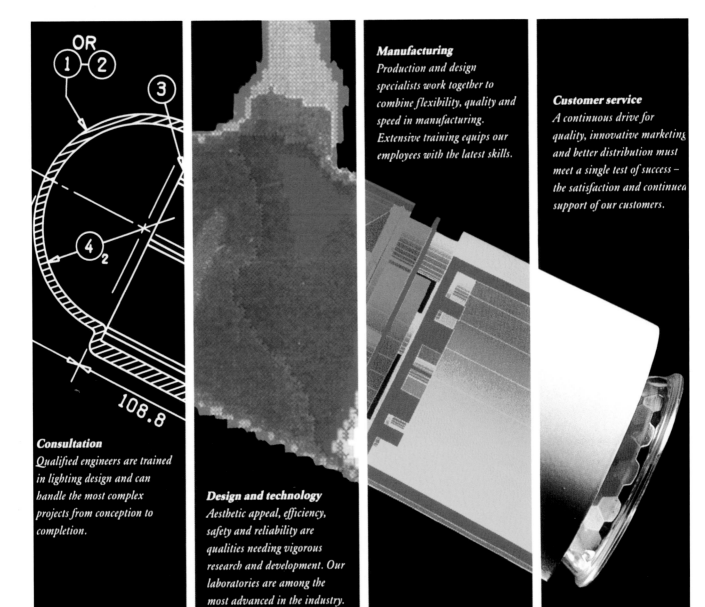

OR
1 2
3
4 2
108.8

Consultation
Qualified engineers are trained in lighting design and can handle the most complex projects from conception to completion.

Design and technology
Aesthetic appeal, efficiency, safety and reliability are qualities needing vigorous research and development. Our laboratories are among the most advanced in the industry.

Manufacturing
Production and design specialists work together to combine flexibility, quality and speed in manufacturing. Extensive training equips our employees with the latest skills.

Customer service
A continuous drive for quality, innovative marketing and better distribution must meet a single test of success – the satisfaction and continued support of our customers.

U.K. 1995
CD: Tor Pettersen
CD, AD, D: Jeff Davis
D: Sarah Davies
DF: Tor Pettersen & Partners Ltd.
CL: Thorn EMI

Diagram emphasising the total solutions capability of Thorn Lighting Group by using a montage of diagrams, photos and thermal images that together form a complete light fitting, the company's main product.
ソーン・ライティング・グループの総合的な問題解決力を強調するダイアグラム。
ダイアグラム、写真、サーモグラフィを合成し、社のメインプロダクトである照明器具を形作った。

TRANSLATING POLICIES INTO PRACTICES

AIR QUALITY

We minimize the use of materials suspected of depleting the ozone layer. All vending and dispensing equipment purchased after December 1994 is free of chlorofluorocarbons.

OPERATIONS

We maintain procedures for managing fuels, cleaning fluids and other materials that can impact the environment if mishandled.

REGULAR AUDITS

All Company-owned production facilities are audited every three years.

WASTE PROGRAMS

Our plants have solid waste management programs covering waste avoidance, minimization, reuse and recycling.

CONSERVATION

We work hard to conserve water. Many of our facilities, for example, use treated wastewater to wash delivery vehicles, irrigate landscaping and satisfy other non-product water needs.

WATER PURITY

Before we discharge wastewater into a natural body of water, we treat that discharge to a level capable of supporting fish life.

MAKING OUR PLASTIC BOTTLE BETTER

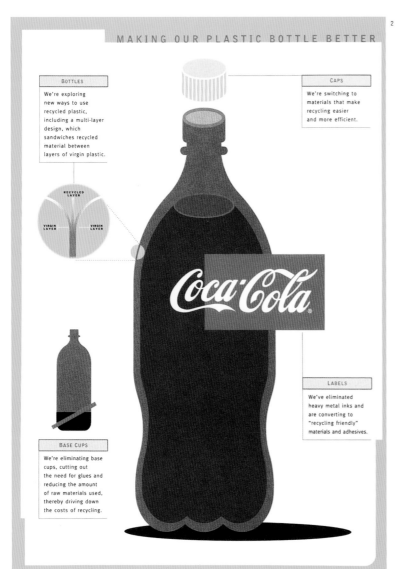

BOTTLES

We're exploring new ways to use recycled plastic, including a multi-layer design, which sandwiches recycled material between layers of virgin plastic.

RECYCLED LAYER

VIRGIN LAYER   VIRGIN LAYER

CAPS

We're switching to materials that make recycling easier and more efficient.

LABELS

We've eliminated heavy metal inks and are converting to "recycling friendly" materials and adhesives.

BASE CUPS

We're eliminating base cups, cutting out the need for glues and reducing the amount of raw materials used, thereby driving down the costs of recycling.

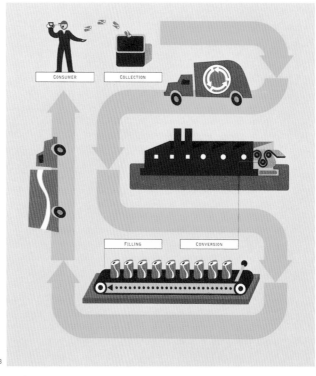

CONSUMER   COLLECTION

FILLING   CONVERSION

3

U.S.A.   1997
CD, AD, D, I: Rex Peteet
I: K. C. Teis
DF: Sibley/Peteet Design
CL: The Coca-Cola Company

This chart illustrates the environmental efforts the Coca-Cola Company is making at the processing and corporate levels. (1)
環境問題に対する、製造工程および企業レベルでのコカ・コーラ社の取り組みを図解。(1)

This chart dissects the various components of a Coke bottle and illustrates the various efforts the Coca-Cola Company is making to protect the environment. (2)
コーラのボトルの解剖図と、環境保護のためにコカ・コーラ社が行っているさまざまな努力を表している。(2)

This chart tracks "a day in the life" of a Coke can and illustrates the life cycle from waste to product on the shelf. (3)
コカ・コーラの廃棄から再製品化までのライフサイクルを示したもの。(3)

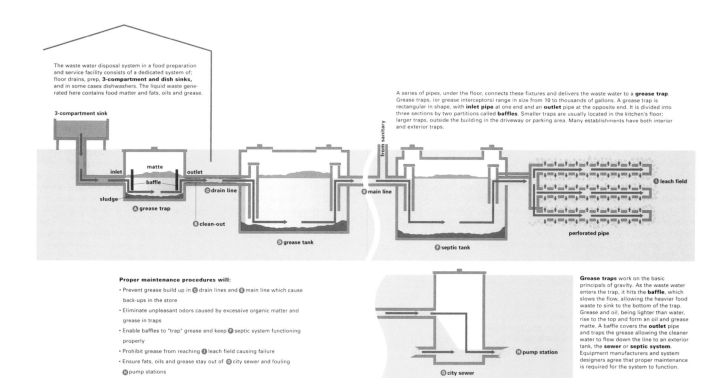

The waste water disposal system in a food preparation and service facility consists of a dedicated system of; floor drains, prep, **3-compartment and dish sinks,** and in some cases dishwashers. The liquid waste generated here contains food matter and fats, oils and grease.

A series of pipes, under the floor, connects these fixtures and delivers the waste water to a **grease trap**. Grease traps, (or grease interceptors) range in size from 10 to thousands of gallons. A grease trap is rectangular in shape, with **inlet pipe** at one end and an **outlet** pipe at the opposite end. It is divided into three sections by two partitions called **baffles**. Smaller traps are usually located in the kitchen's floor; larger traps, outside the building in the driveway or parking area. Many establishments have both interior and exterior traps.

3-compartment sink

inlet matte outlet
baffle
sludge
Ⓐ grease trap
Ⓒ drain line
Ⓑ clean-out
Ⓓ grease tank
from sanitary
Ⓔ main line
Ⓕ septic tank
perforated pipe
Ⓘ leach field

Proper maintenance procedures will:

- Prevent grease build up in Ⓒ drain lines and Ⓔ main line which cause back-ups in the store
- Eliminate unpleasant odors caused by excessive organic matter and grease in traps
- Enable baffles to "trap" grease and keep Ⓕ septic system functioning properly
- Prohibit grease from reaching Ⓘ leach field causing failure
- Ensure fats, oils and grease stay out of Ⓖ city sewer and fouling Ⓗ pump stations
- Comply with local discharge limits and avoid surcharges

Ⓗ pump station
Ⓖ city sewer

Grease traps work on the basic principals of gravity. As the waste water enters the trap, it hits the **baffle**, which slows the flow, allowing the heavier food waste to sink to the bottom of the trap. Grease and oil, being lighter than water, rise to the top and form an oil and grease matte. A baffle covers the **outlet** pipe and traps the grease allowing the cleaner water to flow down the line to an exterior tank, the **sewer** or **septic system**. Equipment manufacturers and system designers agree that proper maintenance is required for the system to function.

1

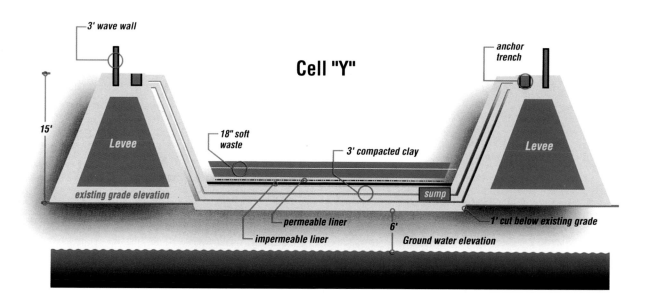

3' wave wall
anchor trench

Cell "Y"

15'
Levee
existing grade elevation
18" soft waste
3' compacted clay
permeable liner
impermeable liner
sump
Levee
1' cut below existing grade
6'
Ground water elevation

2

U.S.A. 1999
CD: Krzysztof Lenk
D: Ryutaro Sakai
DF: Dynamic Diagrams
CL: US Liquids

Schematic of a waste water disposal treatment plant. (1)
廃水処理プラントの概略図。(1)

U.S.A. 1998
CD, AD, D: Scott M. Head
I: Mauro Gomez
CW: Pam Collins
DF: Metal Studio, Inc.
CL: GCA

The "Cell Y" illustration shows the complexity of a landfill. (2)
『Cell Y』の図は、複雑な埋立て地の構造を図解している。(2)

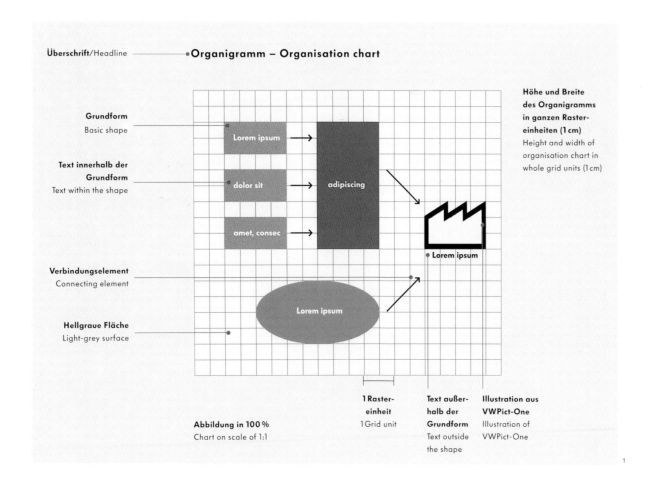

Überschrift/Headline ——— •Organigramm – Organisation chart

Grundform
Basic shape

Text innerhalb der
Grundform
Text within the shape

Verbindungselement
Connecting element

Hellgraue Fläche
Light-grey surface

Höhe und Breite
des Organigramms
in ganzen Raster-
einheiten (1 cm)
Height and width of
organisation chart in
whole grid units (1 cm)

Abbildung in 100 %
Chart on scale of 1:1

1 Raster-
einheit
1 Grid unit

Text außer-
halb der
Grundform
Text outside
the shape

Illustration aus
VWPict-One
Illustration of
VWPict-One

1

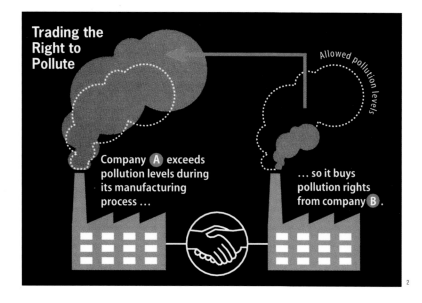

Trading the
Right to
Pollute

Allowed pollution levels

Company A exceeds
pollution levels during
its manufacturing
process ...

... so it buys
pollution rights
from company B.

2

Germany 1998
DF: Meta Design
CL: Volkswagen Ag

*Documentation of typefaces, information charts, and other elements,
to ensure the correct world-wide implementation of the Volkswagen corporate design.* (1)
フォルクスワーゲン社のコーポレイト・デザインが世界中で正しく使用されるよう、
タイプフェイス、情報のチャート、その他の要素について規定したもの。(1)

U.S.A. 1998
AD: Susanna Dulkinys
D, I, DF: Nigel Holmes
CL: Wired

One of a series of diagrams explaining "The New Economy." (2)
「新しい経済」を解説するダイアグラムのシリーズより。(2)

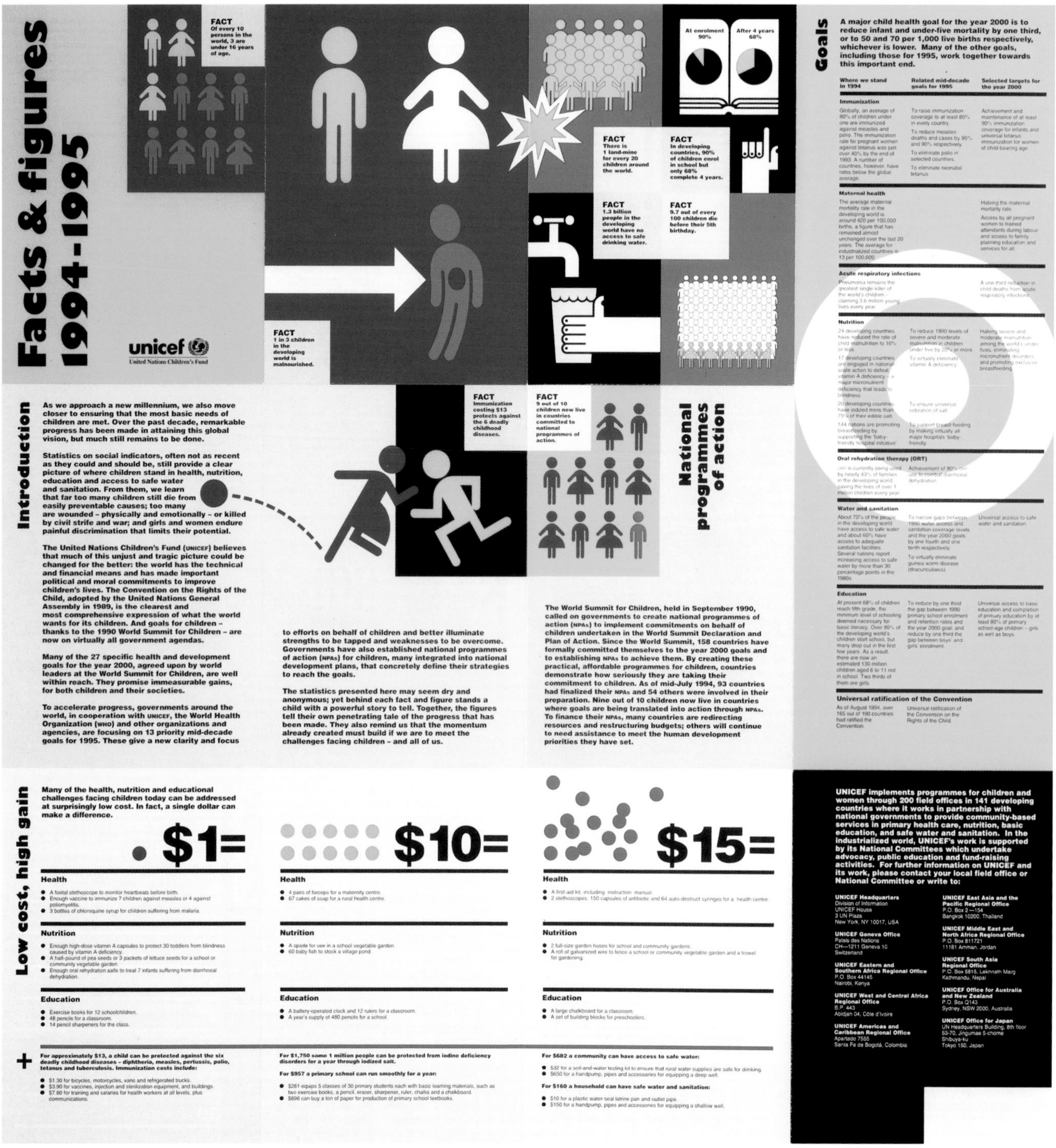
Facts & figures 1994-1995
unicef
United Nations Children's Fund
FACT
Of every 10 persons in the world, 3 are under 16 years of age.
FACT
1 in 3 children in the developing world is malnourished.
FACT
There is 1 land-mine for every 20 children around the world.
FACT
In developing countries, 90% of children enrol in school but only 68% complete 4 years.
At enrolment 90%
After 4 years 68%
FACT
1.3 billion people in the developing world have no access to safe drinking water.
FACT
9.7 out of every 100 children die before their 5th birthday.
FACT
Immunization costing $13 protects against the 6 deadly childhood diseases.
FACT
9 out of 10 children now live in countries committed to national programmes of action.
Introduction
As we approach a new millennium, we also move closer to ensuring that the most basic needs of children are met. Over the past decade, remarkable progress has been made in attaining this global vision, but much still remains to be done.
Statistics on social indicators, often not as recent as they could and should be, still provide a clear picture of where children stand in health, nutrition, education and access to safe water and sanitation. From them, we learn that far too many children still die from easily preventable causes; too many are wounded – physically and emotionally – or killed by civil strife and war; and girls and women endure painful discrimination that limits their potential.
The United Nations Children's Fund (UNICEF) believes that much of this unjust and tragic picture could be changed for the better: the world has the technical and financial means and has made important political and moral commitments to improve children's lives. The Convention on the Rights of the Child, adopted by the United Nations General Assembly in 1989, is the clearest and most comprehensive expression of what the world wants for its children. And goals for children – thanks to the 1990 World Summit for Children – are now on virtually all government agendas.
Many of the 27 specific health and development goals for the year 2000, agreed upon by world leaders at the World Summit for Children, are well within reach. They promise immeasurable gains, for both children and their societies.
To accelerate progress, governments around the world, in cooperation with UNICEF, the World Health Organization (WHO) and other organizations and agencies, are focusing on 13 priority mid-decade goals for 1995. These give a new clarity and focus to efforts on behalf of children and better illuminate strengths to be tapped and weaknesses to be overcome. Governments have also established national programmes of action (NPAs) for children, many integrated into national development plans, that concretely define their strategies to reach the goals.
The statistics presented here may seem dry and anonymous; yet behind each fact and figure stands a child with a powerful story to tell. Together, the figures tell their own penetrating tale of the progress that has been made. They also remind us that the momentum already created must build if we are to meet the challenges facing children – and all of us.
National programmes of action
The World Summit for Children, held in September 1990, called on governments to create national programmes of action (NPAs) to implement commitments on behalf of children undertaken in the World Summit Declaration and Plan of Action. Since the World Summit, 158 countries have formally committed themselves to the year 2000 goals and to establishing NPAs to achieve them. By creating these practical, affordable programmes for children, countries demonstrate how seriously they are taking their commitment to children. As of mid-July 1994, 93 countries had finalized their NPAs and 54 others were involved in their preparation. Nine out of 10 children now live in countries where goals are being translated into action through NPAs. To finance their NPAs, many countries are redirecting resources and restructuring budgets; others will continue to need assistance to meet the human development priorities they have set.
Goals
A major child health goal for the year 2000 is to reduce infant and under-five mortality by one third, or to 50 and 70 per 1,000 live births respectively, whichever is lower. Many of the other goals, including those for 1995, work together towards this important end.
Where we stand in 1994
Related mid-decade goals for 1995
Selected targets for the year 2000
Immunization
Globally, an average of 80% of children under one are immunized against measles and polio. The immunization rate for pregnant women against tetanus was just over 40% by the end of 1993. A number of countries, however, have rates below the global average.
To raise immunization coverage to at least 80% in every country.
To reduce measles deaths and cases by 95% and 90% respectively.
To eliminate polio in selected countries.
To eliminate neonatal tetanus.
Achievement and maintenance of at least 90% immunization coverage for infants and universal tetanus immunization for women of child-bearing age.
Maternal health
The average maternal mortality rate in the developing world is around 420 per 100,000 births, a figure that has remained almost unchanged over the last 20 years. The average for industrialized countries is 13 per 100,000.
Halving the maternal mortality rate.
Access by all pregnant women to trained attendants during labour and access to family planning education and services for all.
Acute respiratory infections
Pneumonia remains the greatest single killer of the world's children – claiming 3.6 million young lives every year.
A one-third reduction in child deaths from acute respiratory infections.
Nutrition
24 developing countries have reduced the rate of child malnutrition to 10% or less.
17 developing countries are engaged in national-scale action to defeat vitamin A deficiency – a major micronutrient deficiency that leads to blindness.
20 developing countries have iodized more than 75% of their edible salt.
144 nations are promoting breastfeeding by supporting the 'baby-friendly hospital initiative'.
To reduce 1990 levels of severe and moderate malnutrition in children under five by 20% or more.
To virtually eliminate vitamin A deficiency.
To ensure universal iodization of salt.
To support breast-feeding by making virtually all major hospitals 'baby-friendly'.
Halving severe and moderate malnutrition among the world's under fives, eliminating micronutrient disorders and promoting exclusive breastfeeding.
Oral rehydration therapy (ORT)
ORT is currently being used by nearly 43% of families in the developing world, saving the lives of over 1 million children every year.
Achievement of 80% ORT use to combat diarrhoeal dehydration.
Water and sanitation
About 70% of the people in the developing world have access to safe water and about 60% have access to adequate sanitation facilities. Several nations report increasing access to safe water by more than 30 percentage points in the 1980s.
To narrow gaps between 1990 water access and sanitation coverage levels and the year 2000 goals by one fourth and one tenth respectively.
To virtually eliminate guinea worm disease (dracunculiasis).
Universal access to safe water and sanitation.
Education
At present 68% of children reach fifth grade, the minimum level of schooling deemed necessary for basic literacy. Over 90% of the developing world's children start school, but many drop out in the first few years. As a result, there are now an estimated 130 million children aged 6 to 11 not in school. Two thirds of them are girls.
To reduce by one third the gap between 1990 primary school enrolment and retention rates and the year 2000 goal, and reduce by one third the gap between boys' and girls' enrolment.
Universal access to basic education and completion of primary education by at least 80% of primary school-age children – girls as well as boys.
Universal ratification of the Convention
As of August 1994, over 165 out of 190 countries had ratified the Convention.
Universal ratification of the Convention on the Rights of the Child.
Low cost, high gain
Many of the health, nutrition and educational challenges facing children today can be addressed at surprisingly low cost. In fact, a single dollar can make a difference.
$1=
Health
A foetal stethoscope to monitor heartbeats before birth.
Enough vaccine to immunize 7 children against measles or 4 against poliomyelitis.
3 bottles of chloroquine syrup for children suffering from malaria.
Nutrition
Enough high-dose vitamin A capsules to protect 30 toddlers from blindness caused by vitamin A deficiency.
A half-pound of pea seeds or 3 packets of lettuce seeds for a school or community vegetable garden.
Enough oral rehydration salts to treat 7 infants suffering from diarrhoeal dehydration.
Education
Exercise books for 12 schoolchildren.
48 pencils for a classroom.
14 pencil sharpeners for the class.
$10=
Health
4 pairs of forceps for a maternity centre.
67 cakes of soap for a rural health centre.
Nutrition
A spade for use in a school vegetable garden.
60 baby fish to stock a village pond.
Education
A battery-operated clock and 12 rulers for a classroom.
A year's supply of 480 pencils for a school.
$15=
Health
A first-aid kit, including instruction manual.
2 stethoscopes, 150 capsules of antibiotic and 64 auto-destruct syringes for a health centre.
Nutrition
2 full-size garden hoses for school and community gardens.
A roll of galvanized wire to fence a school or community vegetable garden and a trowel for gardening.
Education
A large chalkboard for a classroom.
A set of building blocks for preschoolers.
+
For approximately $13, a child can be protected against the six deadly childhood diseases – diphtheria, measles, pertussis, polio, tetanus and tuberculosis. Immunization costs include:
$1.30 for bicycles, motorcycles, vans and refrigerated trucks.
$3.90 for vaccines, injection and sterilization equipment, and buildings.
$7.80 for training and salaries for health workers at all levels, plus communications.
For $1,750 some 1 million people can be protected from iodine deficiency disorders for a year through iodized salt.
For $957 a primary school can run smoothly for a year:
$261 equips 5 classes of 30 primary students each with basic learning materials, such as two exercise books, a pencil, eraser, sharpener, ruler, chalks and a chalkboard.
$696 can buy a ton of paper for production of primary school textbooks.
For $682 a community can have access to safe water:
$32 for a soil-and-water testing kit to ensure that rural water supplies are safe for drinking.
$650 for a handpump, pipes and accessories for equipping a deep well.
For $160 a household can have safe water and sanitation:
$10 for a plastic water-seal latrine pan and outlet pipe.
$150 for a handpump, pipes and accessories for equipping a shallow well.
UNICEF implements programmes for children and women through 200 field offices in 141 developing countries where it works in partnership with national governments to provide community-based services in primary health care, nutrition, basic education, and safe water and sanitation. In the industrialized world, UNICEF's work is supported by its National Committees which undertake advocacy, public education and fund-raising activities. For further information on UNICEF and its work, please contact your local field office or National Committee or write to:
UNICEF Headquarters
Division of Information
UNICEF House
3 UN Plaza
New York, NY 10017, USA
UNICEF Geneva Office
Palais des Nations
CH—1211 Geneva 10
Switzerland
UNICEF Eastern and Southern Africa Regional Office
P.O. Box 44145
Nairobi, Kenya
UNICEF West and Central Africa Regional Office
B.P. 443
Abidjan 04, Côte d'Ivoire
UNICEF Americas and Caribbean Regional Office
Apartado 7555
Santa Fe de Bogotá, Colombia
UNICEF East Asia and the Pacific Regional Office
P.O. Box 2—154
Bangkok 10200, Thailand
UNICEF Middle East and North Africa Regional Office
P.O. Box 811721
11181 Amman, Jordan
UNICEF South Asia Regional Office
P.O. Box 5815, Lekhnath Marg
Kathmandu, Nepal
UNICEF Office for Australia and New Zealand
P.O. Box Q143
Sydney, NSW 2000, Australia
UNICEF Office for Japan
UN Headquarters Building, 8th floor
53-70, Jingumae 5-chome
Shibuya-ku
Tokyo 150, Japan

U.K. 1994
CD, AD, D: Peter Grundy
CD, AD, D, I: Tilly Northedge
DF: Grundy & Northedge
CL: Unicef

An information leaflet/poster showing the plight of children worldwide.
世界の子供たちの窮状を訴えたリーフレットおよびポスター。

Security for intranets is achieved with a **firewall,** which prevents "outsiders" from gaining access to the intranet. "Insiders," however, may cross through the firewall to retrieve data from the net proper.

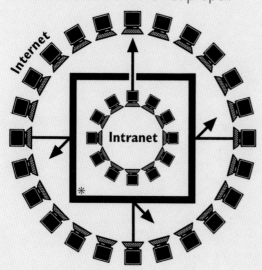

If well-engineered, users of an intranet will be unaware of whether they are "inside" or "outside."

*The firewall works by disabling part of the packet-switching activity of the net.

A **Virtual Private Network (VPN)** is an arrangement between two or more companies to open their firewalls to each other, allowing access to their respective intranets for a limited time—on a specific joint project, for example.

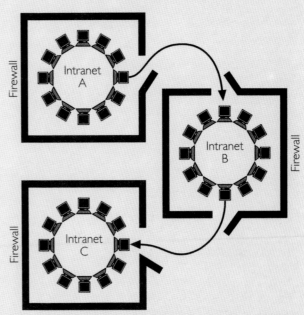

This is also called a **Secure Wide Area Network (SWAN).**

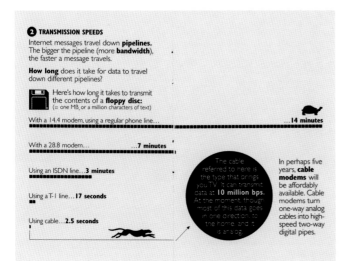

2 TRANSMISSION SPEEDS

Internet messages travel down **pipelines.** The bigger the pipeline (more **bandwidth**), the faster a message travels.

How long does it take for data to travel down different pipelines?

Here's how long it takes to transmit the contents of a **floppy disc:** (= one MB, or a million characters of text)

With a 14.4 modem, using a regular phone line... ...**14 minutes**

With a 28.8 modem... ...**7 minutes**

Using an ISDN line...**3 minutes**

Using a T-1 line...**17 seconds**

Using cable...**2.5 seconds**

The cable referred to here is the type that brings you TV. It can transmit data at **10 million bps.** At the moment, though, most of this data goes in one direction: to the home, and it is analog.

In perhaps five years, **cable modems** will be affordably available. Cable modems turn one-way analog cables into high-speed two-way digital pipes.

7 SECURITY

Security is a pressing concern for both buyers and sellers. Credit card companies and banks are jointly developing **Secure Electronic Transaction (SET)** technologies.

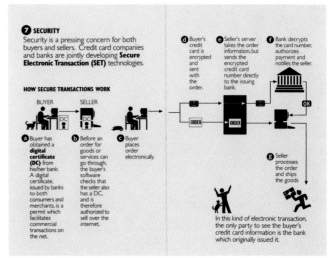

HOW SECURE TRANSACTIONS WORK

BUYER   SELLER

a Buyer has obtained a **digital certificate (DC)** from his/her bank. A digital certificate, issued by banks to both consumers and merchants, is a permit which facilitates commercial transactions on the net.

b Before an order for goods or services can go through, the buyer's software checks that the seller also has a DC, and is therefore authorized to sell over the internet.

c Buyer places order electronically.

d Buyer's credit card is encrypted and sent with the order.

e Seller's server takes the order information, but sends the encrypted credit card number directly to the issuing bank.

f Bank decrypts the card number, authorizes payment and notifies the seller.

g Seller processes the order and ships the goods.

In this kind of electronic transaction, the only party to see the buyer's credit card information is the bank which originally issued it.

U.S.A. 1997
CD, D, I, CW, DF: Nigel Holmes

Pocket-sized book to accompany lectures about how the Internet works.
Designed to provide non-technical people, such as executives, with explanations of common Internet terms and processes.
インターネットについての講義で使用する小冊子より。
非技術系の人々（管理職など）にインターネットの用語やプロセスを説明するためにデザインされたもの。

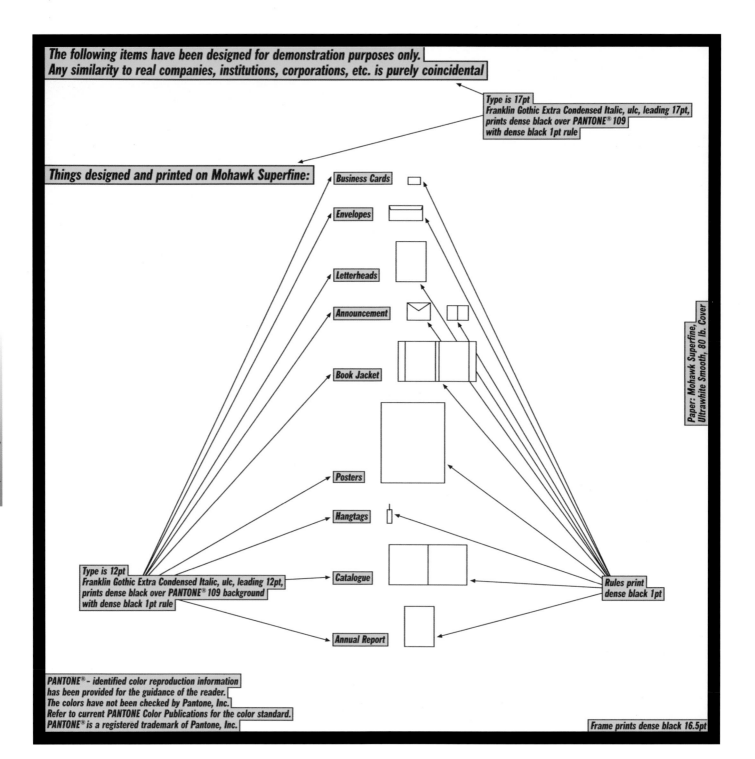

The following items have been designed for demonstration purposes only.
Any similarity to real companies, institutions, corporations, etc. is purely coincidental

Type is 17pt
Franklin Gothic Extra Condensed Italic, ulc, leading 17pt,
prints dense black over PANTONE® 109
with dense black 1pt rule

Things designed and printed on Mohawk Superfine:

Business Cards

Envelopes

Letterheads

Announcement

Book Jacket

Posters

Hangtags

Catalogue

Annual Report

Paper: Mohawk Superfine,
Ultrawhite Smooth, 80 lb. Cover

Type is 12pt
Franklin Gothic Extra Condensed Italic, ulc, leading 12pt,
prints dense black over PANTONE® 109 background
with dense black 1pt rule

Rules print
dense black 1pt

PANTONE® - identified color reproduction information
has been provided for the guidance of the reader.
The colors have not been checked by Pantone, Inc.
Refer to current PANTONE Color Publications for the color standard.
PANTONE® is a registered trademark of Pantone, Inc.

Frame prints dense black 16.5pt

System Diagrams & Scores

028

U.S.A. 1998
AD: Paula Scher
D: Anke Stohlmann/Keith Daigle
DF: Pentagram Design
CL: Mohawk Paper Mills, Inc.

Promotional booklet for a paper stock company, demonstrating potential uses for the company's various shades and weights of paper.
さまざまな色調や重量の紙をどのように使うかを説明した製紙会社のプロモーション用ブックレットより。

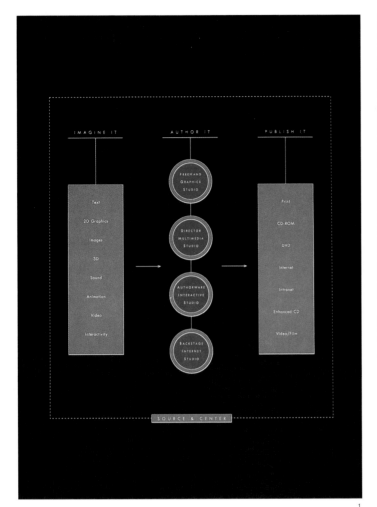

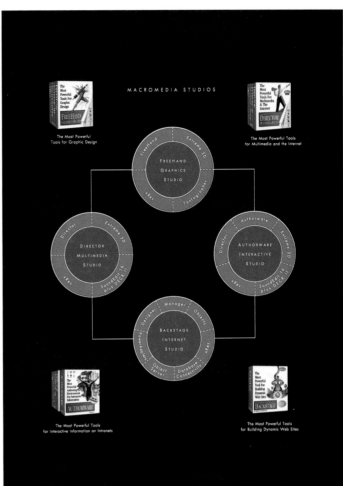

1

2

U.S.A. 1996
CD, AD: Bill Cahan
D: Lian Ng
D, CW: Craig Clark
P: Tony Stromberg
I: Will Davies
CW: Tom Lucente
DF: Cahan & Associates
CL: Macromedia

A diagram showing how all of Macromedia's products work together cohesively, enabling production in different media. (1)
マクロメディア社のあらゆる製品が結集し、さまざまなメディアでのプロダクションが可能になることを表したダイアグラム。(1)

A diagram showing selected Macromedia products, packaged in four distinctive categories. (2)
マクロメディア社の主要製品を4つのカテゴリーで表したダイアグラム。(2)

3つの事業分野
世界に比類なきエレクトロニクス企業へ

地球規模で展開する民生分野、産業分野、部品分野の3事業分野が、それぞれの分野でグローバルなものづくり、ビジネスを実践しています。民生分野では21世紀のライフスタイルを提案する世界No.1の「コンシューマー・エレクトロニクス・メーカー」として、産業分野においては機器、ソフトウェアからシステムインテグレーションなどのすべてに対応する「トータルソリューション企業」として、部品分野ではデジタル化の進展を支える世界最大レンジの部品メーカーとして、各分野は同じ経営理念、ブランド、知財権、経営管理制度、情報システムなどでつながれたひとつのグループとして互いに補完し合い、連携し、有機的にネットワークすることで、「世界に比類なきエレクトロニクス企業」としての、事業ダイナミズムを創造しています。そしてその、ひとつの松下電器は、21世紀へ向けて、地球環境との共存、社会との信頼関係構築、世界の人々の豊かな生活を実現するために、日々新たな価値創造をめざしています。

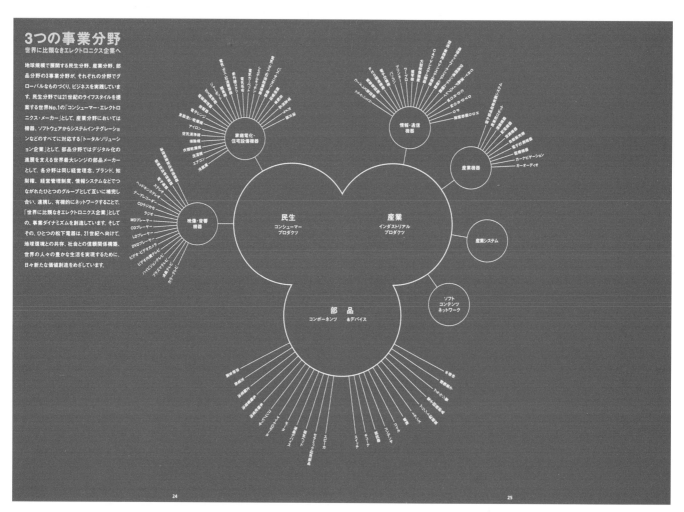

5つの重点事業
デジタルがひらくコミュニケーション

民生・産業・デバイスの3分野で培ってきた高水準のデジタル技術が融合しています。誰にとっても使いやすいインターフェースと快適なコミュニケーション、そして次代のグローバルスタンダードをめざす5つの重点事業です。

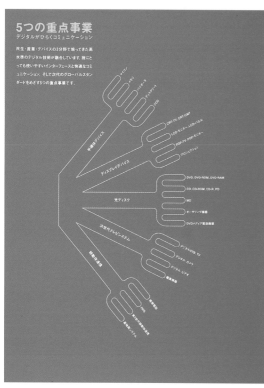

Japan　1998
AD: Shinnoske Sugisaki
DF: Shinnoske Inc.
CL: Matsushita Electric Industrial Co., Ltd.

Diagrams show the varied business fields of general electrics manufacturer Matsushita Electric, and priority areas for their next generation of business.
総合電器メーカー「松下電器」の事業分野と次世代における重点事業を表したダイアグラム。

●武蔵野美術大学短期大学部教育課程構成図

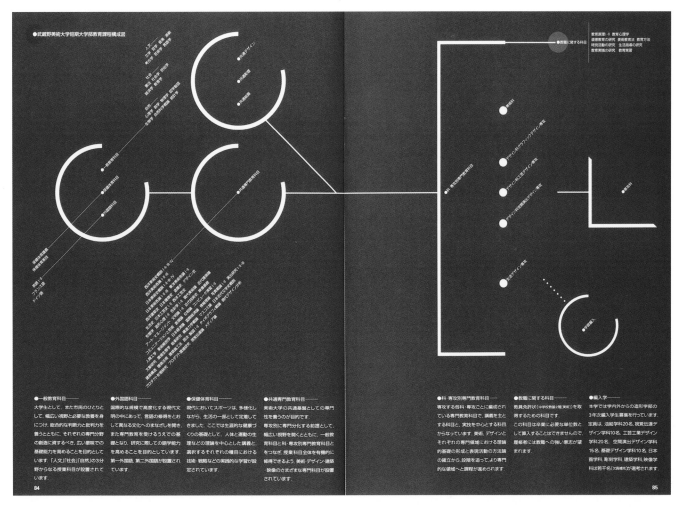

教育原理Ⅰ・Ⅱ　教育心理学
道徳教育の研究　美術教育法　教育方法
特別活動の研究　生活指導の研究
教育実践の研究　教育実習
●教職に関する科目

●一般教育科目——
大学生として、また市民のひとりとして、幅広い視野と必要な教養を身につけ、総合的な判断力と批判力を養うとともに、それぞれの専門分野の創造に資するべき、広い意味での基礎能力を高めることを目的としています。「人文」「社会」「自然」の3分野からなる授業科目が設置されています。

●外国語科目——
国際的な規模で高度化する現代文明の中にあって、言語の修得をとおして異なる文化へのまなざしを開き、また専門教育を受けるうえでの基礎となり、研究に際しての語学能力を高めることを目的としています。第一外国語、第二外国語が設置されています。

●保健体育科目——
現代においてスポーツは、多様化しながら、生活の一部として定着してきました。ここでは生涯的な健康づくりの基礎として、人体と運動の生理などの理論を中心とした講義と、技術・戦略などの実践的な学習が設定されています。

●共通専門教育科目——
美術大学の共通基盤としての専門性を養うのが目的です。専攻別に専門分化する前提として、幅広い視野を開くとともに、一般教育科目と科・専攻別専門教育科目とをつなぎ、授業科目全体を有機的に修得できるよう、美術・デザイン・建築・映像のさまざまな専門科目が設置されています。

●科・専攻別専門教育科目——
専攻する各科・専攻ごとに編成されている専門教育科目で、講義を主とする科目と、実技を中心とする科目からなっています。美術、デザインとそれぞれの専門領域における理論的基礎の形成と表現活動の方法論を修得できるよう、段階を追って、より専門的な領域へと課程が進められます。

●教職に関する科目——
教員免許状（中学校教諭2種〈美術〉）を取得するための科目です。この科目は卒業に必要な単位数として算入することはできませんので、履修者には教職への強い意志が望まれます。

●編入学——
本学では学内外からの造形学部の3年次編入学生募集を行っています。定員は、油絵学科20名、視覚伝達デザイン学科10名、工芸工業デザイン学科20名、空間演出デザイン学科15名、基礎デザイン学科10名、日本画学科、彫刻学科、建築学科、映像学科は若干名（欠員補充）が選考されます。

84

85

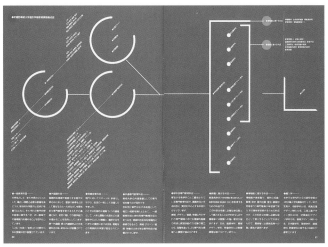

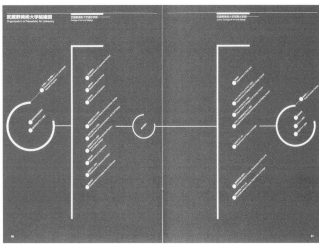

Japan　1996
AD: Mitsuo Katsui
D: Shin Tanaka/Taeko Tanaka
CL: Musashino Art University

Organization charts of the Musashino Art University; and the departments of its College of Art and Design, and Junior College of Art and Design. From the school's promotional brochure.
学校案内より。「武蔵野美術大学」の組織図、「武蔵野美術大学造形学部教育課程」の構成図、「武蔵野美術大学短期大学部教育課程」の構成図。

Poems with a Certain Air

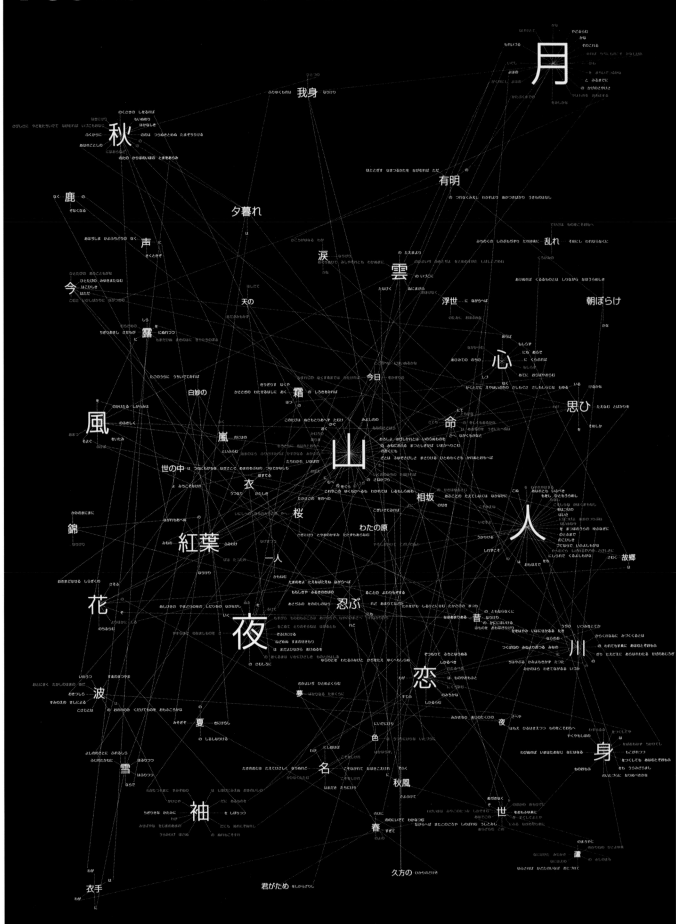

The dicisive character

To get the correct card as fast as you can, you have to memorize the dicisive character.

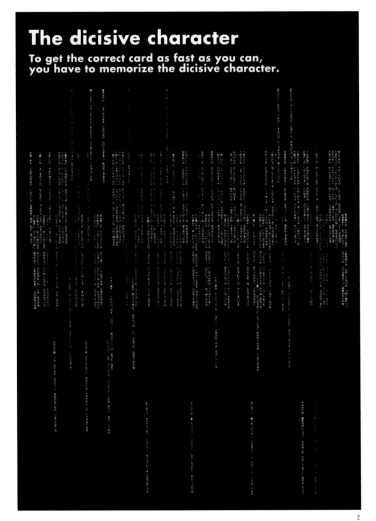

100 people's Relationship

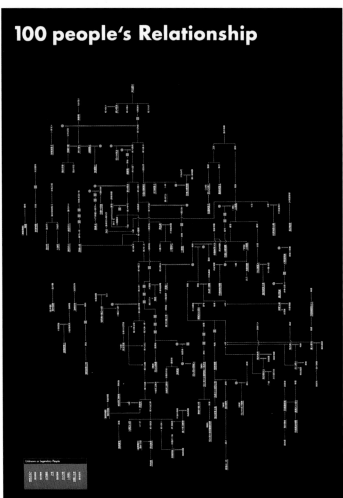

2

3

Japan 1998
AD, D: Naoko Nakui

Diagram indicates frequency of words used in the "Hyakunin Isshu (100 Famous Poems)" playing card game. (1)
「百人一首」に使われている言葉の使用頻度を表したダイアグラム。(1)

Diagram showing which cards are most quickly taken during the Hyakunin Isshu game. (2)
「百人一首」のゲームをしているとき、早く取ることができるカードの順番を表したダイアグラム。(2)

Chart showing the relationships of the 100 people who wrote the poems of the Hyakunin Isshu game. (3)
「百人一首」を詠んだ100人の関係を表した人物相関図。(3)

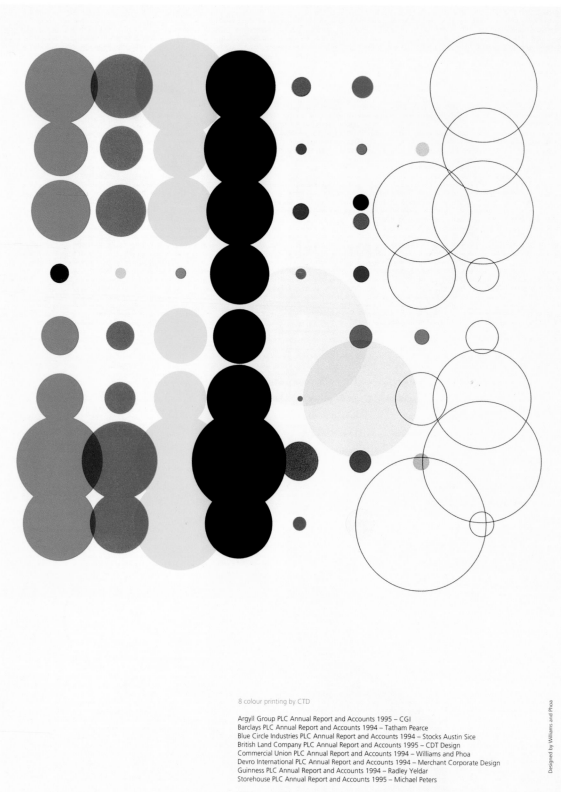

8 colour printing by CTD

Argyll Group PLC Annual Report and Accounts 1995 – CGI
Barclays PLC Annual Report and Accounts 1994 – Tatham Pearce
Blue Circle Industries PLC Annual Report and Accounts 1994 – Stocks Austin Sice
British Land Company PLC Annual Report and Accounts 1995 – CDT Design
Commercial Union PLC Annual Report and Accounts 1994 – Williams and Phoa
Devro International PLC Annual Report and Accounts 1994 – Merchant Corporate Design
Guinness PLC Annual Report and Accounts 1994 – Radley Yeldar
Storehouse PLC Annual Report and Accounts 1995 – Michael Peters

CTD's new Heidelberg Speed Master 8-colour machine means that up to eight colours
can be printed in line, with greater precision and in less time

Contact – Graham Tanner
CTD Printers Limited, Unit 2, Heathlands, Heathlands Close, Twickenham, Middlesex TW1 4BP
Telephone 0181 892 8884, Facsimile 0181 891 5035

Designed by Williams and Phoa

U.K.   1996
AD, D, CW: Clifford Hiscock
DF: Williams and Phoa
CL: CTD Printers Ltd.

*A graphic representation of the comparative amounts of inks (process, special inks, and varnishes)
used on eight key annual reports printed by the company, intended to demonstrate the versatility
of their 8-color printer in a way that will appeal to designers.*
CTDプリンター社の印刷した8つの主なアニュアル・リポートについて、使用されたインク（プロセスカラー、特色、光沢）の量を比較した図。
デザイナーに8色プリンターの柔軟な対応力をアピールするためのもの。

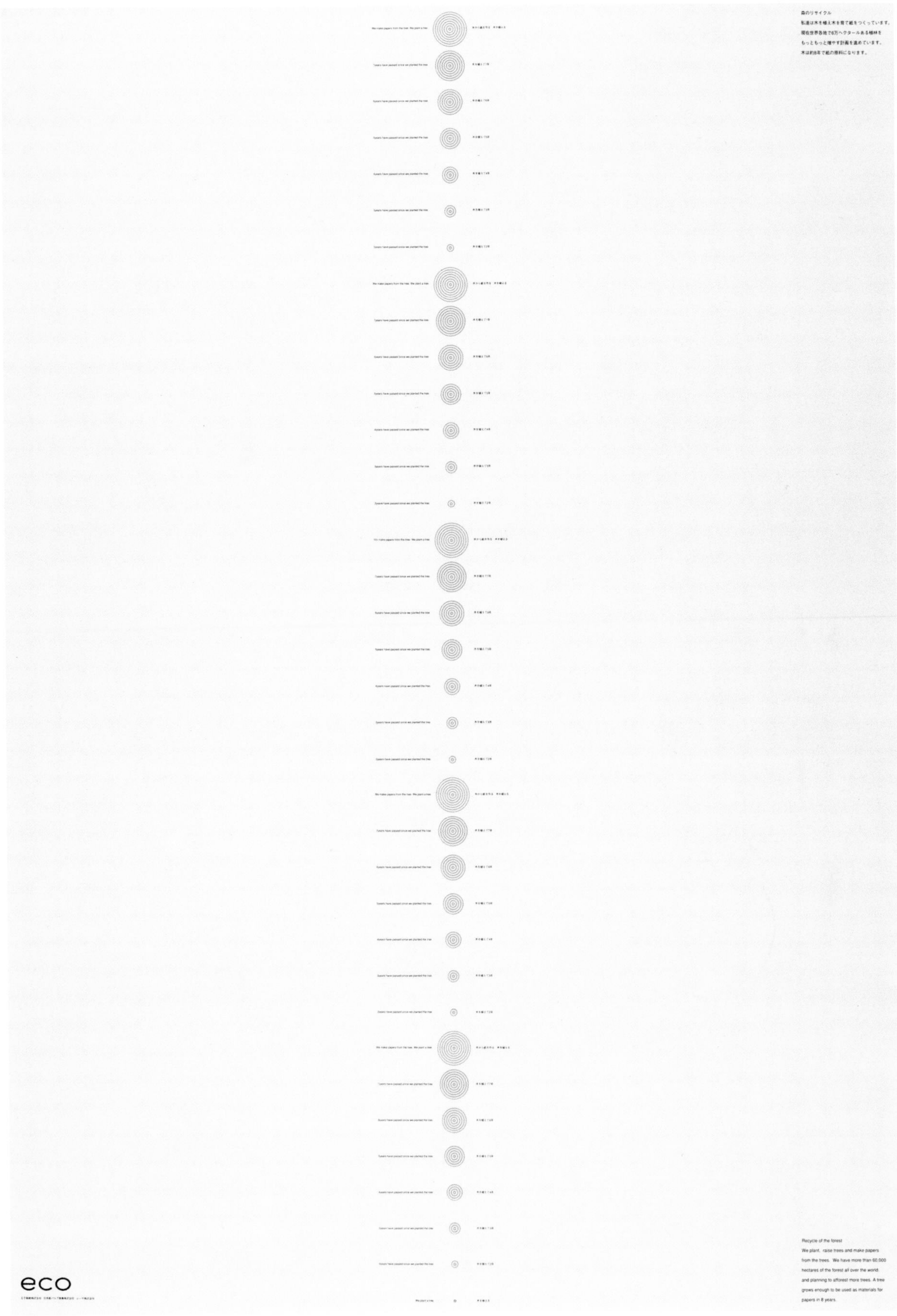

Japan 1999
AD: Akio Okumura
D: Yasuyo Fukumoto
CW: Manami Maeda
DF: Packaging Create Inc.
CL: Musa

A poster made for a paper manufacturing company.
Tree rings illustrate the 8 years that will pass before a tree is used to make paper.
製紙会社「ムーサ」のポスターより。植林した木が最終的に紙になるまでの8年というサイクルを、木の年輪の数で表した。

TAKENAKA CORPORATE GROUP
グループで創造する都市・人間環境 竹中工務店

[TAKENAKA REAL ESTATE CORPORATE BROCHURE—1989]

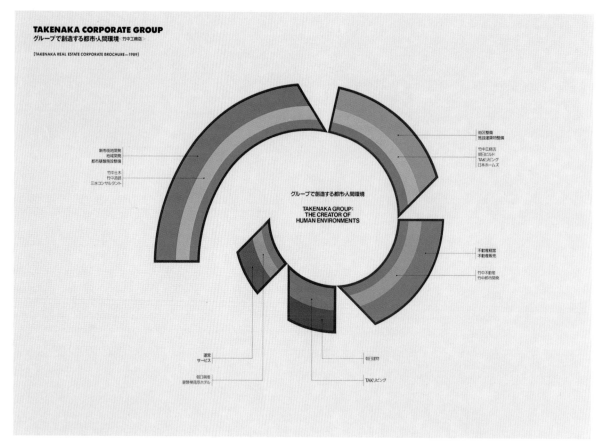

新市街地開発
地域開発
都市基盤施設整備

竹中土木
竹中道路
三水コンサルタント

街区整備
施設建築物整備

竹中工務店
朝日ビルド
TAKリビング
日本ホームズ

グループで創造する都市・人間環境

TAKENAKA GROUP:
THE CREATOR OF
HUMAN ENVIRONMENTS

不動産経営
不動産販売

竹中不動産
竹中都市開発

運営
サービス

朝日興産
磐梯桧原高原ホテル

朝日建物

TAKリビング

TAKENAKA CORPORATE GROUP
グループで創造する都市・人間環境 竹中工務店

[TAKENAKA REAL ESTATE CORPORATE BROCHURE—1989]

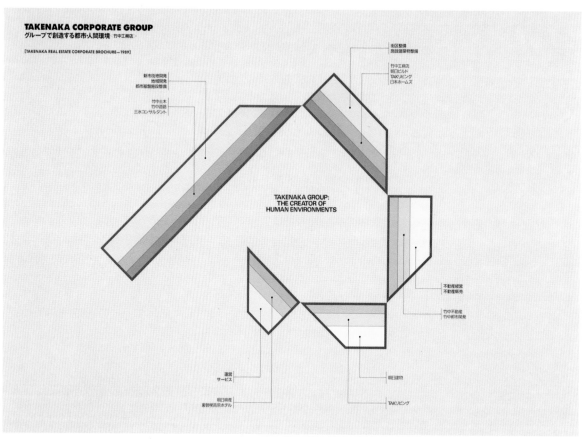

新市街地開発
地域開発
都市基盤施設整備

竹中土木
竹中道路
三水コンサルタント

街区整備
施設建築物整備

竹中工務店
朝日ビルド
TAKリビング
日本ホームズ

TAKENAKA GROUP:
THE CREATOR OF
HUMAN ENVIRONMENTS

不動産経営
不動産販売

竹中不動産
竹中都市開発

運営
サービス

朝日興産
磐梯桧原高原ホテル

朝日建物

TAKリビング

Japan 1989
CD, AD, D: Tetsuya Ohta
CL: Takenaka Real Estate Co., Ltd.

Graphs from a real estate group's corporate brochure that lists the companies in the group and the business activities in which they are involved.

竹中工務店の会社案内より。都市部での人間環境における竹中工務店のかかわり方を表した組織チャート。

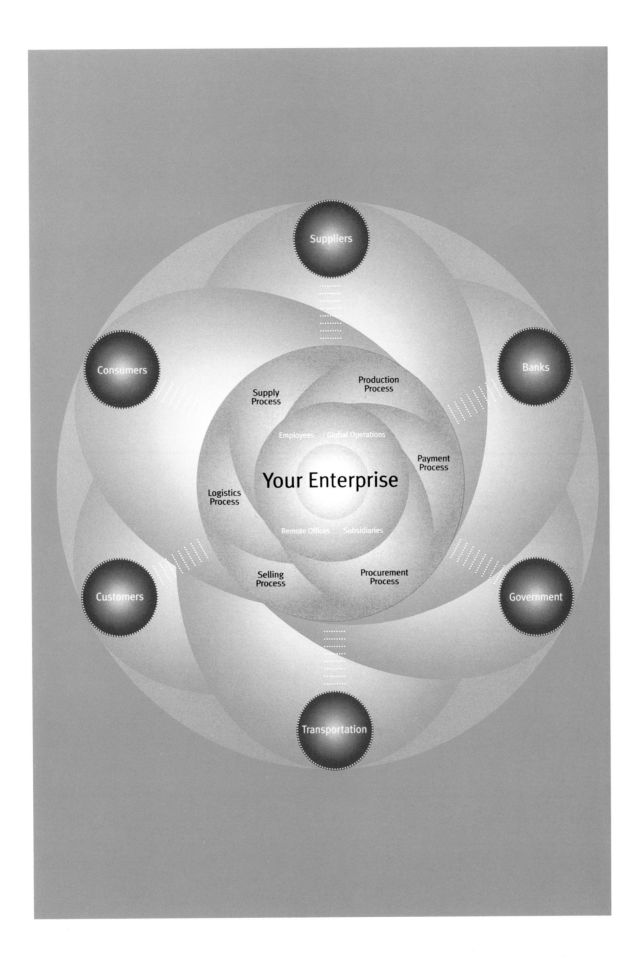

電子商取引の急速な発展と、グローバル市場における企業のクリエイティブで先進的な地位を強調している。

U.S.A. 1998
CD: Kristin Johnson
AD, D, I: Raelene Mercer
CW: Frank Cunningham
DF: Pinkhaus
CL: Sterling Commerce

This graphic highlights the rapid growth of electronic commerce, and emphasizes the company's creative and leading place in that global market.
電子商取引の急速な発展と、グローバル市場における企業のクリエイティブで先進的な地位を強調している。

Michael Birck asked Hambrecht & Quist to join Greylock and Sutter Hill in the first round financing at Tellabs. Cliff Higgerson sponsored the H&Q investment and continued to be associated with the company as venture capitalist, investment banker and analyst. Tellabs goes public in 1980. Today, Tellabs is the 2nd largest U.S. supplier of transmission and switching equipment.

Bill Gibson, Bob Friess, Mike Freidenbach and Cliff Higgerson met in Bill's living room to discuss the start-up venture. Cliff seeded company and helped to raise first round. First product is a bypass microwave 23 GHz radio. Since IPO in 1987, the company has become a leading supplier of microwave products and services used in commercial telecommunications transmission networks worldwide.

IPO 1980 — tellabs

MCI

IPO 1988 — OcTel

IPO 1987 — NET

IPO 1987 — DIGITAL MICROWAVE CORPORATION

IPO 1979 — PARADYNE

IPO 1981 — micom

IPO 1987 — EXECUTONE

IPO 199 — AMERICA Online

IPO 1985 — Telco Systems

75 76 77 78 79 80 81 82 83 84 85

We like to get involved

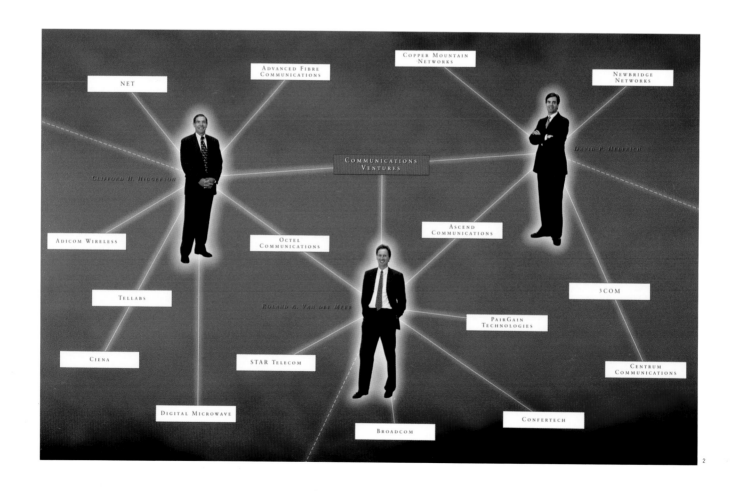

COPPER MOUNTAIN NETWORKS

ADVANCED FIBRE COMMUNICATIONS

NET

NEWBRIDGE NETWORKS

DAVID P. HELFRICH

CLIFFORD H. HIGGERSON

COMMUNICATIONS VENTURES

ADICOM WIRELESS

OCTEL COMMUNICATIONS

ASCEND COMMUNICATIONS

TELLABS

ROLAND A. VAN DER MEER

3COM

CIENA

STAR TELECOM

PAIRGAIN TECHNOLOGIES

CENTRUM COMMUNICATIONS

DIGITAL MICROWAVE

BROADCOM

CONFERTECH

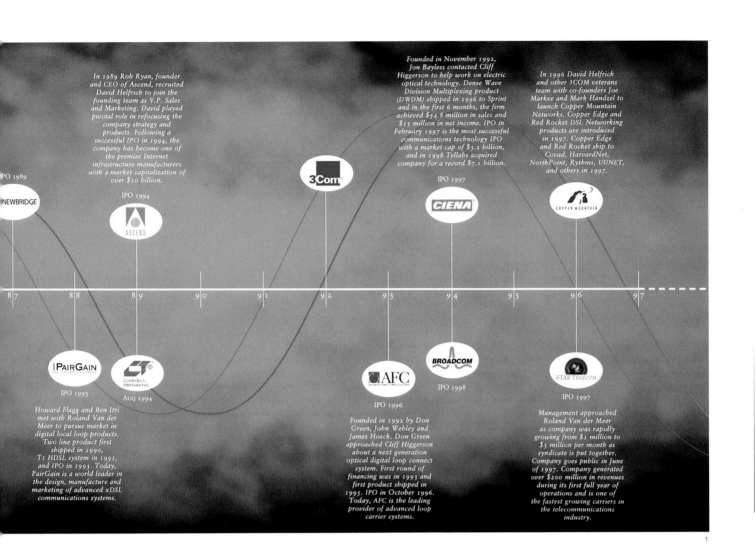

In 1989 Rob Ryan, founder and CEO of Ascend, recruited David Helfrich to join the founding team as V.P. Sales and Marketing. David played pivotal role in refocusing the company strategy and products. Following a successful IPO in 1994, the company has become one of the premier Internet infrastructure manufacturers with a market capitalization of over $10 billion.

Founded in November 1992, Jon Bayless contacted Cliff Higgerson to help work on electric optical technology. Dense Wave Division Multiplexing product (DWDM) shipped in 1996 to Sprint and in the first 6 months, the firm achieved $54.8 million in sales and $15 million in net income. IPO in February 1997 is the most successful communications technology IPO with a market cap of $3.2 billion, and in 1998 Tellabs acquired company for a record $7.1 billion.

In 1996 David Helfrich and other 3COM veterans team with co-founders Joe Markee and Mark Handzel to launch Copper Mountain Networks. Copper Edge and Red Rocket DSL Networking products are introduced in 1997. Copper Edge and Red Rocket ship to Covad, HarvardNet, NorthPoint, Rythms, UUNET, and others in 1997.

IPO 1989 NEWBRIDGE

IPO 1994 ASCEND

3Com

IPO 1997

CIENA

COPPER MOUNTAIN

87 88 89 90 91 92 93 94 95 96 97

PAIRGAIN

ComterTech International

IPO 1993   ACQ 1994

AFC

BROADCOM

STAR TELECOM

IPO 1996   IPO 1998   IPO 1997

Howard Flagg and Ben Itri met with Roland Van der Meer to pursue market in digital local loop products. Two line product first shipped in 1990, T1 HDSL system in 1991, and IPO in 1993. Today, PairGain is a world leader in the design, manufacture and marketing of advanced xDSL communications systems.

Founded in 1992 by Don Green, John Webley and James Hoeck. Don Green approached Cliff Higgerson about a next generation optical digital loop connect system. First round of financing was in 1993 and first product shipped in 1995. IPO in October 1996. Today, AFC is the leading provider of advanced loop carrier systems.

Management approached Roland Van der Meer as company was rapidly growing from $1 million to $3 million per month as syndicate is put together. Company goes public in June of 1997. Company generated over $200 million in revenues during its first full year of operations and is one of the fastest growing carriers in the telecommunications industry.

U.S.A.   1998
CD, AD, D, I: Earl Gee
D, I: Fani Chung
P: Scott Peterson/Ted Mock (2)
DF: Gee + Chung Design
CL: Communications Ventures

Timeline illustrating the evolution of the communications industry from 1975 to 1997 and the major role that Communications Ventures, a venture capital firm, has played in its development. (1)
1975年から1997年にかけての通信産業の発展と、コミュニケーション・ベンチャーズ社（投機会社）がその発展において果たした役割を表した時系列表。(1)

Diagram illustrating the network of industry contacts and communications companies that the three partners helped to launch throughout their careers, and their interrelationships. (2)
3者のパートナーが、それぞれのキャリアと相互提携を通じて着手した業界内および通信会社のネットワークを表している。(2)

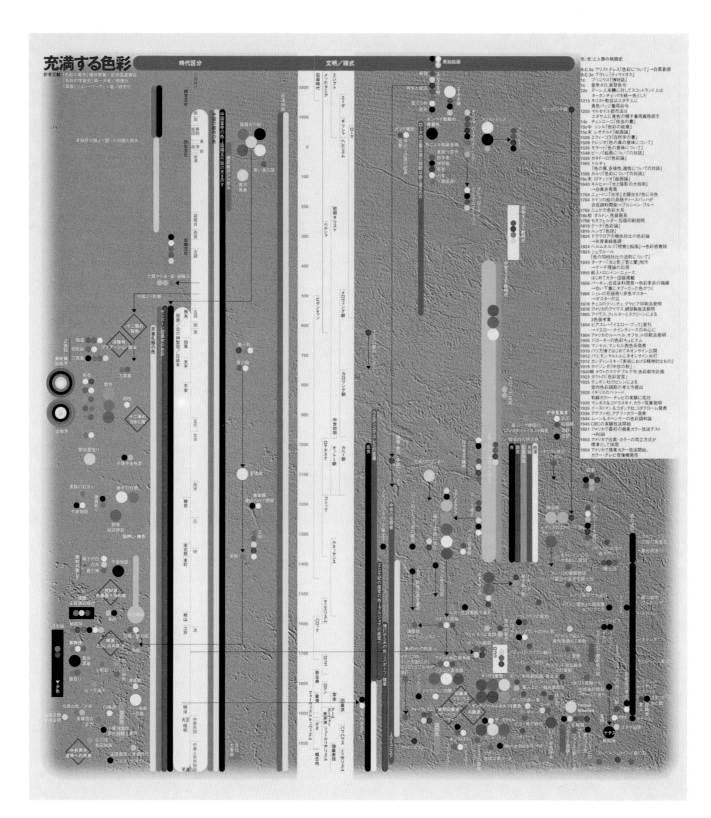

Japan   1998
CD, AD: Yukimasa Matsuda
D: Mayumi Sawachi
CL: INAX Publishing Co., Ltd.

A history of mankind as related to color.
人類の「色彩」に対するこだわりの歴史を色点で構成した図。

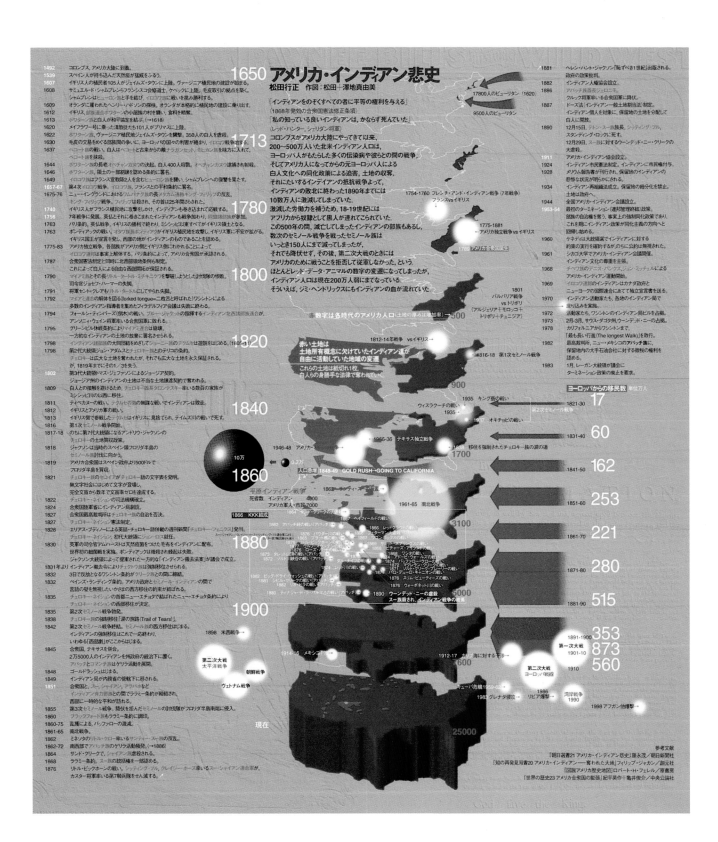

Japan 1998
CD, AD: Yukimasa Matsuda
D: Mayumi Sawachi
CL: INAX Publishing Co., Ltd.

A history map of the U.S.A. showing the invasion by white settlers of the land originally occupied by American Indians.
アメリカ合衆国の歴史を先住民であるアメリカ・インディアン側から見た、白人による北アメリカ侵略の歴史図。

PRODUCT RANGE

NEW PRODUCTS · TELEPHONY · COMPUTERS · SMALL APPLIANCES · AIR-CONDITIONING
PRODUCT EXTENSIONS · WIDESCREEN TV · MULTIMEDIA · DISHWASHERS · FRIDGES
WHITE GOODS · WASHING MACHINES · TVs · VIDEOS · HI-FI
BROWN GOODS

SIMPLE AGREEMENTS
WELCOMING CONVENIENT STORES · CONVENIENT PAYMENT ARRANGEMENTS
FULL SERVICE PROTECTION · EXPERT ADVICE
ABILITY TO CHANGE · UPGRADE OPTION · PROMPT RESPONSE

SERVICE SUPPORT

LONG AND SHORT-TERM HIRE
RENT-TO-OWN
RENT WITH PURCHASE OPTION
HIRE-PURCHASE
ACCESS OPTIONS

Rental provides a choice of products, access options and service support. Future prospects are being enhanced by expanding the choices available to customers, so further increasing Rental's flexibility and broadening its appeal.

1

Cables

Power cables — Medium voltage distribution cables up to 33kV used by Regional Electricity Companies and by industrial users.

General cables — Low voltage cables used in a variety of industrial, commercial and residential applications.

Special cables — Communication, signal conducting and electric cables used in hazardous and demanding environments.

Circuit protection

Medium voltage circuit protection — Products protecting 500v electrical distribution and control circuits from overload including circuit breakers and fused switches.

Low voltage circuit protection and accessories — Products protecting 250v electrical circuits from overload including consumer units and miniature circuit breakers, safety products to protect people from electrocution, and wiring accessories.

Other — Includes the MEM Malaysia range of products, automotive switches, electrical control systems and the repair of electric motors.

Engineering

Plumbing products — Pan-European operations manufacturing and distributing valves for systems used in water and gas supply and for central heating, air conditioning, refrigeration and medical equipment.

Controls and components — Products for the gas supply and appliance markets. Also very high pressure stainless steel fittings, valves and manifolds for use in the petrochemical and process industries and fire fighting products.

Extrusions — Extruded brass and specialised alloy products.

Industrial services

Electric motor repairs and services — Electric motor repairs and supplier of corrosion protective coatings.

Distribution and consumables — Distribution of industrial consumables, electrical products and replacement parts for construction and mining equipment.

Other — Production of high purity electrolytic manganese and manufacture of plumbing and related products.

2

U.K. 1994
CD: Tor Pettersen
CD, AD, D: Jeff Davis
D: Sarah Davies
I: David Baker/David Hunter
DF: Tor Pettersen & Partners Ltd.
CL: Thorn EMI

Diagram showing the three main customer benefits that together make up the Thorn Rentals' offer. Sub rings demonstrate how each benefit is expanding to widen and strengthen Thorn's offer. (1)
ソーン・レンタル社の提案は、
顧客にとって3つの主な利益があることを示した図。
下位のリングは、提案がそれぞれの利益によって
いかに拡大強化されているかを表す。(1)

U.K. 1994
CD: Tor Pettersen
AD, D: David Brown
I: David Hunter
DF: Tor Pettersen & Partners Ltd.
CL: Delta

The chart represents the sales contribution of each business sector, and the delta-shaped bars reflect the company name. (2)
各事業部門の売上げ貢献度を示すチャート。
社名にちなんで、デルタをかたどった
棒グラフを使用した。(2)

Progress towards more sustainable operation:

- Substantial progress made.
- Some management control exercised, data collected.
- Issue not addressed (may not merit high priority), data unavailable.
- Could be outside the control of the business.

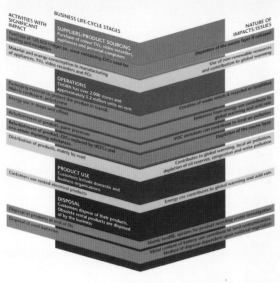

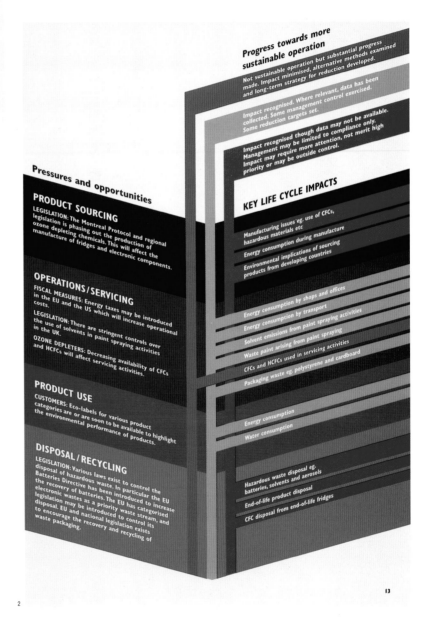

U.K. 1994 (2)/1995 (1)
CD: Tor Pettersen
AD, D: Craig Johnson
I: David Baker
DF: Tor Pettersen & Partners Ltd.
CL: Thorn EMI

Illustrates the progress made, using colour coding, in the key environmental issues of the rental business across the life-cycle of the products and operations.
レンタル・ビジネスにおける製品のライフサイクルと、業務における主な環境問題への取り組み状況を色分けして表したもの。

... OR A WEB OF COLLABORATION ?

The connecting links on this chart represent working business relationships among "competitors" in the U.S. media.

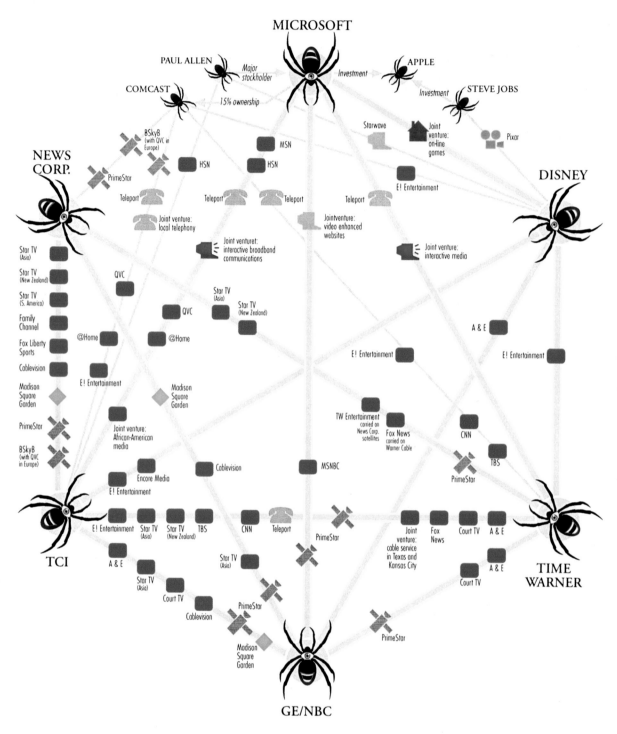

Information correct as of 9/29/97

Notes *1. go here. 2. Notes (bound to be masses of qualifications) go here. 3. masses of qualifications go here. 4. Bound to be masses of qualifications go here. 5. Bound to be qualifications. 6. Bound to be qualifications. 7. Bound to be masses of qualifications go here. 8. Bound to be masses of qualifications go here. 9. Bound to be qualifications. 10. Bound to be masses of qualifications go here. 11. Bound to be masses of qualifications go here.* **Sources:** *Go here. (bound to be masses of qualifications) go here. go here Bound to be masses of qualifications go here Bound to be qualifications Bound to be qualifications Bound to be masses of qualifications go here Bound to be masses of qualifications go here Bound to be qualifications Bound to be masses of qualifications go here Bound to be masses of qualifications go here.*

U.S.A. 1997
AD: Chris Curry
D, I, DF: Nigel Holmes
CL: New Yorker

Connections between six major media companies in the U.S.A., showing that they collaborate as much as they compete.
アメリカの６大メディアの関係図。競争のみでなくコラボレートする関係になっている。

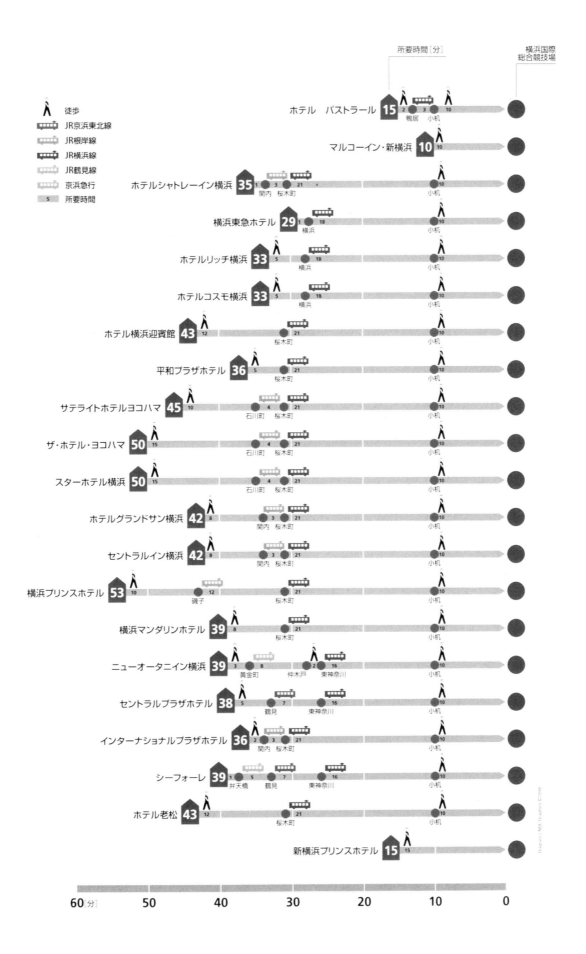

所要時間［分］

横浜国際
総合競技場

徒歩
JR京浜東北線
JR根岸線
JR横浜線
JR鶴見線
京浜急行
5　所要時間

ホテル　パストラール	15		2	鴨居	3	小机	10				
マルコーイン・新横浜	10	10
ホテルシャトレーーイン横浜	35	1 関内	3 桜木町	21	10 小机
横浜東急ホテル	29	1 横浜	18	10 小机
ホテルリッチ横浜	33	5 横浜	18	10 小机
ホテルコスモ横浜	33	5 横浜	18	10 小机
ホテル横浜迎賓館	43	12	桜木町	21	10 小机
平和プラザホテル	36	5 桜木町	21	10 小机
サテライトホテルヨコハマ	45	10 石川町	4 桜木町	21	10 小机
ザ・ホテル・ヨコハマ	50	15 石川町	4 桜木町	21	10 小机
スターホテル横浜	50	15 石川町	4 桜木町	21	10 小机
ホテルグランドサン横浜	42	8 関内	3 桜木町	21	10 小机
セントラルイン横浜	42	8 関内	3 桜木町	21	10 小机
横浜プリンスホテル	53	10 磯子	12 桜木町	21	10 小机
横浜マンダリンホテル	39	8 桜木町	21	10 小机
ニューオータニイン横浜	39	3 黄金町	8 仲木戸	2 東神奈川	16	10 小机
セントラルプラザホテル	38	鶴見	7 東神奈川	16	10 小机
インターナショナルプラザホテル	36	2 関内	3 桜木町	21	10 小机
シーフォーレ	39	1 弁天橋	5 鶴見	7 東神奈川	16	10 小机
ホテル老松	43	12 桜木町	21	10 小机
新横浜プリンスホテル	15	15

60［分］　50　40　30　20　10　0

Japan　1998
AD: Kenzo Nakagawa
D: Satoshi Morikami/Hiromi Maekawa/
　Hiroyuki Inda/Norika Nakayama/Akira Shimizu
I: Hiroyasu Nobuyama
CW: Maki Nakatsuka
DF: NDC Graphics Inc.
CL: Yokohama-shi

From the guidebook for a National Athletic Meet held in Yokohama. A chart indicating the various hotels in which athletes will be staying, and routes and required travel time to the stadium. Arranged by route.

神奈川国体横浜市総合ガイドブックより。
競技に参加する選手たちが宿泊施設から競技会場へ移動するときのルートと所要時間を、ルート別に表している。

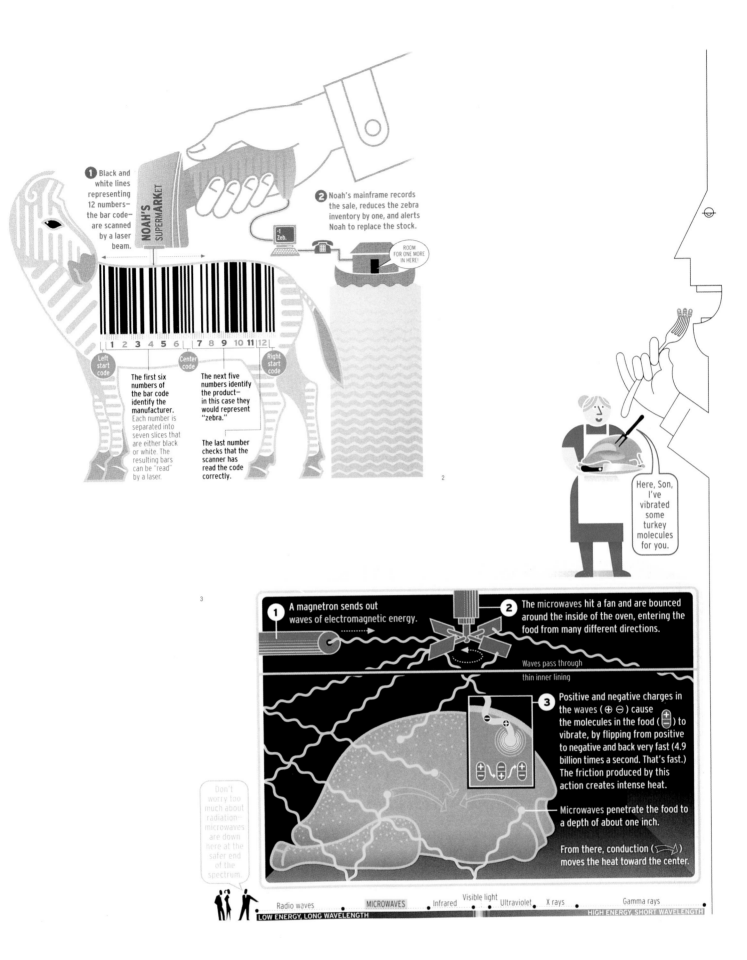

1 Black and white lines representing 12 numbers—the bar code—are scanned by a laser beam.

NOAH'S SUPERMARKET

2 Noah's mainframe records the sale, reduces the zebra inventory by one, and alerts Noah to replace the stock.

-1 Zeb.

ROOM FOR ONE MORE IN HERE!

1 2 3 4 5 6 7 8 9 10 11 12

Left start code

Center code

Right start code

The first six numbers of the bar code identify the manufacturer. Each number is separated into seven slices that are either black or white. The resulting bars can be "read" by a laser.

The next five numbers identify the product—in this case they would represent "zebra."

The last number checks that the scanner has read the code correctly.

2

Here, Son, I've vibrated some turkey molecules for you.

3

1 A magnetron sends out waves of electromagnetic energy.

2 The microwaves hit a fan and are bounced around the inside of the oven, entering the food from many different directions.

Waves pass through

thin inner lining

3 Positive and negative charges in the waves (⊕ ⊖) cause the molecules in the food ( ) to vibrate, by flipping from positive to negative and back very fast (4.9 billion times a second. That's fast.) The friction produced by this action creates intense heat.

Microwaves penetrate the food to a depth of about one inch.

From there, conduction ( ) moves the heat toward the center.

Don't worry too much about radiation—microwaves are down here at the safer end of the spectrum.

Radio waves   MICROWAVES   Infrared   Visible light Ultraviolet   X rays   Gamma rays

LOW ENERGY, LONG WAVELENGTH   HIGH ENERGY SHORT WAVELENGTH

U.S.A.   1997 (2)/1998 (1)(3)
AD: Paul Carstensen
D, I, DF: Nigel Holmes
CW: Nigel Holmes (2)
CL: Attaché

A graphic explanation of how a Bill becomes Law in the U.S.A. Government. (1)
アメリカ政府において、法案が成立し法律となる過程を説明したグラフィック。(1)

Series of diagrams explaining everyday processes: Bar codes, Microwaves. (2)(3)
日常的なテーマを取り上げたシリーズより。バーコード、電子レンジの原理について。(2)(3)

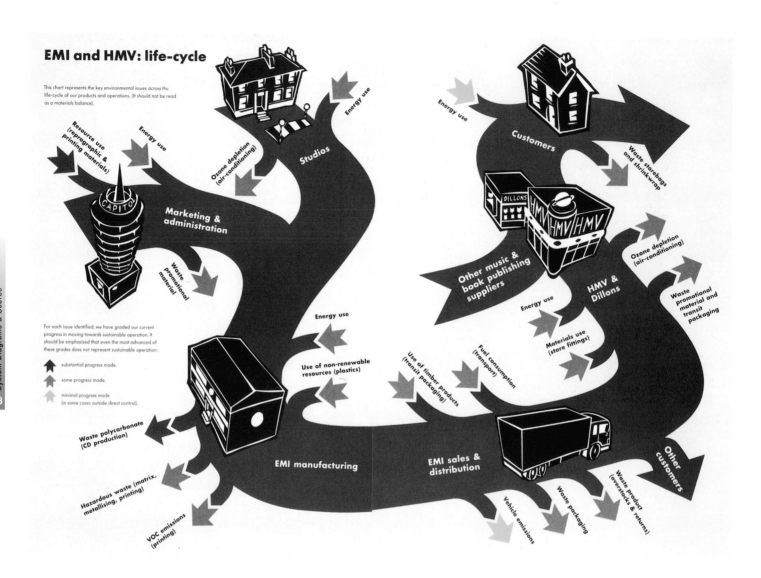

EMI and HMV: life-cycle

This chart represents the key environmental issues across the life-cycle of our products and operations. (It should not be read as a materials balance).

Resource use (reprographic & printing materials)

Energy use

Energy use

Ozone depletion (air-conditioning)

Studios

Energy use

Energy use

Customers

Waste storebags and shrinkwrap

Marketing & administration

Waste promotional material

For each issue identified, we have graded our current progress in moving towards sustainable operation. It should be emphasised that even the most advanced of these grades does not represent sustainable operation:

substantial progress made.

some progress made.

minimal progress made (in some cases outside direct control).

Other music & book publishing suppliers

Ozone depletion (air-conditioning)

Waste promotional material and transit packaging

Energy use

HMV & Dillons

Energy use

Use of non-renewable resources (plastics)

Use of timber products (transit packaging)

Fuel consumption (transport)

Materials use (store fittings)

Waste polycarbonate (CD production)

Other customers

Hazardous waste (matrix, metallising, printing)

EMI manufacturing

EMI sales & distribution

Vehicle emissions

Waste packaging

Waste product (overstocks & returns)

VOC emissions (printing)

U.K. 1996
CD: Tor Pettersen/Jeff Davis
AD, D: Craig Johnson
I: Martina Farrow/David Baker
DF: Tor Pettersen & Partners Ltd.
CL: Thorn EMI

Illustration detailing the progress towards sustainable operation in the music business, across the life cycle of products and operation, in key environmental areas. Colour-coded arrows reflect degrees of progress made, resources used, and emissions/waste.
音楽業界の製品のライフサイクルや業務における、主な環境問題に対する持続可能な取り組みの進行状況を図解した。色分けされた矢印は、進行の程度、使用されたリソース、排出／廃棄されたものを表している。

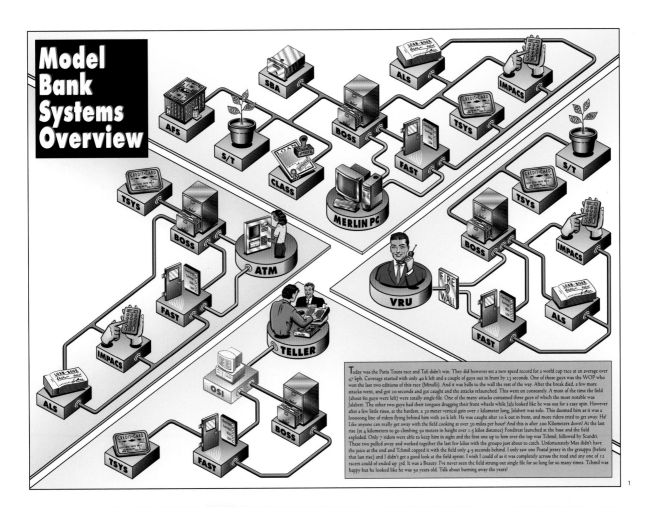

U.S.A. 1999
CD, D: Scott MacNeill
AD: Diane Hunt
DF: MacNeill & Macintosh
CL: Nations Bank, U.S.A.

*A poster for training customer representatives
at Nations Bank. This diagram shows four
different ways a customer can use a complete range
of banking services without actually visiting a bank.* (1)

Nation Bankの窓口係を教育するためのポスター。顧客が銀行に足を運ぶことなく、
あらゆるバンキング・サービスを利用するための４つの方法を図解している。(1)

U.S.A. 1997
AD: Susan Yousem
D, I: Scott MacNeill
DF: MacNeill & Macintosh
CL: Fidelity Investments

*Artwork showing the costs
of different home improvements
typical for U.S.A. homeowners.* (2)

アメリカの住宅所有者にとって
平均的な家の修繕コストを表している。(2)

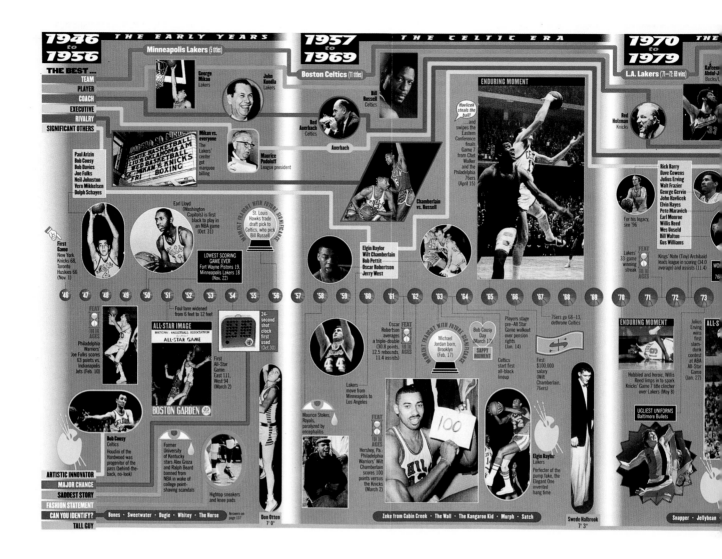

1946 to 1956 — THE EARLY YEARS

Minneapolis Lakers (5 titles)

THE BEST ...
- TEAM
- PLAYER
- COACH
- EXECUTIVE
- RIVALRY
- SIGNIFICANT OTHERS

George Mikan — Lakers
John Kundla — Lakers

Mikan vs. everyone — The Lakers' center got marquee billing

Maurice Podoloff — League president

Paul Arizin
Bob Cousy
Bob Davies
Joe Fulks
Neil Johnston
Vern Mikkelsen
Dolph Schayes

First Game — New York Knicks 68, Toronto Huskies 66 (Nov. 1)

Earl Lloyd (Washington Capitols) is first black to play in an NBA game (Oct. 31)

St. Louis Hawks trade draft pick to Celtics, who pick Bill Russell

MOMENT FREIGHT WITH FUTURE SIGNIFICANCE

LOWEST SCORING GAME EVER — Fort Wayne Pistons 19, Minneapolis Lakers 18 (Nov. 22)

'46 '47 '48 '49 '50 '51 '52 '53 '54 '55 '56

FEAT FOR THE AGES

Philadelphia Warriors' Joe Fulks scores 63 points vs. Indianapolis Jets (Feb. 10)

Foul lane widened from 6 feet to 12 feet

ALL-STAR IMAGE — NATIONAL BASKETBALL ASSOCIATION — ALL-STAR GAME

First All-Star Game: East 111, West 94 (March 2)

24-second shot clock first used (Oct. 30)

BOSTON GARDEN

ARTISTIC INNOVATOR
Bob Cousy — Celtics — Houdini of the Hardwood was progenitor of the pass (behind-the-back, no-look)

MAJOR CHANGE
Former University of Kentucky stars Alex Groza and Ralph Beard banned from NBA in wake of college point-shaving scandals

SADDEST STORY
Hightop sneakers and knee pads

FASHION STATEMENT

CAN YOU IDENTIFY?
Bones · Sweetwater · Dugie · Whitey · The Horse
Answers on page 137

TALL GUY
Don Otten 7' 0"

1957 to 1969 — THE CELTIC ERA

Boston Celtics (11 titles)

Bill Russell — Celtics

Red Auerbach — Celtics

Auerbach

Chamberlain vs. Russell

Elgin Baylor
Wilt Chamberlain
Bob Pettit
Oscar Robertson
Jerry West

'57 '58 '59 '60 '61 '62 '63 '64 '65 '66 '67 '68 '69

Oscar Robertson averages a triple-double (30.8 points, 12.5 rebounds, 11.4 assists)

FEAT FOR THE AGES

Michael Jordan born, Brooklyn (Feb. 17)

SAPPY MOMENT

Bob Cousy Day (March 17)

Players stage pre-All Star Game walkout over pension rights (Jan. 14)

76ers go 68–13, dethrone Celtics

Celtics start first all-black lineup

First $100,000 salary (Wilt Chamberlain, 76ers)

MOMENT FREIGHT WITH FUTURE SIGNIFICANCE

Lakers move from Minneapolis to Los Angeles

Maurice Stokes, Royals, paralyzed by encephalitis

FEAT FOR THE AGES

Hershey, Pa.: Philadelphia Warriors' Wilt Chamberlain scores 100 points versus the Knicks (March 2)

Elgin Baylor — Lakers — Perfecter of the pump fake, the Elegant One invented hang time

UGLIEST UNIFORMS — Baltimore Bullets

Swede Halbrook 7' 3"

Zeke from Cabin Creek · The Wall · The Kangaroo Kid · Murph · Satch

ENDURING MOMENT
Havlicek steals the ball! ...and swipes the Eastern Conference finals' Game 7 from Chet Walker and the Philadelphia 76ers (April 15)

1970 to 1979 — THE

L.A. Lakers (71–72: 69 wins)

Kareem Abdul-J... — Bucks/L...

Red Holzman — Knicks

Rick Barry
Dave Cowens
Julius Erving
Walt Frazier
George Gervin
John Havlicek
Elvin Hayes
Pete Maravich
Earl Monroe
Willis Reed
Wes Unseld
Gus Williams

For his legacy, see '96

Lakers' 33-game winning streak

FEAT FOR THE AGES

Kings' Nate (Tiny) Archibald leads league in scoring (34.0 average) and assists (11.4)

WO...

'70 '71 '72 '73

ENDURING MOMENT
Hobbled and heroic, Willis Reed limps in to spark Knicks' Game 7 title clincher over Lakers (May 8)

Julius Erving wins first slam dunk contest at ABA All-Star Game (Jan. 27)

ALL-S...

Snapper · Jellybean

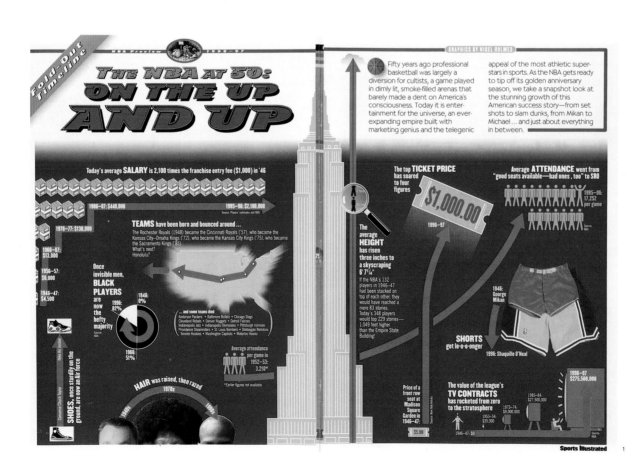

GRAPHICS BY NIGEL HOLMES

Fold-Out Timeline

NBA Preview 1996–97

THE NBA AT 50: ON THE UP AND UP

Fifty years ago professional basketball was largely a diversion for cultists, a game played in dimly lit, smoke-filled arenas that barely made a dent on America's consciousness. Today it is entertainment for the universe, an ever-expanding empire built with marketing genius and the telegenic appeal of the most athletic superstars in sports. As the NBA gets ready to tip off its golden anniversary season, we take a snapshot look at the stunning growth of this American success story—from set shots to slam dunks, from Mikan to Michael ... and just about everything in between.

Today's average **SALARY** is 2,100 times the franchise entry fee ($1,000) in '46

1986–87: $440,000
1995–96: $2,100,000
Source: Players' estimates and NBA

1976–77: $130,000
1966–67: $13,000
1956–57: $6,000
1946–47: $4,500

TEAMS have been born and bounced around ...
The Rochester Royals (1948) became the Cincinnati Royals ('57), who became the Kansas City–Omaha Kings ('72), who became the Kansas City Kings ('75), who became the Sacramento Kings ('85). What's next? Honolulu?

Once invisible men, **BLACK PLAYERS** are now the hefty majority
Source: NBA
1996: 82%
1946: 0%
1968: 51%

...and some teams died
Anderson Packers · Baltimore Bullets · Chicago Stags
Cleveland Rebels · Denver Nuggets · Detroit Falcons
Indianapolis Jets · Indianapolis Olympians · Pittsburgh Ironmen
Providence Steamrollers · St. Louis Bombers · Sheboygan Redskins
Toronto Huskies · Washington Capitols · Waterloo Hawks

Average attendance per game in 1952–53: 3,210*
*Earlier figures not available

SHOES, once sturdily on the ground, are now an Air force
Converse Chuck Taylor

HAIR was raised, then razed
1870s

The top **TICKET PRICE** has soared to four figures
$1,000.00
1996–97

Average **ATTENDANCE** went from "good seats available—bad ones, too" to SRO
1995–96: 17,252 per game
Source: NBA

The average **HEIGHT** has risen three inches to a skyscraping 6'7¼"
If the NBA's 132 players in 1946–47 had been stacked on top of each other, they would have reached a mere 83 stories. Today's 348 players would top 229 stories—1,049 feet higher than the Empire State Building!

1946: George Mikan

SHORTS got lo-o-o-onger
1996: Shaquille O'Neal

Price of a front row seat at Madison Square Garden in 1946–47: $5.00

The value of the league's **TV CONTRACTS** has rocketed from zero to the stratosphere
1953–54: $39,000
1946–47: $0
1973–74: $9,000,000
1983–84: $27,500,000
1995–96: $275,500,000
Source: NBA

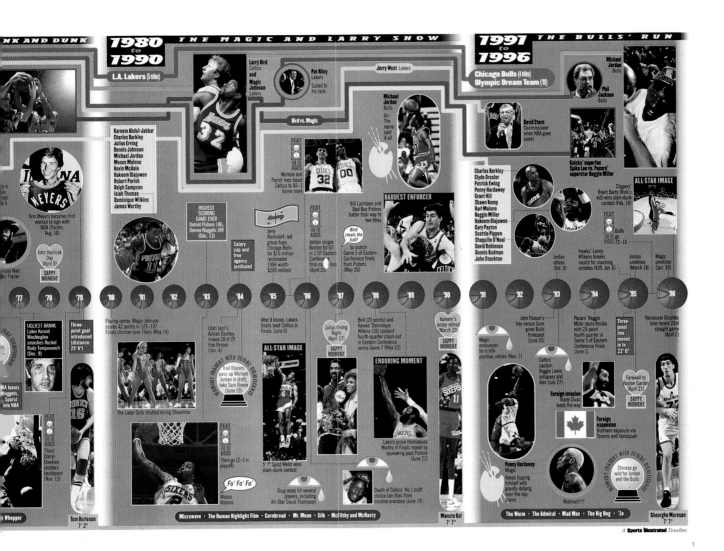

U.S.A.   1996 (1) / 1997 (2)
CD: Steve Hoffman
D, I, DF: Nigel Holmes
CW: Nigel Holmes (2)
CL: Sports Illustrated

Fold-out time-line showing 50 years of basketball in the U.S.A. (1)
アメリカのバスケットボール史50年を年代別に図解した雑誌の折り込みページ。(1)

From a regular column showing aspects of different sports.
This column on cycling includes a course profile of the Tour de France. (2)
さまざまなスポーツを特集する連載記事より。サイクリングに関するこの記事は、ツール・ド・フランスのコースについて説明している。(2)

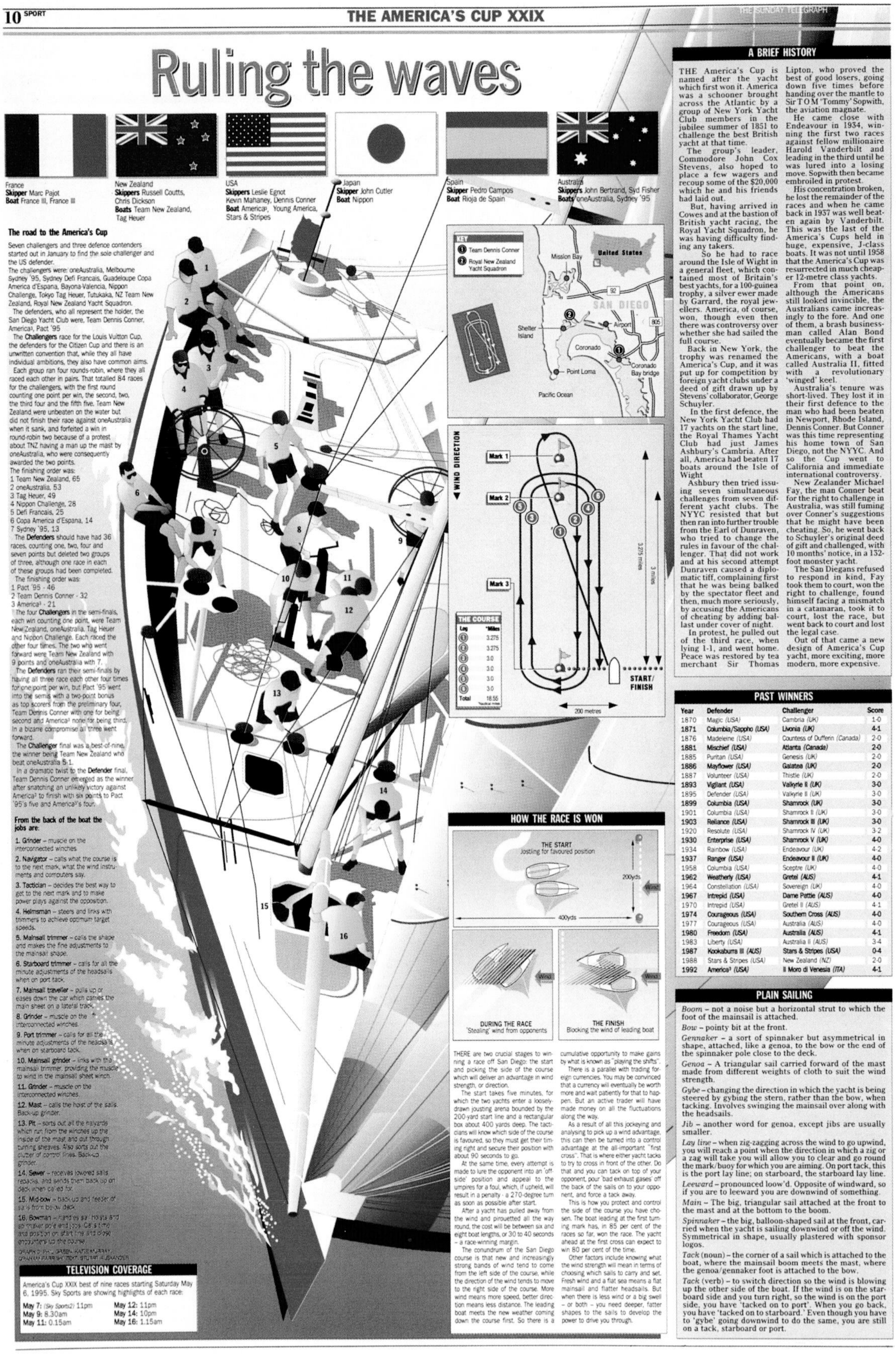

10 SPORT — THE AMERICA'S CUP XXIX — THE SUNDAY TELEGRAPH

Ruling the waves

France
Skipper Marc Pajot
Boat France III, France III

New Zealand
Skippers Russell Coutts, Chris Dickson
Boats Team New Zealand, Tag Heuer

USA
Skippers Leslie Egnot, Kevin Mahaney, Dennis Conner
Boat America³, Young America, Stars & Stripes

Japan
Skipper John Cutler
Boat Nippon

Spain
Skipper Pedro Campos
Boat Rioja de Spain

Australia
Skippers John Bertrand, Syd Fisher
Boats oneAustralia, Sydney '95

The road to the America's Cup

Seven challengers and three defence contenders started out in January to find the sole challenger and the US defender.
The challengers were: oneAustralia, Melbourne Sydney '95, Sydney Defi Francais, Guadeloupe Copa America d'Espana, Bayona-Valencia, Nippon Challenge, Tokyo Tag Heuer, Tutukaka, NZ Team New Zealand, Royal New Zealand Yacht Squadron.

The defenders, who all represent the holder, the San Diego Yacht Club were, Team Dennis Conner, America³, Pact '95

The **Challengers** race for the Louis Vuitton Cup, the defenders for the Citizen Cup and there is an unwritten convention that, while they all have individual ambitions, they also have common aims.

Each group ran four rounds-robin, where they all raced each other in pairs. That totalled 84 races for the challengers, with the first round counting one point per win, the second, two, the third four and the fifth five. Team New Zealand were unbeaten on the water but did not finish their race against oneAustralia when it sank, and forfeited a win in round-robin two because of a protest about TNZ having a man up the mast by oneAustralia, who were consequently awarded the two points.
The finishing order was:
1 Team New Zealand, 65
2 oneAustralia, 53
3 Tag Heuer, 49
4 Nippon Challenge, 28
5 Defi Francais, 25
6 Copa America d'Espana, 14
7 Sydney '95, 13

The **Defenders** should have had 36 races, counting one, two, four and seven points but deleted two groups of three, although one race in each of these groups had been completed.

The finishing order was:
1 Pact '95 - 46
2 Team Dennis Conner - 32
3 America³ - 21

The four **Challengers** in the semi-finals, each win counting one point, were Team New Zealand, oneAustralia, Tag Heuer and Nippon Challenge. Each raced the other four times. The two who went forward were Team New Zealand with 9 points and oneAustralia with 7.

The **Defenders** ran their semi-finals by having all three race each other four times for one point per win, but Pact '95 went into the semis with a two-point bonus as top scorers from the preliminary four, Team Dennis Conner with one for being second and America³ none for being third. In a bizarre compromise all three went forward.

The **Challenger** final was a best-of-nine, the winner being Team New Zealand who beat oneAustralia 5-1.

In a dramatic twist to the **Defender** final, Team Dennis Conner emerged as the winner after snatching an unlikely victory against America³ to finish with six points to Pact '95's five and America³'s four.

From the back of the boat the jobs are:

1. **Grinder** – muscle on the interconnected winches.
2. **Navigator** – calls what the course is to the next mark, what the wind instruments and computers say.
3. **Tactician** – decides the best way to get to the next mark and to make power plays against the opposition.
4. **Helmsman** – steers and links with trimmers to achieve optimum target speeds.
5. **Mainsail trimmer** – calls the shape and makes the fine adjustments to the mainsail shape.
6. **Starboard trimmer** – calls for all the minute adjustments of the headsails when on port tack.
7. **Mainsail traveller** – pulls up or eases down the car which carries the main sheet on a lateral track.
8. **Grinder** – muscle on the interconnected winches.
9. **Port trimmer** – calls for all the minute adjustments of the headsails when on starboard tack.
10. **Mainsail grinder** – links with the mainsail trimmer, providing the muscle to wind in the mainsail sheet winch.
11. **Grinder** – muscle on the interconnected winches.
12. **Mast** – calls the hoist of the sails. Back-up grinder.
13. **Pit** – sorts out all the halyards which run from the winches up the inside of the mast and out through turning sheaves. Also sorts out the clutter of control lines. Back-up grinder.
14. **Sewer** – receives lowered sails, repacks, and sends them back up on deck when called for.
15. **Mid-bow** – back-up and feeder of sails from below deck.
16. **Bowman** – handles sail hoists and spinnaker pole end jobs. Calls time and position on start line and close encounters up the course.

TELEVISION COVERAGE

America's Cup XXIX best of nine races starting Saturday May 6, 1995. Sky Sports are showing highlights of each race:

May 7: (Sky Sports2) 11pm
May 9: 8.30am
May 11: 0.15am
May 12: 11pm
May 14: 10pm
May 16: 1.15am

KEY
1 Team Dennis Conner
2 Royal New Zealand Yacht Squadron
Mission Bay
United States
SAN DIEGO
Airport
Shelter Island
Coronado
Coronado Bay bridge
Point Loma
Pacific Ocean
WIND DIRECTION
Mark 1
Mark 2
Mark 3
START/ FINISH
3.275 miles
3 miles
200 metres

THE COURSE Leg	*Miles
1	3.275
2	3.275
3	3.0
4	3.0
5	3.0
6	3.0
Total	18.55

*Nautical miles

HOW THE RACE IS WON

THE START
Jostling for favoured position
200yds
400yds
Wind
DURING THE RACE
'Stealing' wind from opponents
THE FINISH
Blocking the wind of leading boat

THERE are two crucial stages to winning a race off San Diego: the start and picking the side of the course which will deliver an advantage in wind strength, or direction.

The start takes five minutes, for which the two yachts enter a loosely-drawn jousting arena bounded by the 200-yard start line and a rectangular box about 400 yards deep. The tacticians will know which side of the course is favoured, so they must get their timing right and secure their position with about 90 seconds to go.

At the same time, every attempt is made to lure the opponent into an 'off-side' position and appeal to the umpires for a foul, which, if upheld, will result in a penalty - a 270-degree turn as soon as possible after start.

After a yacht has pulled away from the wind and pirouetted all the way round, the cost will be between six and eight boat lengths, or 30 to 40 seconds – a race-winning margin.

The conundrum of the San Diego course is that new and increasingly strong bands of wind tend to come from the left side of the course, while the direction of the wind tends to move to the right side of the course. More wind means more speed, better direction means less distance. The leading boat meets the new weather coming down the course first. So there is a cumulative opportunity to make gains by what is known as "playing the shifts".

There is a parallel with trading foreign currencies. You may be convinced that a currency will eventually be worth more and wait patiently for that to happen. But an active trader will have made money on all the fluctuations along the way.

As a result of all this jockeying and analysing to pick up a wind advantage, this can then be turned into a control advantage at the all-important "first cross". That is where either yacht tacks to try to cross in front of the other. Do that and you can tack on top of your opponent, pour 'bad exhaust gases' off the back of the sails on to your opponent, and force a tack away.

This is how you protect and control the side of the course you have chosen. The boat leading at the first turning mark has, in 85 per cent of the races so far, won the race. The yacht ahead at the first cross can expect to win 80 per cent of the time.

Other factors include knowing what the wind strength will mean in terms of choosing which sails to carry and set. Fresh wind and a flat sea means a flat mainsail and flatter headsails. But when there is less wind or a big swell – or both – you need deeper, fatter shapes to the sails to develop the power to drive you through.

A BRIEF HISTORY

THE America's Cup is named after the yacht which first won it. America was a schooner brought across the Atlantic by a group of New York Yacht Club members in the jubilee summer of 1851 to challenge the best British yacht at that time.

The group's leader, Commodore John Cox Stevens, also hoped to place a few wagers and recoup some of the $20,000 which he and his friends had laid out.

But, having arrived in Cowes and at the bastion of British yacht racing, the Royal Yacht Squadron, he was having difficulty finding any takers.

So he had to race around the Isle of Wight in a general fleet, which contained most of Britain's best yachts, for a 100-guinea trophy, a silver ewer made by Garrard, the royal jewellers. America, of course, won, though even then there was controversy over whether she had sailed the full course.

Back in New York, the trophy was renamed the America's Cup, and it was put up for competition by foreign yacht clubs under a deed of gift drawn up by Stevens' collaborator, George Schuyler.

In the first defence, the New York Yacht Club had 17 yachts on the start line, the Royal Thames Yacht Club had just James Ashbury's Cambria. After all, America had beaten 17 boats around the Isle of Wight.

Ashbury then tried issuing seven simultaneous challenges from seven different yacht clubs. The NYYC resisted that but then ran into further trouble from the Earl of Dunraven, who tried to change the rules in favour of the challenger. That did not work and at his second attempt Dunraven caused a diplomatic tiff, complaining first that he was being balked by the spectator fleet and then, much more seriously, by accusing the Americans of cheating by adding ballast under cover of night.

In protest, he pulled out of the third race, when lying 1-1, and went home. Peace was restored by tea merchant Sir Thomas Lipton, who proved the best of good losers, going down five times before handing over the mantle to Sir T O M 'Tommy' Sopwith, the aviation magnate.

He came close with Endeavour in 1934, winning the first two races against fellow millionaire Harold Vanderbilt and leading in the third until he was lured into a losing move. Sopwith then became embroiled in protest.

His concentration broken, he lost the remainder of the races and when he came back in 1937 was well beaten again by Vanderbilt. This was the last of the America's Cups held in huge, expensive, J-class boats. It was not until 1958 that the America's Cup was resurrected in much cheaper 12-metre class yachts.

From that point on, although the Americans still looked invincible, the Australians came increasingly to the fore. And one of them, a brash businessman called Alan Bond eventually became the first challenger to beat the Americans, with a boat called Australia II, fitted with a revolutionary 'winged' keel.

Australia's tenure was short-lived. They lost it in their first defence to the man who had been beaten in Newport, Rhode Island, Dennis Conner. But Conner was this time representing his home town of San Diego, not the NYYC. And so the Cup went to California and immediate international controversy.

New Zealander Michael Fay, the man Conner beat for the right to challenge in Australia, was still fuming over Conner's suggestions that he might have been cheating. So, he went back to Schuyler's original deed of gift and challenged, with 10 months' notice, in a 132-foot monster yacht.

The San Diegans refused to respond in kind, Fay took them to court, won the right to challenge, found himself facing a mismatch in a catamaran, took it to court, lost the race, but went back to court and lost the legal case.

Out of that came a new design of America's Cup yacht, more exciting, more modern, more expensive.

PAST WINNERS

Year	Defender	Challenger	Score
1870	Magic (USA)	Cambria (UK)	1-0
1871	Columbia/Sappho (USA)	Livonia (UK)	4-1
1876	Madeleine (USA)	Countess of Dufferin (Canada)	2-0
1881	Mischief (USA)	Atlanta (Canada)	2-0
1885	Puritan (USA)	Genesis (UK)	2-0
1886	Mayflower (USA)	Galatea (UK)	2-0
1887	Volunteer (USA)	Thistle (UK)	2-0
1893	Vigilant (USA)	Valkyrie II (UK)	3-0
1895	Defender (USA)	Valkyrie II (UK)	3-0
1899	Columbia (USA)	Shamrock (UK)	3-0
1901	Columbia (USA)	Shamrock II (UK)	3-0
1903	Reliance (USA)	Shamrock III (UK)	3-0
1920	Resolute (USA)	Shamrock IV (UK)	3-2
1930	Enterprise (USA)	Shamrock V (UK)	4-0
1934	Rainbow (USA)	Endeavour (UK)	4-2
1937	Ranger (USA)	Endeavour II (UK)	4-0
1958	Columbia (USA)	Sceptre (UK)	4-0
1962	Weatherly (USA)	Gretel (AUS)	4-1
1964	Constellation (USA)	Sovereign (UK)	4-0
1967	Intrepid (USA)	Dame Pattie (AUS)	4-0
1970	Intrepid (USA)	Gretel II (AUS)	4-1
1974	Courageous (USA)	Southern Cross (AUS)	4-0
1977	Courageous (USA)	Australia (AUS)	4-0
1980	Freedom (USA)	Australia (AUS)	4-1
1983	Liberty (USA)	Australia II (AUS)	3-4
1987	Kookaburra III (AUS)	Stars & Stripes (USA)	0-4
1988	Stars & Stripes (USA)	New Zealand (NZ)	2-0
1992	America³ (USA)	Il Moro di Venesia (ITA)	4-1

PLAIN SAILING

Boom – not a noise but a horizontal strut to which the foot of the mainsail is attached.

Bow – pointy bit at the front.

Gennaker – a sort of spinnaker but asymmetrical in shape, attached, like a genoa, to the bow or the end of the spinnaker pole close to the deck.

Genoa – A triangular sail carried forward of the mast made from different weights of cloth to suit the wind strength.

Gybe – changing the direction in which the yacht is being steered by gybing the stern, rather than the bow, when tacking. Involves swinging the mainsail over along with the headsails.

Jib – another word for genoa, except jibs are usually smaller.

Lay line – when zig-zagging across the wind to go upwind, you will reach a point when the direction in which a zig or a zag will take you will allow you to clear and go round the mark/buoy for which you are aiming. On port tack, this is the port lay line; on starboard, the starboard lay line.

Leeward – pronounced loow'd. Opposite of windward, so if you are to leeward you are downwind of something.

Main – The big, triangular sail attached at the front to the mast and at the bottom to the boom.

Spinnaker – the big, balloon-shaped sail at the front, carried when the yacht is sailing downwind or off the wind. Symmetrical in shape, usually plastered with sponsor logos.

Tack (noun) – the corner of a sail which is attached to the boat, where the mainsail boom meets the mast, where the genoa/gennaker foot is attached to the bow.

Tack (verb) – to switch direction so the wind is blowing up the other side of the boat. If the wind is on the starboard side and you turn right, so the wind is on the port side, you have 'tacked on to port'. When you go back, you have 'tacked on to starboard.' Even though you have to 'gybe' going downwind to do the same, you are still on a tack, starboard or port.

U.K. 1995
Graphics Editor: Phillip J Green
Graphics Artists: Katie Murray/Grapham Parish
CL: The Sunday Telegraph

Graphic explaining the job of each crew member, a location map, race map, and the tactics used by competing teams.
ヨットレースにおける各クルーの仕事、開催地マップ、コース・マップおよび他チームの戦略について図解。

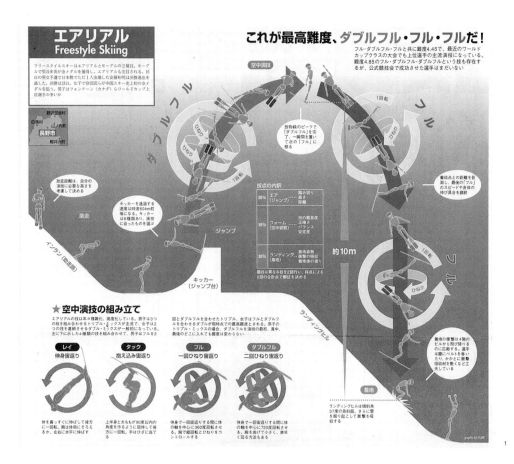

エアリアル
Freestyle Skiing

フリースタイルスキーはエアリアルとモーグルの2種目。モーグルで里谷多英が金メダルを獲得し、エアリアルも注目される。16日の男女予選で日本勢は決勝進出を逃した。決勝は18日。女子で徐囲ら中国スキー史上初の金メダルを狙う。男子はフォンテーン（カナダ）らワールドカップ上位選手の争いか

これが最高難度、ダブルフル・フル・フルだ！

フル・ダブルフル・フルと共に難度4.45で、最近のワールドカップクラスの大会でも上位選手の主流演技になっている。難度4.85のフル・ダブルフル・ダブルフルという技も存在するが、公式競技会で成功させた選手はまだいない

空中演技

ダブルフル　フル

フル

放物線のピークで「ダブルフル」を完了、一瞬間を置いて次の「フル」に移る

約10m

助走距離は、自分の演技に必要な高さを考慮して決める

キッカーを通過する速度は時速60km前後になる。キッカーは6種類あり、演技に合ったものを選ぶ

着地点との距離を目測し、最後の「フル」のスピードや身体の伸び具合を調節

採点の内訳

20%	エア（ジャンプ）	踏み切り 高さ 距離
50%	フォーム（空中姿勢）	技の難易度 正確さ バランス 安定度
30%	ランディング（着地）	着地姿勢 衝撃の吸収 着地後の滑り

競技は異なる技を2回行い、採点による2回の合計点で順位を決める

助走

インラン（助走路）

キッカー（ジャンプ台）

ランディングヒル

着地

着地の衝撃は4階のビルから飛び降りるのに匹敵する。選手は腰にベルトを巻いたり、かかとに衝撃吸収材を敷くなど工夫している

ランディングヒルは傾斜角37度の急斜面。さらに雪を掘り起こして衝撃を緩和する

ランディングヒルは傾斜角37度の急斜面。さらに雪を掘り起こして衝撃を緩和する

★空中演技の組み立て

エアリアルの技は年々複雑化、高度化している。男子は3つの技を組み合わせるトリプル・ミックスが主流で、女子は2つの技を連続させるダブル・ミックスが一般的になっている。主に下に示した4種類の技を組み合わせ、男子はフルを2

| レイ | タック | フル | ダブルフル |
| 伸身宙返り | 抱え込み宙返り | 一回ひねり宙返り | 二回ひねり宙返り |

体を真っすぐに伸ばして後方に一回転。腕は体側にそろえるか、左右に水平に伸ばす

上半身と太ももが90度以内の角度をたもつように屈伸して後方に一回転。手はひざに当てる

伸身で一回宙返りする間に体の軸を中心に360度回転させる。腕は縦回転とひねりをコントロールする

伸身で一回宙返りする間に体の軸を中心に720度回転させる。胸を曲げて小さく、素早く回る方法もある

graphic by TUBE

1

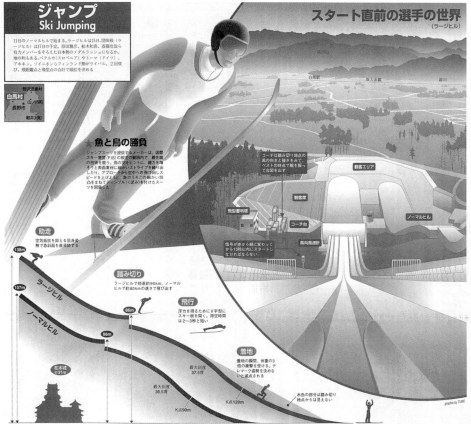

ジャンプ
Ski Jumping

11日のノーマルヒルで始まる。ラージヒルは15日、団体戦（ラージヒル）は17日の予定。原田雅彦、船木和喜、斎藤浩哉ら有力メンバーをそろえた日本のメダルラッシュになるか。地の利もある。ペテルカ（スロベニア）やトーマ（ドイツ）、アホネン、ソイニネンらフィンランド勢がライバル。2回飛び、飛距離点と飛型点の合計で順位を決める

スタート直前の選手の世界
（ラージヒル）

魚と鳥の勝負

ジャンプスーツを提供するメーカーは、国際スキー連盟（FIS）の規定の範囲内で、最大限の技術を競う。魚の羽をヒントに、揚力を生み出そうと素材を縦に細かいストライプを織り出したり、アプローチから空中への飛び出しにスピードを上げるよう、魚のうろこの細かい凹凸をまねてディンプル（くぼみ）を付けたスーツを開発など

助走
空気抵抗を抑える屈身姿勢で急斜面を直滑降する

踏み切り
ラージヒルで時速90km、ノーマルヒルで約80kmの速さで飛び出す

飛行
浮力を得るためにV字型にスキー板を開く。滞空時間は2〜3秒と短い

着地
着地の瞬間、体重の3倍の衝撃を受ける。テレマーク姿勢を決めるかどうかなど減点される

コーチは踏み切り地点の風の向きと強さをみて、ベストの時点で腕を振って合図を出す

信号が赤から緑に変わってから15秒以内にスタートしなければならない

観客エリア

観客席

飛型審判塔

飛型審判塔

コーチ台

風向風速計

ノーマルヒル

ラージヒル
138m

107m

ノーマルヒル

86m

66m

水色の部分は踏み切り地点からは見えない

最大斜度 37.5度

最大斜度 36.5度

K点120m

K点90m

松本城 約31m

graphic by TUBE

2

Japan 1998
CD: Hiroyuki Kimura
D: Ryu Sato
DF: Tube Graphics
CL: The Shinano Mainichi Shimbun

Illustrations showing the movements of athletes competing in the Freestyle Skiing "Aerial" event of the Nagano Winter Olympics. Moves that are commonly undertaken are also identified and explained. (1)

長野冬季オリンピックで「エアリアル」の技を披露する選手の動きと、技の名称を具体的に図解。(1)

View from the Ski Jumping starting platform, as seen by athletes competing in said event in the Nagano Winter Olympics. (2)

長野冬季オリンピックの「ジャンプ」で競技する選手たちがスタート台から見る景色を図解。(2)

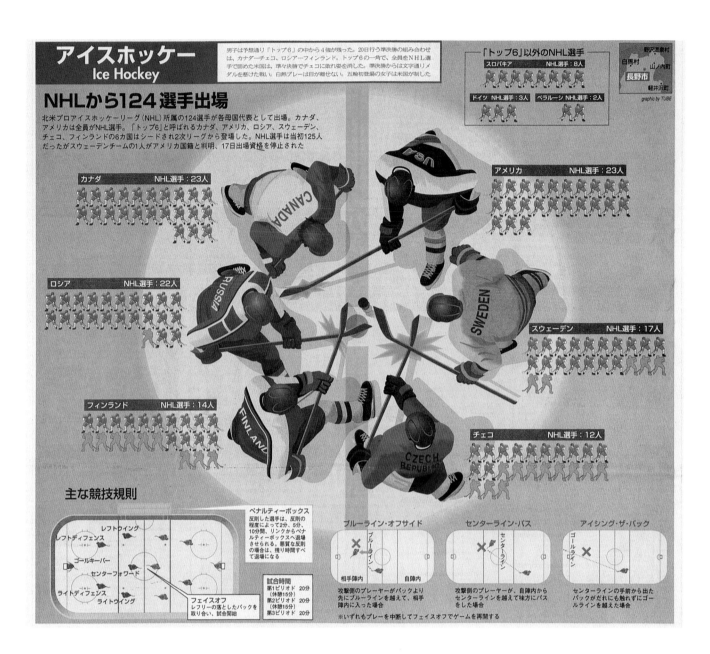

アイスホッケー
Ice Hockey

男子は予想通り「トップ6」の中から4強が残った。20日行う準決勝の組み合わせは、カナダ―チェコ、ロシア―フィンランド。トップ6の一角で、全員をNHL選手で固めた米国は、準々決勝でチェコに敗れ姿を消した。準決勝からは文字通りメダルを懸けた戦い。白熱プレーは目が離せない。五輪初登場の女子は米国が制した

NHLから124選手出場

北米プロアイスホッケーリーグ（NHL）所属の124選手が各母国代表として出場。カナダ、アメリカは全員がNHL選手。「トップ6」と呼ばれるカナダ、アメリカ、ロシア、スウェーデン、チェコ、フィンランドの6カ国はシードされ2次リーグから登場した。NHL選手は当初125人だったがスウェーデンチームの1人がアメリカ国籍と判明、17日出場資格を停止された

「トップ6」以外のNHL選手

| スロバキア | NHL選手：8人 |
| ドイツ　NHL選手：3人 | ベラルーシ　NHL選手：2人 |

野沢温泉村
白馬村　山ノ内町
長野市
軽井沢町

graphic by TUBE

カナダ	NHL選手：23人
アメリカ	NHL選手：23人
ロシア	NHL選手：22人
スウェーデン	NHL選手：17人
フィンランド	NHL選手：14人
チェコ	NHL選手：12人

主な競技規則

レフトウイング
レフトディフェンス
ゴールキーパー
センターフォワード
ライトディフェンス
ライトウイング

フェイスオフ
レフリーの落としたパックを取り合い、試合開始

ペナルティーボックス
反則した選手は、反則の程度によって2分、5分、10分間、リンクからペナルティーボックスへ退場させられる。悪質な反則の場合は、残り時間すべて退場になる

試合時間
第1ピリオド　20分
（休憩15分）
第2ピリオド　20分
（休憩15分）
第3ピリオド　20分

ブルーライン・オフサイド
ブルーライン
相手陣内　　自陣内
攻撃側のプレーヤーがパックより先にブルーラインを越えて、相手陣内に入った場合

センターライン・パス
センターライン
攻撃側のプレーヤーが、自陣内からセンターラインを越えて味方にパスをした場合

アイシング・ザ・バック
ゴールライン
センターラインの手前から出たパックがだれにも触れずにゴールラインを越えた場合

※いずれもプレーを中断してフェイスオフでゲームを再開する

Japan　1998
CD: Hiroyuki Kimura
D: Nozomi Hatakeyama
DF: Tube Graphics
CL: The Shinano Mainichi Shimbun

Illustration showing the number of NHL players competing as members of their home country's Men's Ice Hockey team, in the 1998 Nagano Winter Olympics.

長野冬季オリンピックの「アイスホッケー（男子）」に各国代表として出場した、NHL（北米プロアイスホッケーリーグ）所属選手の数を国別に表したグラフと、主な競技規則を図解した主題図。

クロスカントリー
Cross-Country Skiing

男子はビョルン・ダーリらノルウェー勢が強い。女子はエレーナ・ビャルベ（ロシア）、ステファーニア・ベルモンド（イタリア）らが有力。日本は男女のリレーで五輪距離史上初の入賞を目指す。青木富美子の活躍にも期待したい

種目別　コースの距離とスタートとの高低差　グラフ上の❶〜❹は鳥観図の記号と対応する

男子50kmフリー（同じコースを3周する）　▼はメーン会場

女子30kmフリー（同じコースを2周する）

男子30kmクラシカル（同じコースを2周する）

女子15kmクラシカル

男子15kmフリー【パシュート】

女子10kmフリー【パシュート】　女子5kmクラシカル

男子10kmクラシカル

女子4×5kmリレー
第1・第2走者【クラシカル】　第3・第4走者【フリー】

男子4×10kmリレー（1走者が1周5kmのコースを2周する）
第1・第2走者【クラシカル】　第3・第4走者【フリー】

スノーハープ

白馬クロスカントリー競技場は愛称スノーハープ。38.6haの敷地にA、Bともに4.8km、C（7.8km）の3コースを設け、メーン会場内の周回コースと合わせて総延長は18.6kmある。3コースを組み合わせるため、選手がメーン会場に戻る回数が増え、観戦しやすい。各コースともアップダウンがきつく、難度は高い。

Bコース

Aコース

全コースの中で最大の標高差67m、長さ約570mの長い上り坂が続く。クラシカルならグリップワックスの出来が成績を大きく左右。「最高の見せ場。声援が大きな力に」

❶ 標高差約40m、長さ約440mの上り坂

❷

Cコース

❸

❹　メーン会場　●スタート
●フィニッシュ

国道148号へ

標高差約50m、長さ約480mの上り坂。直後に約200mを一気に下る。大きなカーブがあり、上りの疲労の影響が露に出やすい

標高差約30mを上り下りする。最大で20%の傾斜。Cコースを3周する複合個人では、疲労がたまった選手を待ち受ける最後の難関。（このコースを使うのは女子10km、男子15km、複合）

野沢温泉村
白馬村　山ノ内町
長野市
軽井沢町

南神城駅、国道148号へ

graphic by TUBE

※図は実際よりも標高差を強調しています。
また、目の錯覚を利用して立体に見せるため、南斜面が陰になっています

Japan　1998
CD: Hiroyuki Kimura
D: Sachiko Hagiwara
DF: Tube Graphics
CL: The Shinano Mainichi Shimbun

A bird's-eye view of the Nagano Winter Olympics' Cross-Country Skiing course.
Distances, and course profiles which include elevations, show the difficulty of the courses.
長野冬季オリンピックのクロスカントリーコースの全体を、ふかん図で表現。
さらに、コースの距離とスタート地点との高低差の情報を入れ、レースの過酷さを表した。

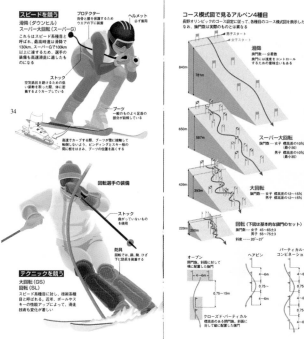

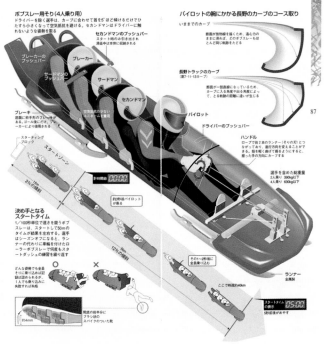

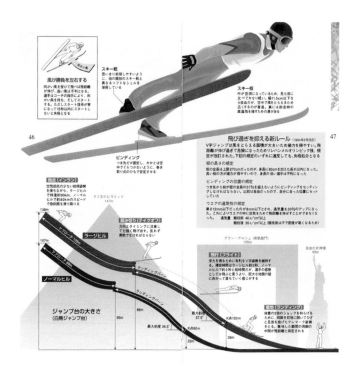

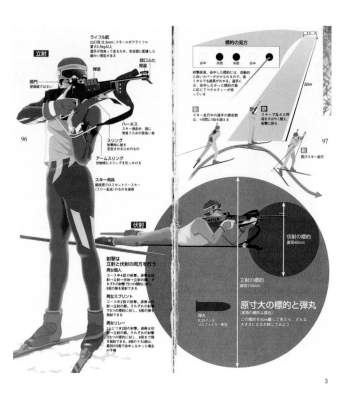

Japan　1998
CD: Hiroyuki Kimura
D: Ryu Sato (1)/Sachiko Hagiwara (2)(3)/
　　Hiroko Enomoto (4)
DF: Tube Graphics
CL: NAOC/The Shinano Mainichi Shimbun

From the Nagano Winter Olympics Official Guidebook.
Diagrams clearly explain the rules of each event, and show what equipment is required.
長野冬季オリンピックの公式ガイドブックより。各競技のルールや道具のしくみを詳細に図解説明した主題図。

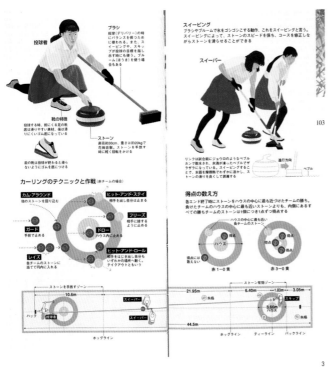

Japan 1998
CD: Hiroyuki Kimura
D: Naomi Sugita (1)/Sachiko Hagiwara (2)/
Nozomi Hatakeyama (3)(4)
DF: Tube Graphics
CL: NAOC/The Shinano Mainichi Shimbun

From the Nagano Winter Olympics Official Guidebook.
Diagrams clearly explain the rules of each event, and show what equipment is required.
長野冬季オリンピックの公式ガイドブックより。各競技のルールや道具のしくみを詳細に図解説明した主題図。

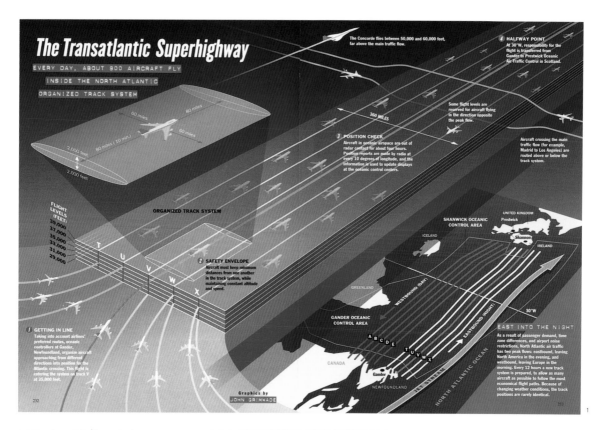

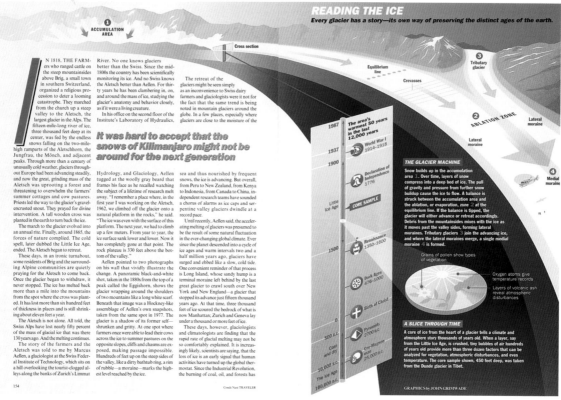

U.S.A. 1996
AD: Robert Best
I: John Grimwade
CL: Condé Nast Traveler

Diagram of the air traffic system over the North Atlantic Ocean. (1)
北大西洋上空の航空交通についてのダイアグラム。(1)

U.S.A. 1995
AD: Diana Laguardia
D: Christin Gangi
I: John Grimwade
CL: Condé Nast Traveler

Anatomy of a glacier, explaining some of the types of stories,
many of which are thousands of years old, that can be told by a core of ice. (2)
氷山の構造図。何千年に及ぶものも多い階層の種類と、それらが氷の芯によって測定できることを説明している。(2)

Graphs & Tables

Pie Charts, Bar Graphs, Line Graphs, Tables

円グラフ、棒グラフ、折線グラフ、比較統計グラフ

Selected Works

入選作品

応募点数 Entered
1544

大賞 Grand Prix

ベストワーク Best Work 18

入選点数 Selected
322

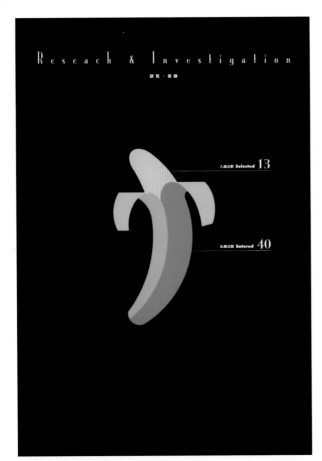

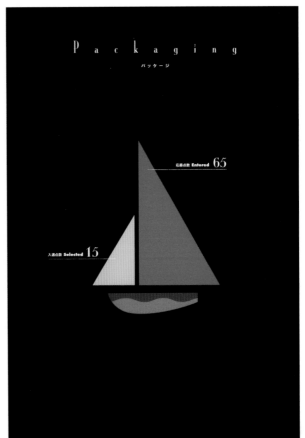

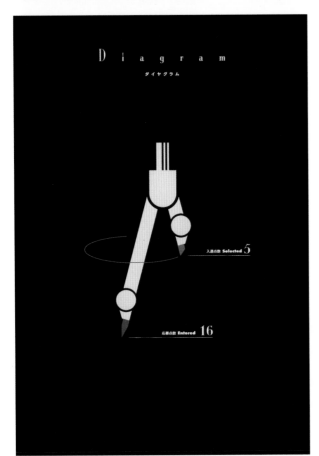

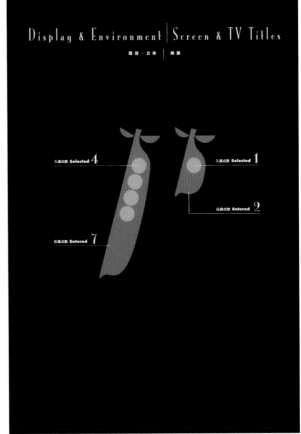

Japan 1996
AD: Kenzo Nakagawa
D: Hiroyasu Nobuyama/Satoshi Morikami/Hiromi Maekawa
DF: NDC Graphics Inc.
CL: Japan Typography Association

Graphs showing the number of works submitted, and the number of works selected, for inclusion in a typography design annual.
書籍『日本タイポグラフィ年鑑1996』より。タイポグラフィ年鑑への作品応募点数と入選点数を、部門別に表したグラフ。

Logotype & Symbolmark

ロゴタイプ・シンボルマーク

応募点数 **Entered** 956

入選点数 **Selected** 156

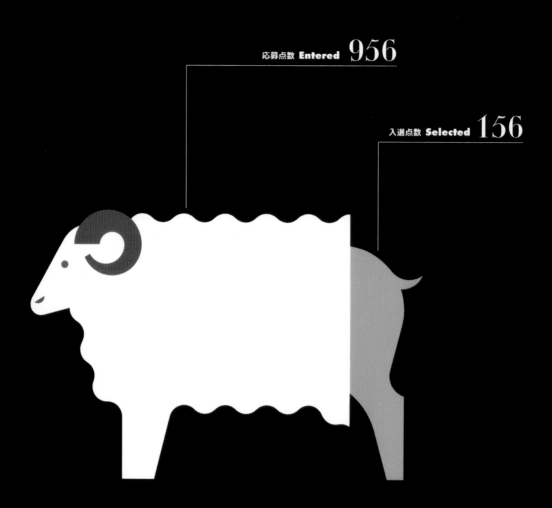

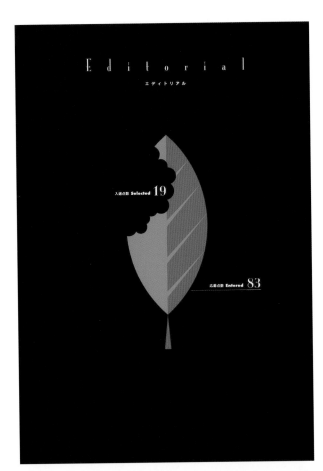

Editorial
エディトリアル

入選点数 Selected 19

応募点数 Entered 83

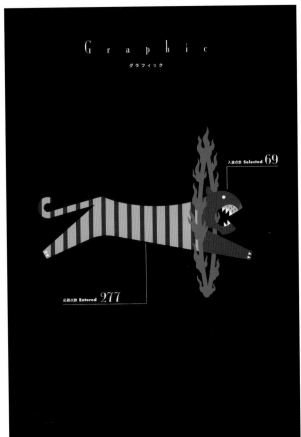

Graphic
グラフィック

入選点数 Selected 69

応募点数 Entered 277

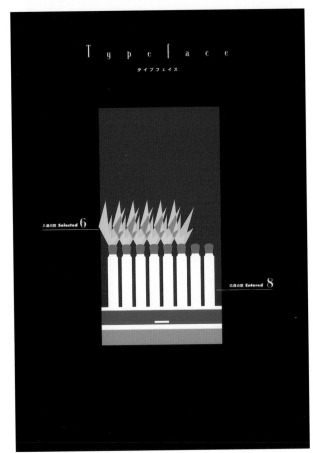

Typeface
タイプフェイス

入選点数 Selected 6

応募点数 Entered 8

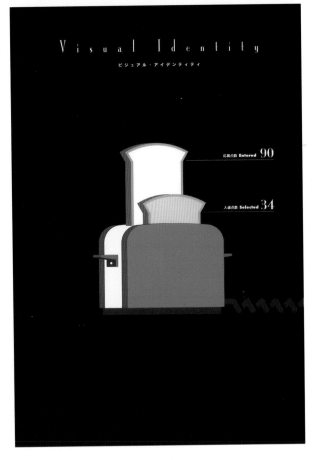

Visual Identity
ビジュアル・アイデンティティ

応募点数 Entered 90

入選点数 Selected 34

Japan 1996
AD: Kenzo Nakagawa
D: Hiroyasu Nobuyama/Satoshi Morikami/Hiromi Maekawa
DF: NDC Graphics Inc.
CL: Japan Typography Association

Graphs showing the number of works submitted, and the number of works selected, for inclusion in a typography design annual.
書籍『日本タイポグラフィ年鑑1996』より。タイポグラフィ年鑑への作品応募点数と入選点数を、部門別に表したグラフ。

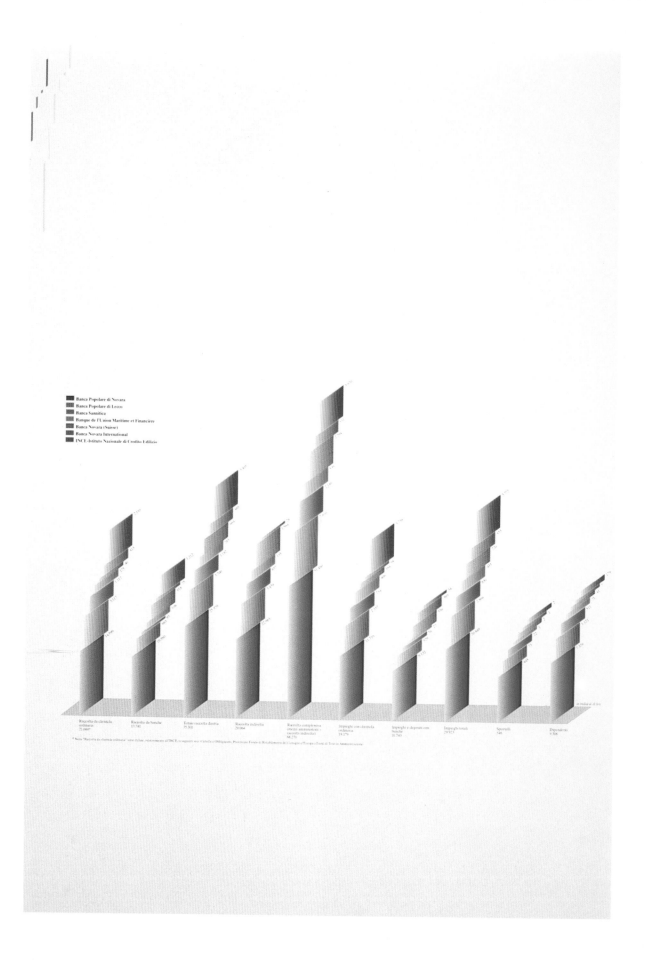

Italy   1994
CD: Enrico Sempi
AD, D: Antonella Trevisan
DF: Tangram Strategic Design
CL: Banca Popolare di Novara

This flame graphic diagram was created for the Banca Popolare di Novara's Annual Report.
It illustrates the revenues of the banks in the Group.
ノバラ・グループのポポラーレ・ディ・ノバラ銀行の売上高について、炎をかたどったグラフで表したもの。アニュアル・リポートに使用された。

Impieghi totali

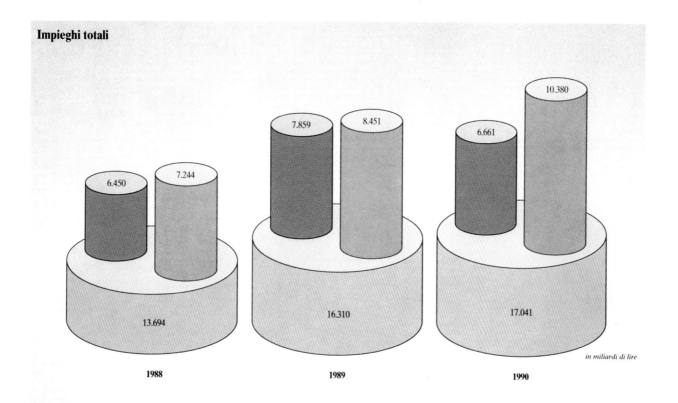

6.450 7.244 13.694 **1988**

7.859 8.451 16.310 **1989**

6.661 10.380 17.041 **1990**

in miliardi di lire

▓ **Impieghi per cassa con clientela ordinaria** ▓ **Impieghi e depositi con banche** ▒ **Impieghi totali**

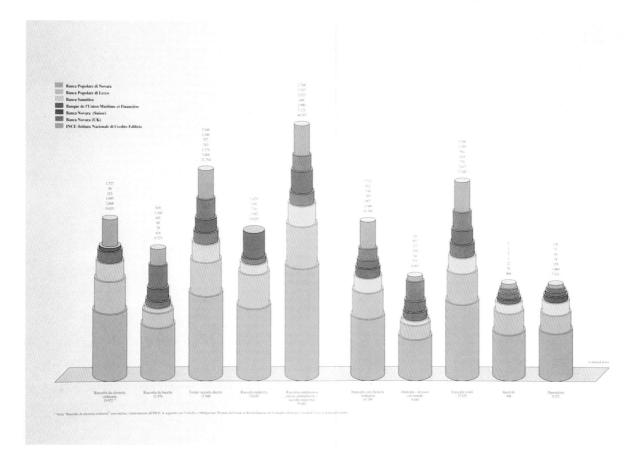

Italy   1994
CD, AD, D: Enrico Sempi
DF: Tangram Strategic Design
CL: Banca Popolare di Novara

*From the bank's Annual Report, these diagrams illustrate the revenues of the banks
in the Banca Popolare di Novara Group, and the bank's distribution of investments.*
ノバラ・グループのポポラーレ・ディ・ノバラ銀行の売上高と投資配分についてのグラフ。

Strategy at work

3 Improving quality of earnings

In the past, the earnings of The Royal Bank of Scotland Group were subject to considerable fluctuations because of their substantial dependence on the UK economy. We have achieved greater stability through a better spread of the Group's earnings, with a larger proportion now coming from Direct Line and Citizens and, within the Bank, from products like mortgages and life assurance. Also, we have improved the quality of our loan portfolio.

Diversifying earnings

Income 1995 (£2.0bn)

Substantial increases in the contributions from Direct Line and Citizens illustrate the diversity of the Group's income sources with a reduced proportion of income from the core UK banking operation.

Income 1991 (£1.2bn)

■ Branch Banking Division
■ Corporate and Institutional Banking Division
■ Operations Division
■ Direct Line
■ Citizens
■ Charterhouse (sold 1993)

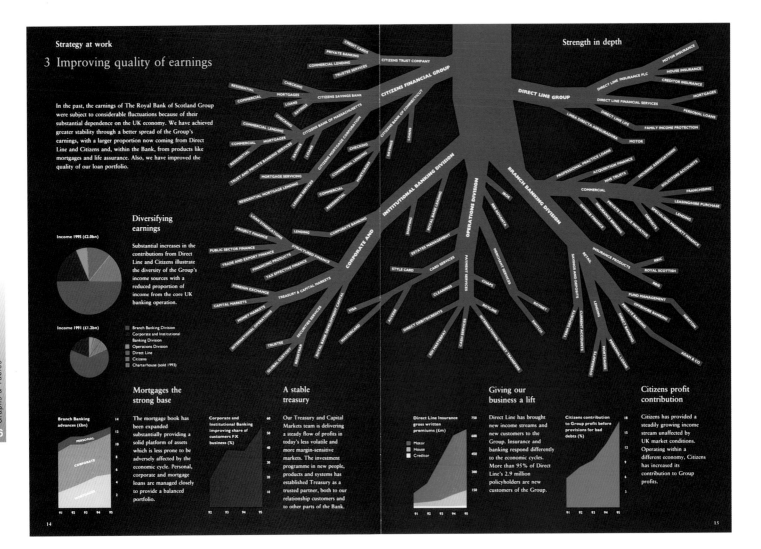

Strength in depth

Mortgages the strong base

Branch Banking advances (£bn)

The mortgage book has been expanded substantially providing a solid platform of assets which is less prone to be adversely affected by the economic cycle. Personal, corporate and mortgage loans are managed closely to provide a balanced portfolio.

A stable treasury

Corporate and Institutional Banking improving share of customers FX business (%)

Our Treasury and Capital Markets team is delivering a steady flow of profits in today's less volatile and more margin-sensitive markets. The investment programme in new people, products and systems has established Treasury as a trusted partner, both to our relationship customers and to other parts of the Bank.

Giving our business a lift

Direct Line Insurance gross written premiums (£m)

■ Motor
■ House
■ Creditor

Direct Line has brought new income streams and new customers to the Group. Insurance and banking respond differently to the economic cycles. More than 95% of Direct Line's 2.9 million policyholders are new customers of the Group.

Citizens profit contribution

Citizens contribution to Group profit before provisions for bad debts (%)

Citizens has provided a steadily growing income stream unaffected by UK market conditions. Operating within a different economy, Citizens has increased its contribution to Group profits.

14   15

U.K. 1995
CD: Tor Pettersen
AD, D: David Brown
D: Ann Kenmure
I: David Keen/David Baker
DF: Tor Pettersen & Partners Ltd.
CL: Royal Bank of Scotland

This graphic represents all of the company's diverse revenue streams, and shows how the revenue is channeled through the five main divisions.
スコットランド・ロイヤル銀行のさまざまな収益ラインと5つの主要部門へのマネー・フローを表したグラフィック。

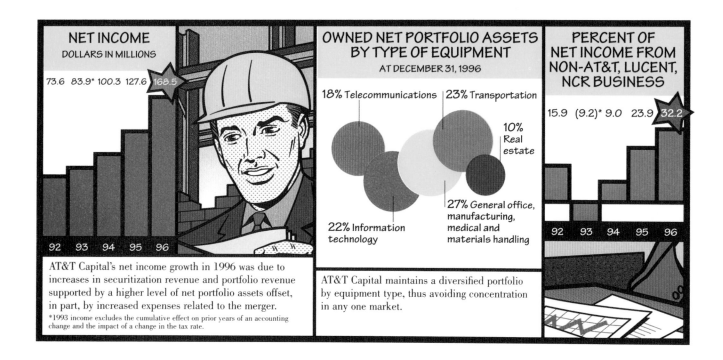

NET INCOME
DOLLARS IN MILLIONS

73.6 83.9* 100.3 127.6 168.5

92 93 94 95 96

AT&T Capital's net income growth in 1996 was due to increases in securitization revenue and portfolio revenue supported by a higher level of net portfolio assets offset, in part, by increased expenses related to the merger.

*1993 income excludes the cumulative effect on prior years of an accounting change and the impact of a change in the tax rate.

OWNED NET PORTFOLIO ASSETS BY TYPE OF EQUIPMENT
AT DECEMBER 31, 1996

18% Telecommunications

23% Transportation

10% Real estate

27% General office, manufacturing, medical and materials handling

22% Information technology

AT&T Capital maintains a diversified portfolio by equipment type, thus avoiding concentration in any one market.

PERCENT OF NET INCOME FROM NON-AT&T, LUCENT, NCR BUSINESS

15.9 (9.2)* 9.0 23.9 32.2

92 93 94 95 96

SPREAD OF RESIDUAL POSITION
AT DECEMBER 31, 1996

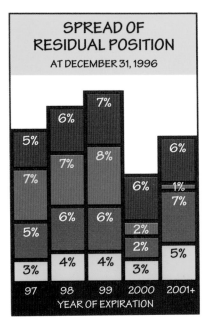

| 97 | 98 | 99 | 2000 | 2001+ |
YEAR OF EXPIRATION

5% 6% 7% 6%
7% 7% 8% 6% 1%
5% 6% 6% 6% 7%
2%
5% 2% 5%
3% 4% 4% 3%

- 30% Telecommunications
- 25% Information technology
- 26% Transportation
- 19% General office, manufacturing, medical and materials handling

CUSTOMER MIX OF OWNED AND MANAGED PORTFOLIO ASSETS
AT DECEMBER 31, 1996

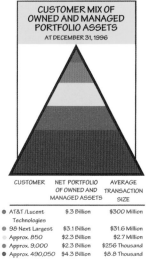

CUSTOMER	NET PORTFOLIO OF OWNED AND MANAGED ASSETS	AVERAGE TRANSACTION SIZE
AT&T /Lucent Technologies	$.3 Billion	$300 Million
98 Next Largest	$3.1 Billion	$31.6 Million
Approx. 850	$2.3 Billion	$2.7 Million
Approx. 9,000	$2.3 Billion	$256 Thousand
Approx. 490,050	$4.3 Billion	$8.8 Thousand

KEY FINANCIAL MEASURES
COMPOUND ANNUAL GROWTH RATES
1985-1996

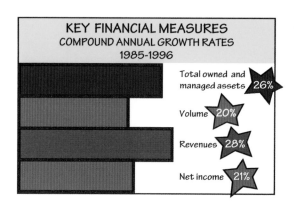

Total owned and managed assets 26%

Volume 20%

Revenues 28%

Net income 21%

U.S.A. 1997
CD, AD: Stephen Ferrari
D: Monica Gotz
DF: The Graphic Expression, Inc.
CL: AT&T Capital Corporation

The AT&T Capital annual report's editorial message was, "Where we are today: A story unfolds." Comic strip illustrations were used to present the corporate strategy with a unique visual approach that was continued in the displays of financial measures.

AT＆Tキャピタル社のアニュアル・リポートのメッセージは「私たちが今日いるところ：明らかにされたストーリー」であった。
企業戦略と企業財政をユニークな視覚的アプローチで説明するために、コミックのスタイルが採用された。

Sales

In millions of dollars

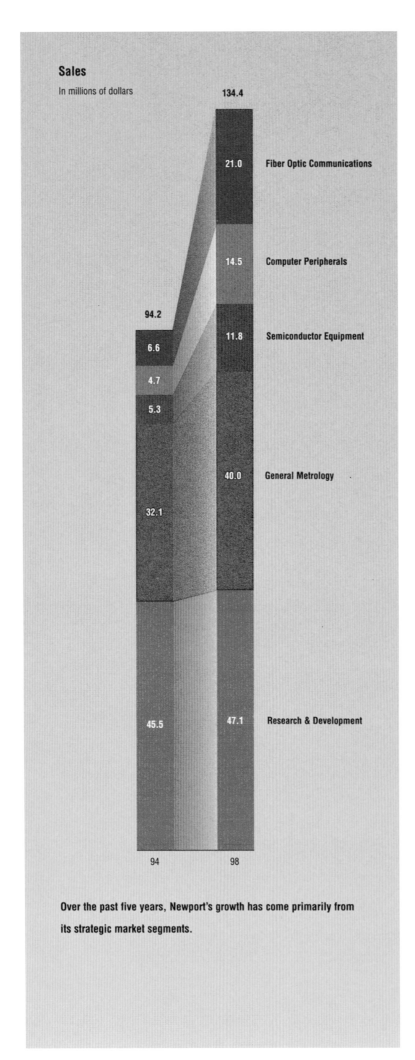

134.4

21.0 — Fiber Optic Communications

14.5 — Computer Peripherals

94.2

11.8 — Semiconductor Equipment

6.6

4.7

5.3

40.0 — General Metrology

32.1

45.5   47.1 — Research & Development

94   98

Over the past five years, Newport's growth has come primarily from its strategic market segments.

Sales

Percentage by market segment

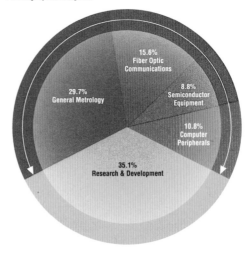

15.6% Fiber Optic Communications

8.8% Semiconductor Equipment

29.7% General Metrology

10.8% Computer Peripherals

35.1% Research & Development

In 1998, Newport's sales to industrial markets represented 65% of total sales.

Sales

In millions of dollars

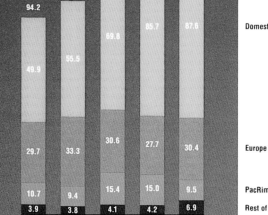

		Label
94.2		
102.0		
119.9		
132.6		
134.4		

Domestic
Europe
PacRim
Rest of World

94 95 96 97 98

Income from Operations

In millions of dollars

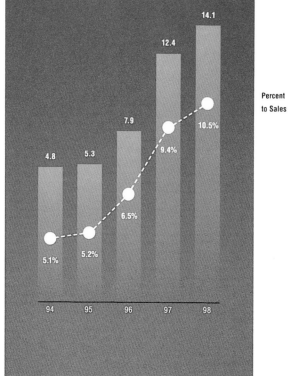

Percent to Sales

94 95 96 97 98

SG&A Expenses

In millions of dollars

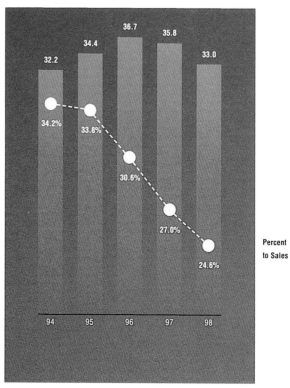

Percent to Sales

94 95 96 97 98

R&D Expenses

In millions of dollars

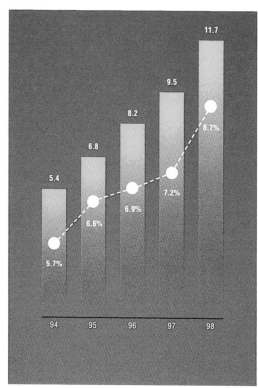

Percent to Sales

94 95 96 97 98

U.S.A. 1999
CD, AD, D: Carl Seltzer
CW: Cecilia A. Wilkinson
DF: Carl Seltzer Design Office
CL: Newport Corporation

Graphs illustrating changes in different areas of corporate income and expenses. From an annual report.
企業の収益と支出の推移を分野別に表したグラフ。アニュアル・リポートより。

メセナ活動における資金援助が大きく上昇

メセナ白書1996で、「メセナ活動をおこなっている」と答えた企業のうち、資金援助額に回答のあった174社の額を前年度の数字と比較してみると、昨年調査より有効回答企業数が減少したにもかかわらず総額では8億9491万円増、平均2119万円増と大きく上昇し、92年より続いてきた資金援助額の減少傾向に歯止めがかかりました。とくに「資金援助額の大きい企業」に「前年度よりも増額した」ケースが多く、メセナ活動をめぐる環境は最悪期を脱し、力を取り戻してきました。この傾向を維持していけるかどうか、また好不況に左右されないメセナ活動を定着させることができるかどうかが、これからの課題となるでしょう。

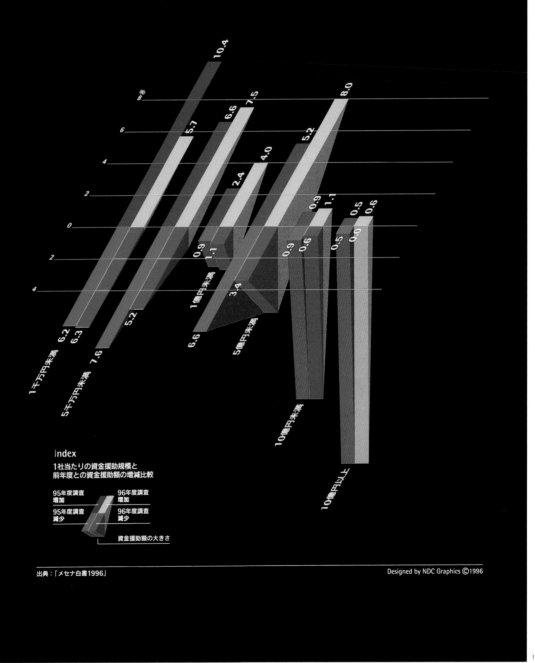

Index

1社当たりの資金援助規模と
前年度との資金援助額の増減比較

95年度調査	96年度調査
増加	増加
95年度調査	96年度調査
減少	減少

資金援助額の大きさ

出典：「メセナ白書1996」

Designed by NDC Graphics ©1996

Japan 1995-1997
AD: Kenzo Nakagawa
D: Satoshi Morikami/Norika Nakayama
DF: NDC Graphics Inc.
CL: Association for Corporate Support of the Arts

Results of a 1996 poll of corporations, indicating the amount of money spend in support of the arts. Comparisons are made with 1995 figures. [1]
メセナ活動を行っている企業に対して1996年に実施された「資金援助規模」のアンケート結果を、1995年と比較して見せたグラフ。[1]

Graph shows artists' and spectators' opinions regarding whether or not corporate-owned cultural facilities are contributing to the popularization of art and culture. [2]
「企業が所有する芸術・文化施設が芸術や文化の普及に貢献しているかどうか」を観客とアーティストに聞いた結果を示したグラフ。[2]

企業の芸術文化施設はアートに貢献してる？

企業が所有する芸術文化施設について、観客とアーティストにききました。まず「企業の芸術文化施設はアートと観客の出会いを身近にしたか」とたずねたところ、観客もアーティストも約8割が好意的な回答をしました。アートを享受する機会を豊かにしてくれたという点では貢献度がかなり認められているようです。ところが「新しい才能の発掘・育成に貢献していると思うか」という質問には、観客は4割が「そう思う」と答えているのにアーティストは4割が「あまりそうは思わない」と答え、対照的です。若い才能の理解層はまだまだ豊かで未発達？と考えれば、心強い限りです。

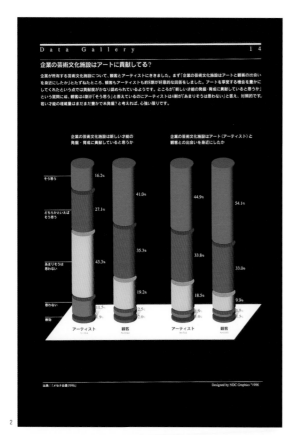

企業の芸術文化施設は新しい才能の
発掘・育成に貢献していると思うか

企業の芸術文化施設はアート（アーティスト）と
観客との出会いを身近にしたか

出典「メセナ白書1996」　　　　Designed by NDC Graphics ©1996

日本企業による海外でのメセナ活動

今年の「メセナ白書」の特集は「世界のメセナ」。日本企業の海外でのメセナ活動について調査したところ、回答企業の半数弱が、過去5年以内に海外でメセナ活動をおこなったことがあるという。その実施理由としてもっとも多かったのは「現地法人による企業市民活動の一環」。一方、活動の財源や決定権がどこにあるか、との質問には、ほぼ過半数の企業が、現地法人にはなく、日本の本社にあると答えた。地域に根ざした企業市民活動とは、現地に精通したスタッフと市民とのコミュニケーションを通じて実現させるべきものでは？本社と海外拠点との連携がおこなわれることを願う。

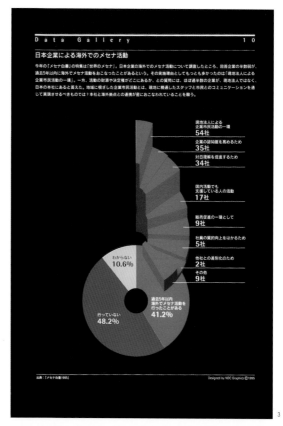

出典「メセナ白書1995」　　　　Designed by NDC Graphics ©1995

この1年間にプロの舞台や作品を直接鑑賞しましたか？

総理府が昨年、全国の5000人を対象におこなった世論調査です。テレビやビデオ、本などで見るのではなく、わざわざ足を運んでプロの公演や作品を直接見たかと答えた人が、昨年はなんと2人に1人！アートに生で接する機会は大都市ほど多く、また女性の割合が男性を上回っているということでしょうか。やはり、という項目でしょうか。総数で美術や映画を抜いて堂々トップに輝いたのは音楽。でも大都市では映画鑑賞がいちばん身近な存在のようです。また、全般に男性は「映画好き」。一方女性は、音楽、美術の鑑賞者が多くなっていますが、複数の分野に足を運んでいる様子もうかがえます。

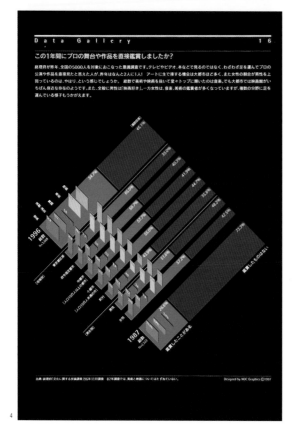

出典「総理府　文化に関する世論調査」96年11月調査　87年度調査は、美術と映画についてはたずねていない。　　　　Designed by NDC Graphics ©1997

国会議員対象「芸術・文化活動とNPO法」に関するアンケート

1997年1月実施／芸術文化振興連絡会議（PAN）

先の国会にてNPO法案が審議されました。ところで、この法案と芸術団体との関係はどのようなものでしょうか。法案審議にあたった当の国会議員を対象に実施したアンケートによると、回答にあたったほぼすべての議員が「芸術文化が人間の生活に欠かせない」と考えており、また85.6%の議員が「非営利目的の芸術文化活動は社会的に意義をもった公益性の高い活動だ」と考えています。つまり芸術団体も同法案の対象団体として強く認識されているといえそうです。さらに非営利目的の芸術文化活動に対する税制措置を講じることについては、74.3%の議員が「ぜひ必要」と答えているのも大いに注目したいところ。

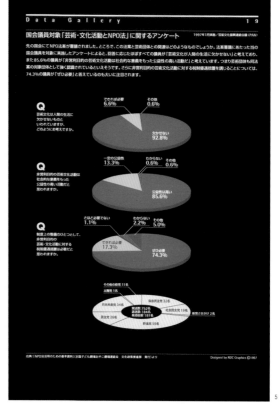

出典「NPO法活用のための基本資料」〈全国子ども劇場おやこ劇場連絡会　文化政策推進課　発行〉より　　　　Designed by NDC Graphics ©1997

Japan　1995-1997
AD: Kenzo Nakagawa
D: Satoshi Morikami/Norika Nakayama
DF: NDC Graphics Inc.
CL: Association for Corporate Support of the Arts

*A pie chart indicating the percent of Japanese corporations
that have been involved in overseas activities in support of the arts, and their reasons for doing so.* (3)
海外でメセナ活動を実施したことがある日本企業の割合と、行っていない企業の割合を表したグラフ。(3)

*Graph showing the percentage of Japanese who experienced live art or cultural events in a 1-year period.
Separated by category of event, as well as respondent's age and the size of their city of residence.* (4)
日本国民が1年間にどのくらいの割合で積極的に生の芸術や文化にふれているかを、項目別に表したグラフ。(4)

*This chart shows the results of a poll taken of Japanese Diet members, asking their opinion concerning
"Art and Cultural Activities and the Nonprofit Organizations law."* (5)
日本の国会議員を対象に行われた「芸術・文化活動とNPO法」に関するアンケート結果をまとめたグラフ。(5)

メセナ
白書
1996
[社]企業メセナ協議会 編

ISBN4-478-30051-8

C0034 P3000E

◆ダイヤモンド社

定価3000円[本体2913円]

9784478300510

1910034030005

企業の芸術文化施設で発表したことはありますか

[アーティストへのアンケート調査]

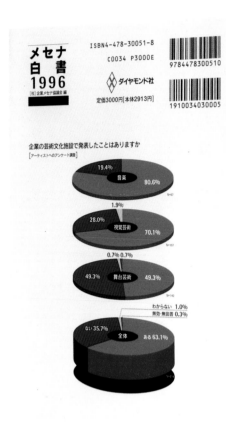

メセナ
白書
1996
[社]企業メセナ協議会 編

メセナ活動
実施状況

メセナ活動を
行っている 66.8%

行っていない 33.2%

ダイヤモンド社
300518

メセナ白書 1996

[社]企業メセナ協議会 編

特集：企業の芸術文化施設

企業が所有する文化施設の種類

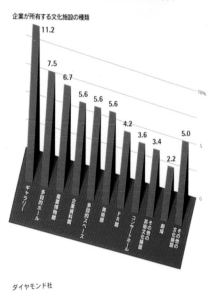

ダイヤモンド社

メセナ
白書
1997
[社]企業メセナ協議会 編

ISBN4-478-30054-2

C0034 ¥3000E

◆ダイヤモンド社

定価(本体3000円+税)

9784478300541

1920034030004

1社あたりの平均支援件数と資金援助額

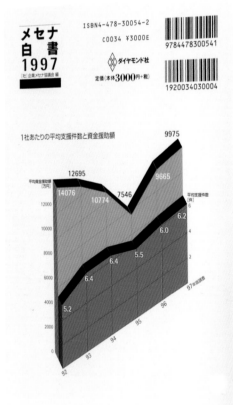

メセナ
白書
1997
[社]企業メセナ協議会 編

メセナ活動
実施状況

メセナ活動を
行っている 70.8%

行っていない 29.2%

ダイヤモンド社
300542

メセナ白書 1997

[社]企業メセナ協議会 編

特集：企業の顕彰・コンクール事業

顕彰事業の目的

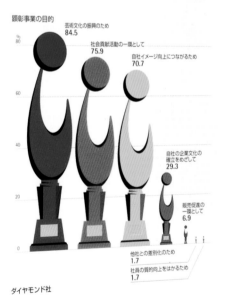

ダイヤモンド社

Japan 1996-1997
AD: Kenzo Nakagawa
D: Satoshi Morikami/Norika Nakayama
DF: NDC Graphics Inc.
CL: Association for Corporate Support of the Arts

Covers of the "Mecenat Report."
Graphs of data related to corporate and local government activities in support of the arts.
書籍『メセナ白書』の表紙カバーより。企業のメセナ活動の実態をさまざまなデータをもとに表したグラフ。

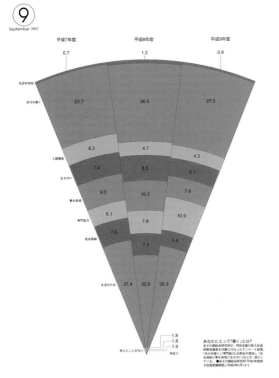

SYRIEZ
⑨
September 1997

会計人のためのコンサルティング情報誌　[月刊 シリエズ]

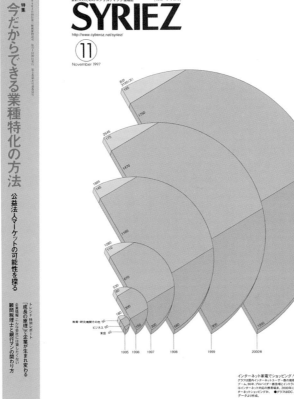

特集
今だからできる業種特化の方法
公益法人マーケットの可能性を探る
顧問税理士と銀行との関わり方

あなたにとって「働く」とは？

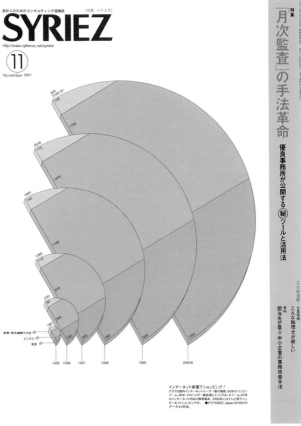

SYRIEZ
⑪
November 1997
http://www.cyberoz.net/syriez/

会計人のためのコンサルティング情報誌　[月刊 シリエズ]

特集
「月次監査」の手法革命
優良事務所が公開する㊙ツールと活用法

こんな税理士が欲しい
関与先が喜ぶ中小企業の業務改善手法

インターネット家電でショッピング！

SYRIEZ
⑩
October 1997

会計人のためのコンサルティング情報誌　[月刊 シリエズ]

特集
全国の中小企業4,000社に聞く
「税理士を替えたい」理由

会計事務所のアイデアボックス

次期社長候補との関係は良好？

SYRIEZ
⑫
December 1997

会計人のためのコンサルティング情報誌　[月刊 シリエズ]

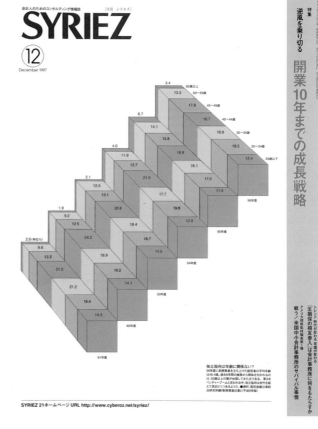

特集
逆風を乗り切る
開業10年までの成長戦略

独立指向は年齢に関係ない？

SYRIEZ 21ホームページ URL http://www.cyberoz.net/syriez/

Japan　1997
AD: Toshiyuki Ohkubo
D: Yasutomo Tashiro/Naomi Tokuno
DF: Ohkubo Design Office
CL: SYRIEZ

Covers of "Syriez," a consulting information magazine for accountants. Each month's issue features a graph, with themes such as "Reasons for Working," "Changes in the Number of Internet Users," "How I Met My Business Partner," and "Does Age Matter when Starting a New Business?"

会計人のためのコンサルティング情報誌『SYRIES』の表紙より。
「働く理由」「国内インターネットユーザー数の推移」「ビジネスパートナーと知り合ったきっかけ」
「新規事業を立ち上げた経営者の年齢別割合」を表したグラフ。

ESCALA E QUALIDADE DE PRODUÇÃO
(Volumes da Fábrica de Software)

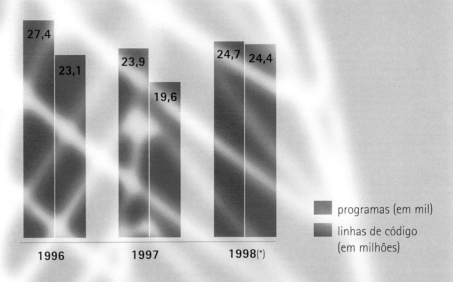

27,4 23,1   23,9 19,6   24,7 24,4

1996   1997   1998(*)

■ programas (em mil)

■ linhas de código
(em milhões)

1

PORTAS PARA O SÉCULO XXI**
Números de Linhas Convertidas (em milhões)

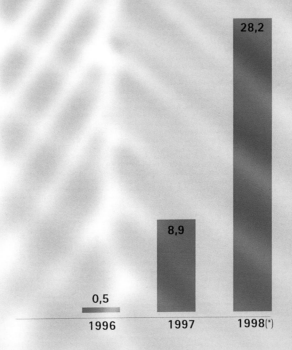

28,2

8,9

0,5

1996   1997   1998(*)

2

(*) Previsão
(* *) Bug do Milênio

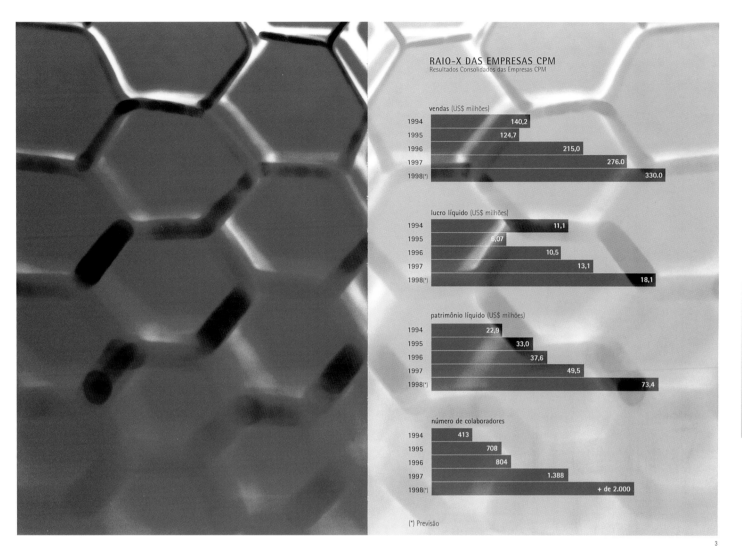

RAIO-X DAS EMPRESAS CPM
Resultados Consolidados das Empresas CPM

vendas (US$ milhões)

1994	140,2
1995	124,7
1996	215,0
1997	276.0
1998(*)	330.0

lucro líquido (US$ milhões)

1994	11,1
1995	6,07
1996	10,5
1997	13,1
1998(*)	18,1

patrimônio líquido (US$ milhões)

1994	22,9
1995	33,0
1996	37,6
1997	49,5
1998(*)	73,4

número de colaboradores

1994	413
1995	708
1996	804
1997	1.388
1998(*)	+ de 2.000

(*) Previsão

3

Brazil 1998
CD, AD, D: Rico Lins
AD: Mariana Bernd
P: Roberto Stelzer
CW: Ana Marcia Vainsencher
DF: Rico Lins Studio
CL: CPM

Illustrates the industry concept (programs, volume and code lines) applied to the production of software. (1)
ソフトウエア生産に採用された業界コンセプト（プログラム、量、コード体系）をグラフ化したもの。(1)

Indicates the expansion of demand for the "2000 Kit" (for conversion of code lines to enable computers to cope with the Y2K problem), a product from the software plant of CPM Sistemas. (2)
CPMシステマズ社のソフトウエア部門の製品『2000年対応キット』（コンピューターの2000年問題を解決するためコードラインを変換するもの）の需要の伸びを示したグラフ。(2)

Shows some of the main economic and financial indicators for the companies (sales and net profits), their solidity (assets and their growth), as well as their characteristics and number of employees. (3)
会社の財政状態を表す指標（売上高と純利益）、安定性（資産と成長）、および会社の特色と従業員数を示したグラフ。(3)

1. Vergleich/Comparison

Überschrift – Headline

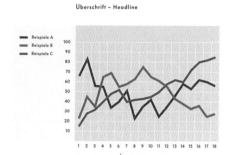

Überschrift – Headline

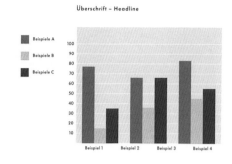

Überschrift – Headline

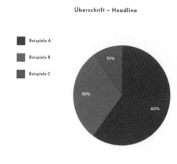

2. Hervorhebung/Emphasis

Überschrift – Headline

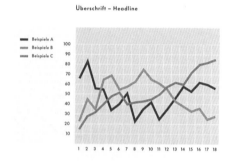

Überschrift – Headline

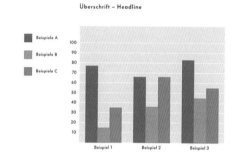

Überschrift – Headline

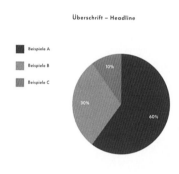

1. Version mit grauen Hintergrundflächen/Version with grey background

Überschrift – Headline

Überschrift – Headline

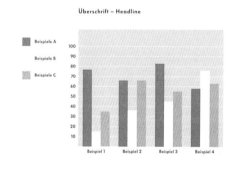

Überschrift – Headline

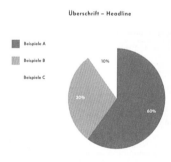

Germany   1998
DF: Meta Design
CL: Volkswagen Ag

Documentation of typefaces, information charts, and other elements,
to ensure the correct world-wide implementation of the Volkswagen corporate design.
フォルクスワーゲン社のコーポレイト・デザインが世界中で正しく使用されるよう、タイプフェイス、情報のチャート、
その他の要素について規定したもの。

1 Construction

Employment

Construction employment and orders (1987-95)

New orders (£bn) / Employment (thousands)

1987 1988 1989 1990 1991 1992 1993 1994 1995

● Construction Industry employment
● Value of new orders

(Source: RICS Economic Model, DoE)

Liquidations in the construction industry (England and Wales) (1988-92)

	1988	1989	1990	1991	1992
Liquidations in the construction industry	1,471	1,638	2,445	3,373	3,830
Total liquidations in England and Wales	9,427	10,456	15,051	21,827	24,425
Construction %	16	16	16	15	16

number

(Source: DTI)

FACT
Over 80% of construction firms have less than 3 employees.

Number of construction firms by size (1991)

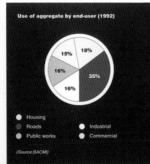

49.7%
1.2%
10.4%
34.0%
4.6%

● 1 employee
● 2-3 employees
● 4-7 employees
● 8-34 employees
● over 34 employees

(Source: Housing and Construction Statistics, DoE)

Output

Housebuilding completions in Great Britain

	1987	1992
Private sector	183,736	139,964
Housing associations	12,571	24,967
Public sector	20,089	4,596

(Source: Housing and Construction Statistics, DoE)

FACT
Jubilee Line Extension:
16 km in length
£1.8bn investment
22,000 jobs
100,000 tonnes of cement required over 3 years
500,000 cubic m of concrete needed
22,500 precast concrete tunnel and shaft linings.
(Source: Financial Times)

FACT
Construction output (current prices)
1987   £37,528m
1990   £55,307m
1992   £47,392m
(Source: Housing and Construction Statistics, DoE)

FACT
Second Severn Crossing:
1,168 m in length
£300m investment (private finance)
1,200 jobs
320,000 cubic m of concrete needed
30,000 tonnes of reinforced steel
Completion 1996.
(Source: Western Mail)

Quantity surveyors workload statistics (1986-93)

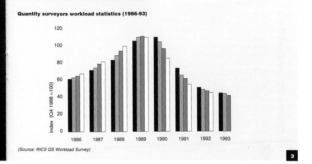

Index (Q4 1988 =100)

1986 1987 1988 1989 1990 1991 1992 1993

(Source: RICS QS Workload Survey)

2

3

Graphs & Tables

077

6 Minerals

Aggregate

Value of mineral production in 1991 (UK)

	£m
Oil	7,468
Natural gas	3,583
Coal	4,102
Industrial and Construction minerals	1,806
Metalliferous minerals	8
Total	**16,967**

(Source: British Geological Survey)

Use of aggregate by end-user (1992)

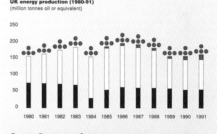

18%
15%
16%
35%
16%

● Housing
● Roads
● Public works
● Industrial
● Commercial

(Source: BACMI)

Employment in (GB) minerals industry (1989-92)

	Coal, oil and natural gas extraction and processing	Metal manufacturing, ore and other mineral extraction
1989	167,000	372,000
1990	157,000	385,000
1991	150,000	337,000
1992	131,000	319,000

(Source: CSO)

FACT
Over the last 35 years, demand for aggregate has risen at an average annual rate of some 3% from 88m tonnes in 1955 to 246m tonnes in 1991.
(Source: CSO)

FACT
The government projects that we will need between 5,900 and 6,500m tonnes of aggregate over the next 20 years. In 1991 England and Wales consumed 200m tonnes.
(Source: BACMI)

FACT
In Great Britain each person on average uses the equivalent of 4.4 tonnes of aggregate, 1.5 tonnes of oil and gas and 1 tonne of coal per year.
(Source: BACMI)

FACT
50-60 tonnes of aggregate are used in the construction of an average house and up to 200,000 tonnes in every mile of motorway.
(Source: BACMI)

Energy

UK energy production (1980-91)
(million tonnes oil or equivalent)

1980 1981 1982 1983 1984 1985 1986 1987 1988 1989 1990 1991

● Coal   ○ Petroleum   ● Natural gas   *(Source: DTI)*

FACT
The construction of the Channel Tunnel will have used over 10m tonnes of aggregate.
(Source: BACMI)

Coal Imports

	Volume (m tonnes)	Value (£m)
1987	9.78	368
1992	20.30	704

(Source: Digest of UK Energy Statistics 1993, DTI)

Energy consumption by final user (1992)

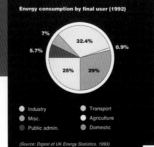

7%
32.4%
0.9%
5.7%
25%
29%

● Industry
● Misc.
● Public admin.
● Transport
● Agriculture
● Domestic

(Source: Digest of UK Energy Statistics, 1993)

18

19

U.K.   1998
CD, AD: Tilly Northedge
D, I: Graeme Kendren
DF: Grundy & Northedge
CL: Royal Institute of Chartered Surveyors

Graphs showing results of various studies pertaining to the construction industry.
建設業界に関する実態調査の結果をまとめたグラフ。

FINANCIAL HIGHLIGHTS

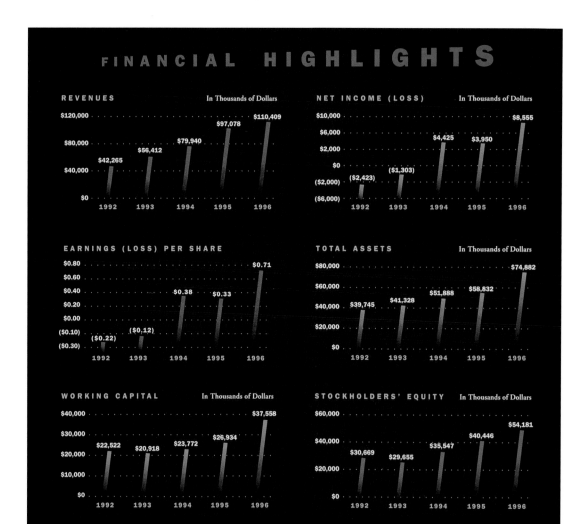

REVENUES   In Thousands of Dollars

$120,000
$80,000 $56,412 $79,940 $97,078 $110,409
$42,265
$40,000
$0
1992 1993 1994 1995 1996

NET INCOME (LOSS)   In Thousands of Dollars

$10,000 $8,555
$6,000 $4,425 $3,950
$2,000
$0
($2,000)   ($2,423)   ($1,303)
($6,000)
1992 1993 1994 1995 1996

EARNINGS (LOSS) PER SHARE

$0.80 $0.71
$0.60
$0.40 $0.38 $0.33
$0.20
$0.00
($0.10)   ($0.12)
($0.22)
($0.30)
1992 1993 1994 1995 1996

TOTAL ASSETS   In Thousands of Dollars

$80,000 $74,882
$60,000 $51,888 $58,832
$40,000 $39,745 $41,328
$20,000
$0
1992 1993 1994 1995 1996

WORKING CAPITAL   In Thousands of Dollars

$40,000 $37,558
$30,000 $26,934
$22,522 $20,918 $23,772
$20,000
$10,000
$0
1992 1993 1994 1995 1996

STOCKHOLDERS' EQUITY   In Thousands of Dollars

$60,000 $54,181
$40,000 $35,547 $40,446
$30,669 $29,655
$20,000
$0
1992 1993 1994 1995 1996

12

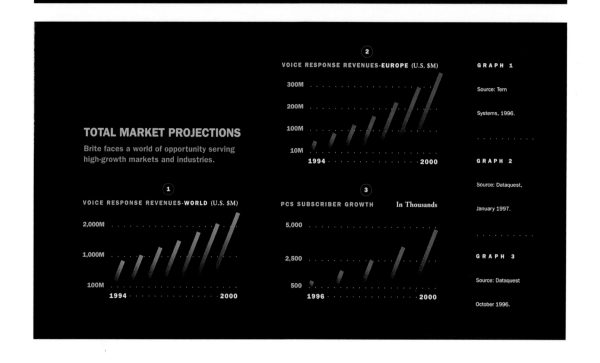

TOTAL MARKET PROJECTIONS

Brite faces a world of opportunity serving high-growth markets and industries.

VOICE RESPONSE REVENUES–WORLD (U.S. $M) ①

2,000M
1,000M
100M
1994 2000

VOICE RESPONSE REVENUES–EUROPE (U.S. $M) ②

300M
200M
100M
10M
1994 2000

PCS SUBSCRIBER GROWTH   In Thousands ③

5,000
2,500
500
1996 2000

GRAPH 1

Source: Tern

Systems, 1996.

GRAPH 2

Source: Dataquest,

January 1997.

GRAPH 3

Source: Dataquest

October 1996.

U.S.A. 1997
CD, AD: Sonia Greteman
AD, D: James Strange
CW: Deanna Harms
DF: Greteman Group
CL: Brite

Graphs for the annual report of a large telecommunications company.
通信会社のアニュアル・リポートのためのグラフ。

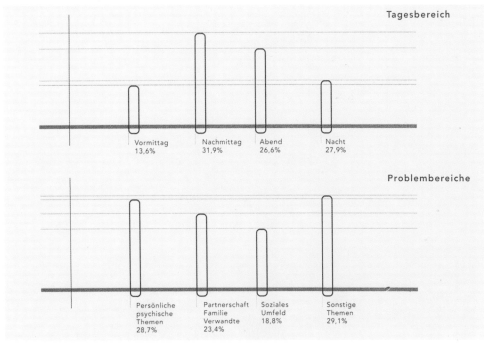

CARD RECEIVABLES – YEAR END (HK$ MILLION)
年底之信用咭應收欠賬（港幣百萬元）

RETURN ON AVERAGE ASSETS (%)
資產回報率（百分率）

NET PROFIT AFTER TAX (HK$ MILLION)
除税後溢利（港幣百萬元）

LOAN LOSS RATIO (%)
貸款損失比率（百分率）

1

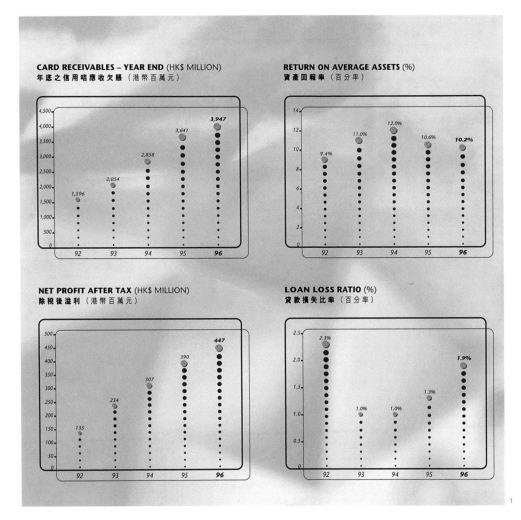

Tagesbereich

Vormittag 13,6% Nachmittag 31,9% Abend 26,6% Nacht 27,9%

Problembereiche

Persönliche psychische Themen 28,7% Partnerschaft Familie Verwandte 23,4% Soziales Umfeld 18,8% Sonstige Themen 29,1%

2

China 1997
CD, AD: Kan Tai-Keung
AD: Freeman Lau Siu Hong
AD, D: Chau So Hing
D: Joseph Leung Chun Wai
P: C. K. Wong
DF: Kan & Lau Design Consultants
CL: Manhattan Card Co., Ltd.

*As the company is a leading credit card issuer,
the charts' borders take the shape of
a credit card with rounded edges.
The customer profile is young and energetic,
which is reflected in the lively chart design.* (1)
クレジット会社のため、角の丸い枠を用いて
クレジットカードの形を模したグラフ。
顧客は若く元気な世代が多く、デザインも
いきいきとしたものにした。(1)

Austria 1998
AD, D: Peter Felder
D: René Dalpra
CW: Rarhara Bohle
DF: Felder Grafikdesign
CL: Telefonseelsorge Vorarlberg

*Graph showing
telephone company data
relating to usage of their
telephone lines.* (2)
電話局が電話回線の
使用に関する調査をまとめたグラフ。(2)

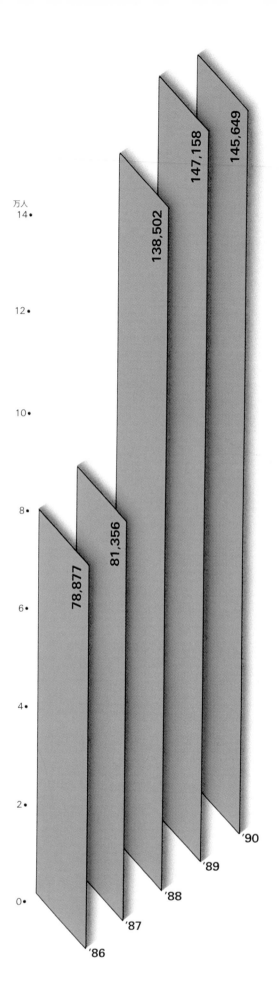

万人
14
12
10
8
6
4
2
0

78,877 '86
81,356 '87
138,502 '88
147,158 '89
145,649 '90

Japan 1990
CD, AD, D: Tetsuya Ohta
CL: Saison Group

Number of workers in Saison Group is detailed in these bar graphs. From an Annual Report.
セゾングループのアニュアルリポートより。総従業員数を表した棒グラフ。

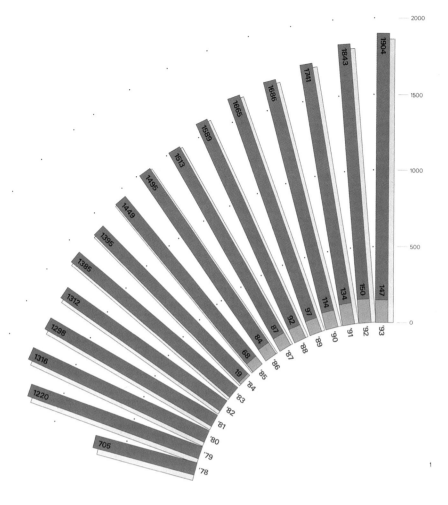

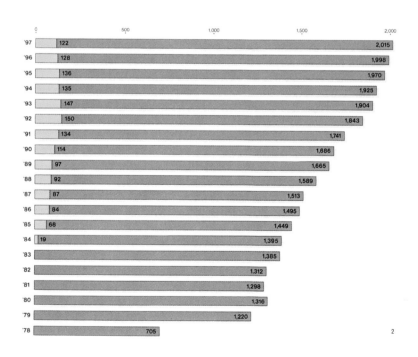

Japan 1993 (1)/1997 (2)
CD, AD, D: Tetsuya Ohta
CL: JAGDA

These bar graphs show the total number of Japan Graphic Designers Association (JAGDA) members.
JAGDA案内より。会員数の推移を表した棒グラフ。

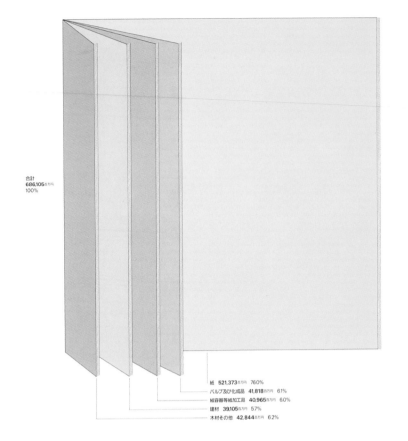

合計
686,105百万円
100%

紙　521,373百万円　76.0%
パルプ及び化成品　41,818百万円　6.1%
紙容器等紙加工品　40,965百万円　6.0%
建材　39,105百万円　5.7%
木材その他　42,844百万円　6.2%

1

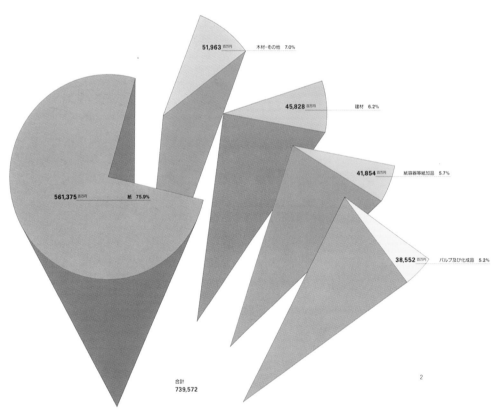

51,963百万円　木材・その他　7.0%

45,828百万円　建材　6.2%

41,854百万円　紙容器等紙加品　5.7%

38,552百万円　パルプ及び化成品　5.2%

561,375百万円　紙　75.9%

合計
739,572

2

Japan　1993 (1)/1995 (2)
CD, AD, D: Tetsuya Ohta
CL: Nippon Paper Industries

A plane graph and 3-dimensional pie chart showing sales of paper. From a corporate informational brochure.
日本製紙の会社案内より。紙の売上高を表した平面グラフと立体グラフ。

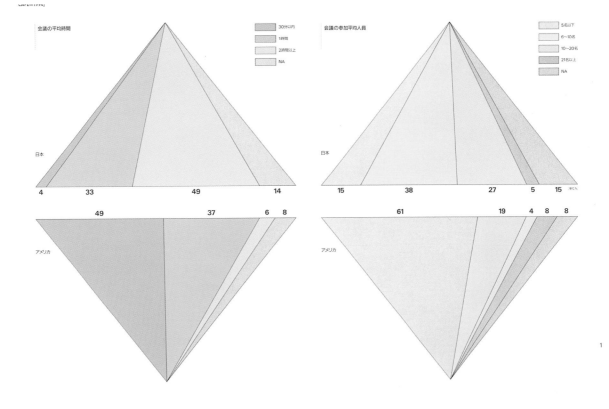

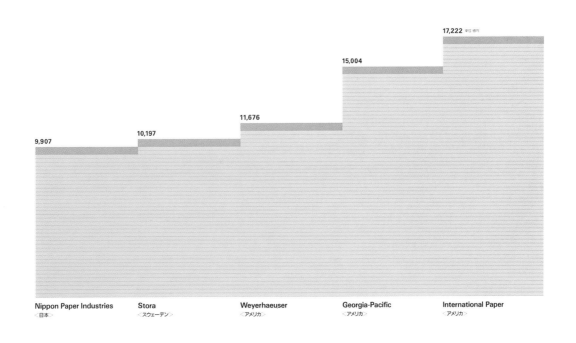

Japan 1994
CD, AD, D: Tetsuya Ohta
CL: Okamura (1) / Nippon Paper Industries (2)

Graph compares differences between meetings held in Japan vs. the U.S.A. (1)
オカムラのPR誌より。日本とアメリカの会議内容に関するデータの違いを表した相似グラフ。(1)

A graph that compares sales of paper in Japan with sales in other countries. (2)
日本製紙の会社案内より。世界各国の紙の売上高を日本と比較した棒グラフ。(2)

$129
MILLION
PRODUCT SALES

$37
MILLION
PROFITS

8,000,000
NUMBER OF MUSE SYSTEMS SOLD WORLDWIDE

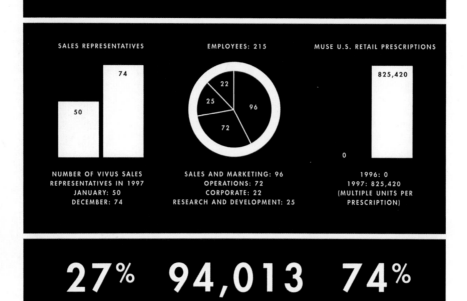

SALES REPRESENTATIVES

74

50

EMPLOYEES: 215

22
25
96
72

MUSE U.S. RETAIL PRESCRIPTIONS

825,420

0

NUMBER OF VIVUS SALES
REPRESENTATIVES IN 1997
JANUARY: 50
DECEMBER: 74

SALES AND MARKETING: 96
OPERATIONS: 72
CORPORATE: 22
RESEARCH AND DEVELOPMENT: 25

1996: 0
1997: 825,420
(MULTIPLE UNITS PER
PRESCRIPTION)

27% **94,013** **74%**

PERCENTAGE OF
GROWTH IN ED OFFICE
VISITS TO UROLOGISTS

NUMBER OF CALLS TO INFO LINES
CONSUMER 1-888-367-MUSE
PROFESSIONAL 1-888-345-MUSE

PERCENTAGE OF MUSE
PRESCRIPTIONS COVERED
BY THIRD PARTY PAYERS

U.S.A. 1998
CD, AD: Bill Cahan
D, I, CW: Kevin Roberson
CW: Jennifer Schraeder
DF: Cahan & Associates
CL: Vivus

This at-a-glance chart includes financial highlights as well as sales figures and consumer hotline information.
企業財政の重要項目を、売上高と消費者ホットラインの利用者数とともに、一見してわかるように示した図。

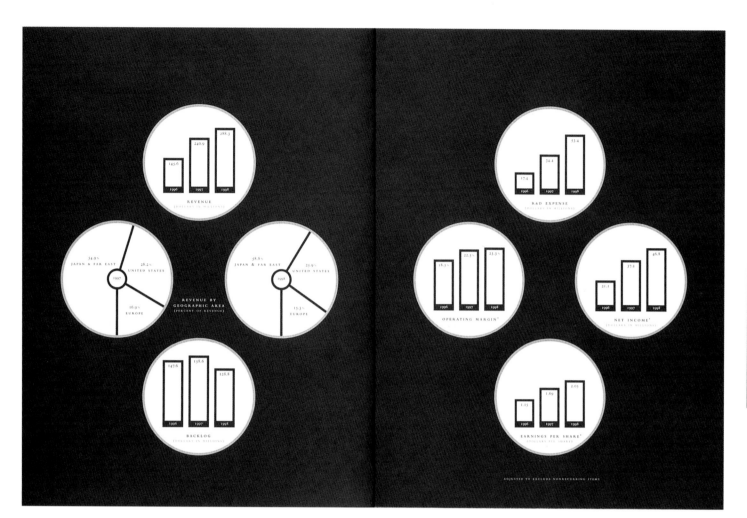

U.S.A.   1998
CD, AD: Bill Cahan
D: Lian Ng
DF: Cahan & Associates
CL: Etec Systems

Etec's financial charts for the 1998 fiscal year. From an annual report.
Etecシステムズ社の1998年度の企業財政を表したグラフ。アニュアル・リポートより。

RETOOLING
SERVICE & SUPPORT

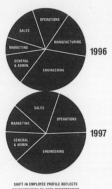

SHIFT IN EMPLOYEE PROFILE REFLECTS
CONCENTRATION ON CORE COMPETENCIES.

THE NETWORK COMPUTING
PYRAMID

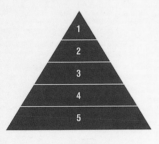

1. SUPER SERVERS
2. MID-RANGE SERVERS
3. PC SERVERS
4. ENTRY LEVEL PC DESKTOP SERVERS
5. DESKTOP PCs AND WORKSTATIONS

PREPARATION

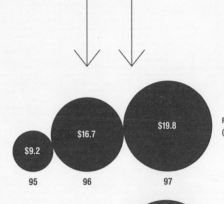

R&D EXPENDITURES
(IN MILLIONS)

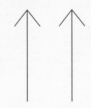

ESTIMATED RAID MARKET
(IN BILLIONS)

SOURCE: IDC 1997 WORLDWIDE DISK SUBSYSTEMS
FORECAST AND MARKET REVIEW (AUGUST, 1997)

OPPORTUNITY

MYLEX 97

U.S.A. 1998
CD, AD: Bill Cahan
D, I, CW: Bob Dinetz
CW: Joanna di Paolo
DF: Cahan & Associates
CL: Mylex

These charts depict the company's move away from manufacturing from 1996 to 1997. (1)
1996年から97年にかけての、製造部門の縮小と移行を示した円グラフ。(1)

This diagram indicates the market breakdown for the company's products. (2)
主要製品の市場分析を示したダイアグラム。(2)

These charts explain Mylex's increased research and development expenditures by showing similar increases in market opportunity over the same time period. (3)
マイレックス社の研究開発投資の増加を、同時期の市場機会の拡大を示すことによって説明した図。(3)

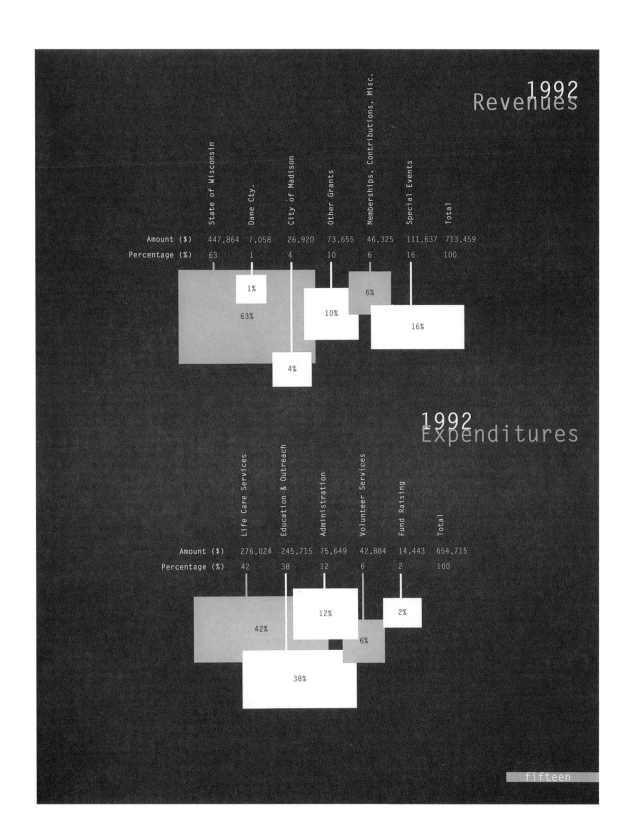

1992 Revenues

	State of Wisconsin	Dane Cty.	City of Madison	Other Grants	Memberships, Contributions, Misc.	Special Events	Total
Amount ($)	447,864	7,058	26,920	73,655	46,325	111,637	713,459
Percentage (%)	63	1	4	10	6	16	100

63% 1% 4% 10% 6% 16%

1992 Expenditures

	Life Care Services	Education & Outreach	Administration	Volunteer Services	Fund Raising	Total
Amount ($)	276,024	245,715	75,649	42,884	14,443	654,715
Percentage (%)	42	38	12	6	2	100

42% 38% 12% 6% 2%

fifteen

U.S.A. 1993
AD, D: Kevin Wade
P: Katherine Walker
CW: Madison AIDS Support Network
DF: Planet Design Company
CL: Madison AIDS Support Network

Graphs that break down 1992 revenues and expenditures
(the dollar amount for each item is shown, as well as its percentage of the total).
1992年度の収入および支出の内訳（各項目の金額と全体に占める割合）を表したグラフ。

O
(OPERATING LEVERAGE)

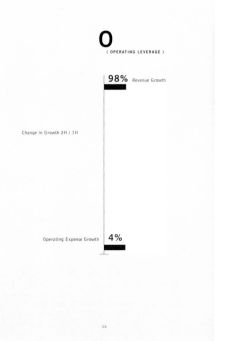

98% Revenue Growth

Change in Growth 2H / 1H

Operating Expense Growth **4%**

16

Mitral Valve

Aortic Valve

1 Vessel

2 Vessel

> 3 Vessel

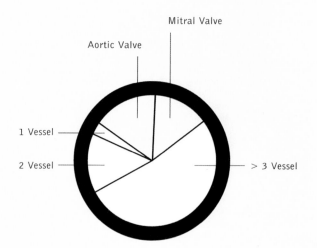

R
(REVENUE IN MILLIONS)

$23.4 Fiscal Year Total

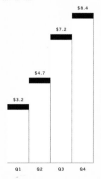

$8.4

$7.2

$4.7

$3.2

Q1   Q2   Q3   Q4

15

Heartport is well-positioned to capitalize on the large market opportunity for minimally invasive heart surgery due to the wide applicability and excellent clinical outcomes possible with its technology.

23

U.S.A. 1998
CD, AD: Bill Cahan
D, I: Kevin Roberson
P: Ken Probst
CW: Heartport
DF: Cahan & Associates
CL: Heartport

From the 1997 annual report of a medical equipment manufacturer.
Graphs detail revenue and earnings, as well as market information.
医療機器会社の1997年度のアニュアル・リポートに収録された収益や市場に関するグラフ。

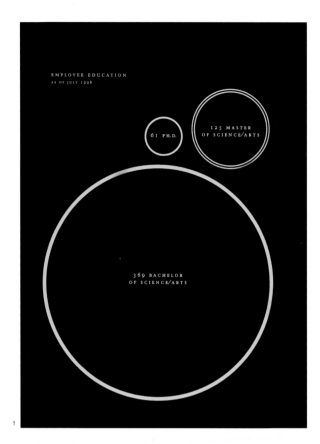

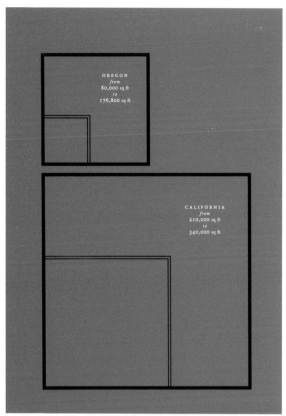

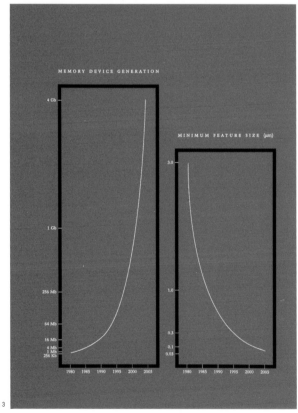

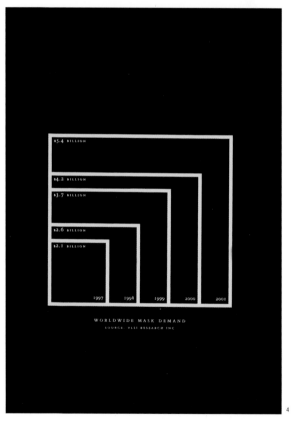

U.S.A. 1998
CD, AD: Bill Cahan
D: Lian Ng
DF: Cahan & Associates
CL: Etec Systems

A diagram showing the education level of the company's employees. (1)
従業員の教育レベルを示した図。(1)

A diagram showing the company's facilities expansion program. (2)
施設拡張計画を説明した図。(2)

This graph demonstrates the inverse relation between feature size and memory capacity. From an annual report. (3)
製品の仕様とメモリ容量の逆比例の関係を表したグラフ。アニュアル・リポートより。(3)

Shows the increasing worldwide demand for mask, used in semiconductor manufacture. (4)
半導体製造において、マスクの需要が世界的に増加していることを示した図。(4)

ca· 9000 Stueck Spritzen

ca· 4000 Liter Infusionsloesungen

ca· 2500 Stueck Infusionsleitungen

10000
8250
7500
6250
5000
3750
2500
1250
0

836 Gasnarkosen

286 rein medikamentoese Narkosen

962 Teilnarkosen

3186 Narkosestunden

684 Notfaelle

1684 geplante Eingriffe

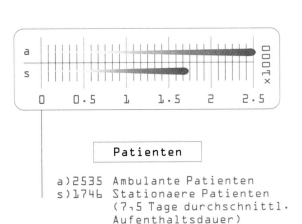

a
s
×1000

0   0·5   1   1·5   2   2·5

Patienten

a) 2535 Ambulante Patienten
s) 1746 Stationaere Patienten
         (7,5 Tage durchschnittl.
         Aufenthaltsdauer)

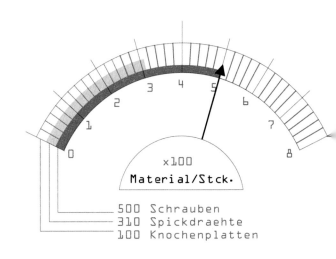

0   1   2   3   4   5   6   7   8

×100
Material/Stck.

500 Schrauben
310 Spickdraehte
100 Knochenplatten

Switzerland 1997
CD, AD, D: Lucia Frey/Heinz Wild
P: Pascal Wüest
CW: Kurt Schori
DF: Wild & Frey
CL: Spital Wil

The graphs and diagrams from a hospital's annual report show some very unusual and entertaining statistics, such as the annual use of orange juice, bread, bandages, stitches, diapers, milk bottles, and much more. They also help describe the large infrastructure and the logistics involved.

オレンジジュース、パン、包帯、糸、オムツ、ほ乳びんなどの年間消費量を表した、珍しい、楽しい統計。
これらはまた、基盤のインフラや経営についても知る手がかりとなる。病院のアニュアル・リポートより。

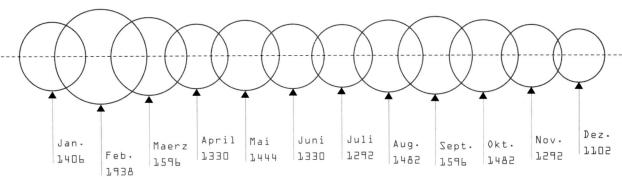

Windelverbrauch 1996

Jan.
1406

Feb.
1938

Maerz
1596

April
1330

Mai
1444

Juni
1330

Juli
1292

Aug.
1482

Sept.
1596

Okt.
1482

Nov.
1292

Dez.
1102

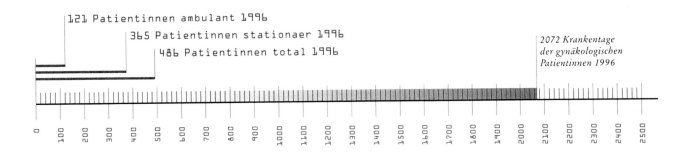

121 Patientinnen ambulant 1996

365 Patientinnen stationaer 1996

486 Patientinnen total 1996

2072 Krankentage der gynäkologischen Patientinnen 1996

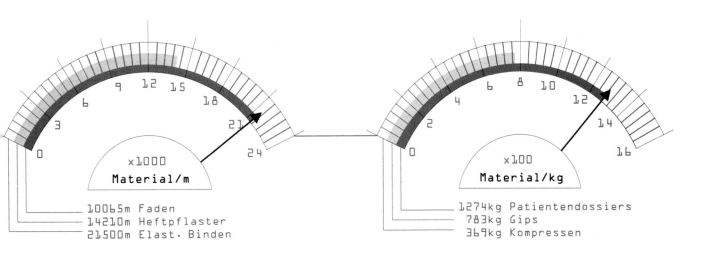

×1000
Material/m

10065m Faden
14210m Heftpflaster
21500m Elast. Binden

×100
Material/kg

1274kg Patientendossiers
783kg Gips
369kg Kompressen

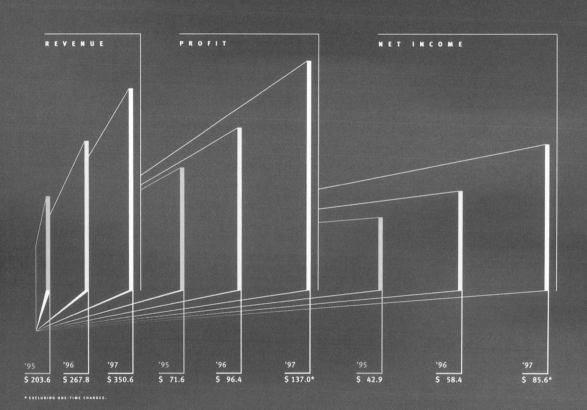

REVENUE   PROFIT   NET INCOME

'95   '96   '97   '95   '96   '97   '95   '96   '97
$ 203.6 $ 267.8 $ 350.6 $ 71.6 $ 96.4 $ 137.0* $ 42.9 $ 58.4 $ 85.6*

* EXCLUDING ONE-TIME CHARGES.

A YEAR OF GROWTH FOR ELECTRONIC COMMERCE.

COMPANIES WHICH HAD NEVER BEFORE USED ELECTRONIC COMMERCE RECOGNIZED THE URGENT NEED TO DO SO. COMPANIES THAT
HAD BEEN EMPLOYING ELECTRONIC COMMERCE EXTENDED IT TO A BROADER RANGE OF FUNCTIONS. COMPANIES WITH LIMITED
EXPERTISE AND BUDGETS BEGAN REAPING THE BENEFITS OF ELECTRONIC COMMERCE THROUGH THE INTERNET. AND EC CONTINUED
TO SPREAD RAPIDLY THROUGHOUT ENTERPRISES AND INDUSTRIES ALL AROUND THE WORLD.

A YEAR OF EXPANSION FOR STERLING COMMERCE.

WE GREW THROUGH STRATEGIC ACQUISITIONS. WE GREW THROUGH AGGRESSIVE EXPANSION INTO MORE AND MORE COUNTRIES AROUND
THE GLOBE. WE GREW BY INTRODUCING NEW PRODUCTS INCLUDING A NUMBER OF INTERNET-RELATED BUSINESS-TO-BUSINESS
SOLUTIONS. WE GREW BY DEEPENING OUR PENETRATION INTO EMERGING INDUSTRIES. WE GREW THROUGH EXPANDING APPLICATIONS
AND SERVICES WITHIN OUR EXISTING CUSTOMER BASE. WE GREW BY PARTNERING WITH PREMIER SUPPLIERS OF COMPLEMENTARY
PRODUCTS AND SERVICES.

1

U.S.A. 1998
CD: Kristin Johnson (1)/Claudia Kis (2)
AD, D, I: Claudia Kis
CW: Frank Cunningham
DF: Pinkhaus
CL: Sterling Commerce

Each graphics highlights the rapid growth of electronic commerce, and emphasizes the company's creative and leading place in that global market. (1)(2)
各図は電子商取引の急速な発展と、グローバル市場における企業のクリエイティブで先進的な地位を強調している。(1)(2)

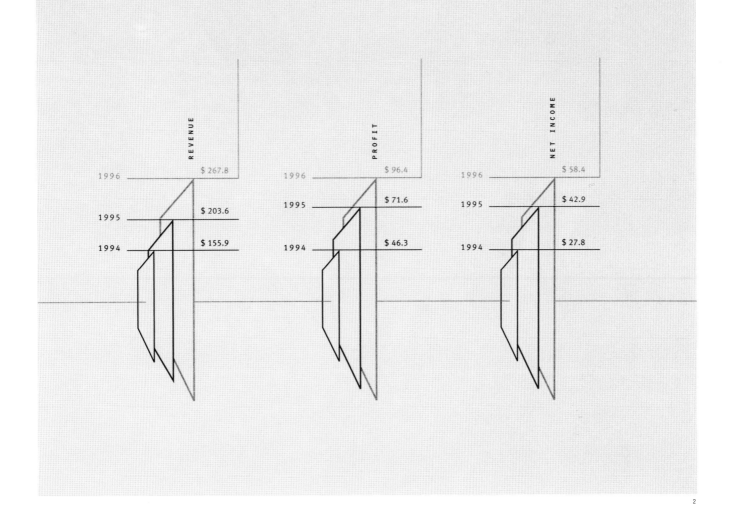

REVENUE

1996	$ 267.8
1995	$ 203.6
1994	$ 155.9

PROFIT

1996	$ 96.4
1995	$ 71.6
1994	$ 46.3

NET INCOME

1996	$ 58.4
1995	$ 42.9
1994	$ 27.8

2

SOUTHWEST AIRLINES CO. ♥ OUR SIX SECRETS OF SUCCESS

PASSENGERS CARRIED PER EMPLOYEE
Scheduled Service Only

2,450 2,597 2,633 2,676 2,379
3,000
2,000
1,000
0
91 92 93 94 95

PASSENGER REVENUE PER PASSENGER MILE
Scheduled Service Only

11.22¢ 11.78¢ 11.77¢ 11.56¢ 11.83¢
15¢
10¢
5¢
0¢
91 92 93 94 95

3

U.S.A. 1996
CD: Tim McClure/GSD&M Advertising
AD, D: Rex Peteet
D: K. C. Teis/Matt Heck
I: Peter Kramer
DF: Sibley/Peteet Design
CL: Southwest Airlines

This graph is simple 3-dimensional chart that convey financial information. (3)
シンプルな3次元グラフで企業財政に関する情報を伝えたもの。(3)

Financial Highlights
Starbucks Corporation

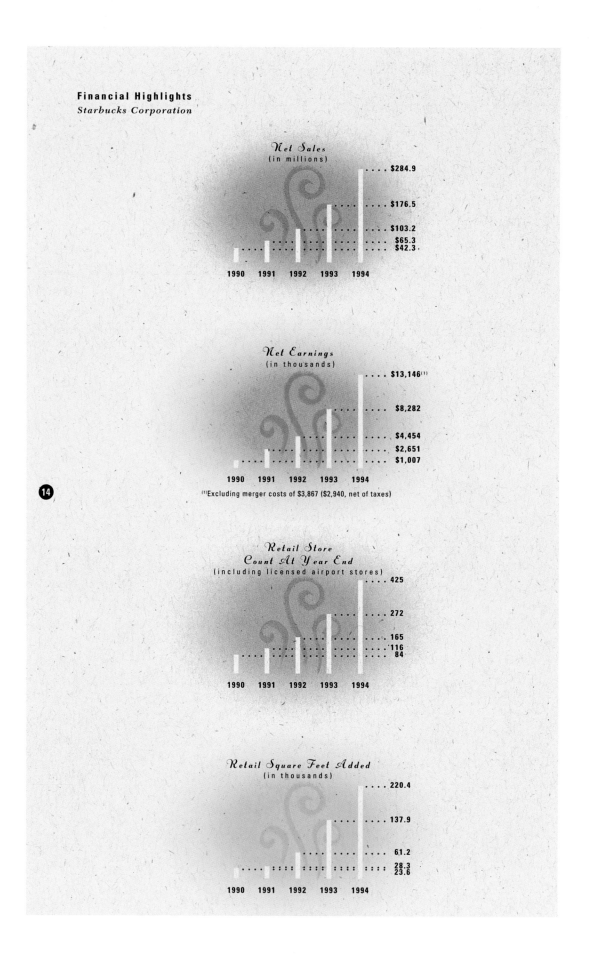

Net Sales
(in millions)

.... $284.9

.... $176.5

.... $103.2
.... $65.3
.... $42.3

1990 1991 1992 1993 1994

Net Earnings
(in thousands)

.... $13,146[1]

.... $8,282

.... $4,454
.... $2,651
.... $1,007

1990 1991 1992 1993 1994

[1]Excluding merger costs of $3,867 ($2,940, net of taxes)

Retail Store
Count At Year End
(including licensed airport stores)

.... 425

.... 272

.... 165
.... 116
84

1990 1991 1992 1993 1994

Retail Square Feet Added
(in thousands)

.... 220.4

.... 137.9

.... 61.2
28.3
23.6

1990 1991 1992 1993 1994

U.S.A. 1995
AD, D: Jack Anderson
D: Julie Lock/Mary Chin Hutchison
P: Michael Baciu
I: Linda Frichtel
CW: Pamela Mason Davey
DF: Hornall Anderson Design Works, Inc.
CL: Starbucks Coffee Company

These graphs from the Starbucks 1994 Annual Report contain financial highlights of the company's earnings scales.
To lend a warmer, friendlier feel to typically cold financial graphs,
elegant patterns of coffee steam accent the background, reflecting the familiar mark found on Starbucks packaging.
スターバックス社の1994年度アニュアル・リポートより。会社の収益について主要なポイントを表すもの。
一般的に素っ気ないものになりがちな財政データのグラフを、温かく、フレンドリーなものにするため、
背景にコーヒーの湯気で、スターバックスのパッケージングでおなじみのマークを想起させるエレガントなパターンを採用した。

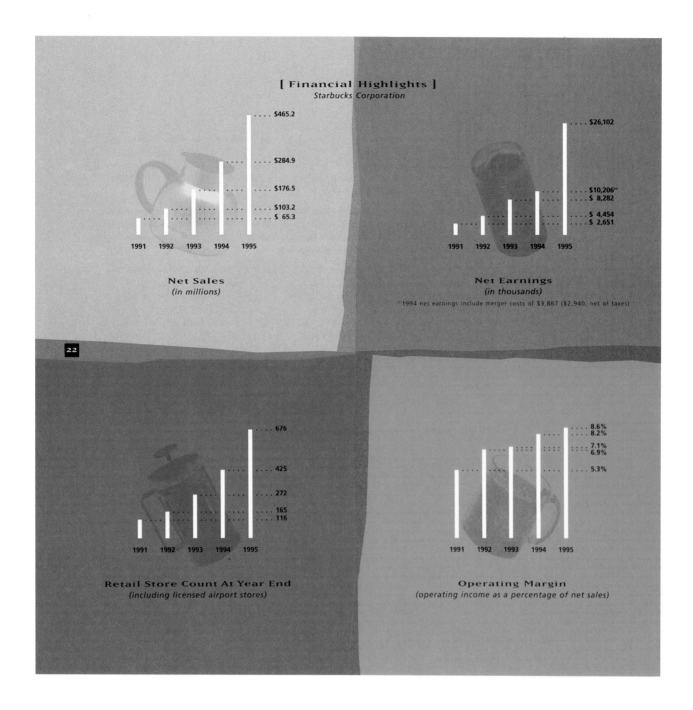

[**Financial Highlights**]
Starbucks Corporation

.... $465.2

.... $284.9

.... $176.5

.... $103.2
.... $ 65.3

1991 1992 1993 1994 1995

Net Sales
(in millions)

.... $26,102

.... $10,206⁽¹⁾
.... $ 8,282

.... $ 4,454
.... $ 2,651

1991 1992 1993 1994 1995

Net Earnings
(in thousands)
⁽¹⁾1994 net earnings include merger costs of $3,867 ($2,940, net of taxes)

.... 676

.... 425

.... 272

.... 165
.... 116

1991 1992 1993 1994 1995

Retail Store Count At Year End
(including licensed airport stores)

.... 8.6%
.... 8.2%

.... 7.1%
.... 6.9%

.... 5.3%

1991 1992 1993 1994 1995

Operating Margin
(operating income as a percentage of net sales)

U.S.A. 1996
AD, D: Jack Anderson
D: Julie Lock/Heidi Favour
P: Alan Abromowitz
CW: Pamela Mason Davey
DF: Hornall Anderson Design Works, Inc.
CL: Starbucks Coffee Company

These charts from the Starbucks 1995 Annual Report contain financial data used to update the company's shareholders and employees on their success and profits.
Black and white photos of coffee cups and carafes are used as background images for each of the four individual graphs.

スターバックス社の1995年度アニュアル・リポートより。会社の成功と利益について株主と従業員に報告するため、財政状況を表したチャート。
4つのグラフそれぞれに、コーヒーカップとカラフェのモノクロ写真がバックグラウンド・イメージとして使用されている。

22

Graphs & Tables

095

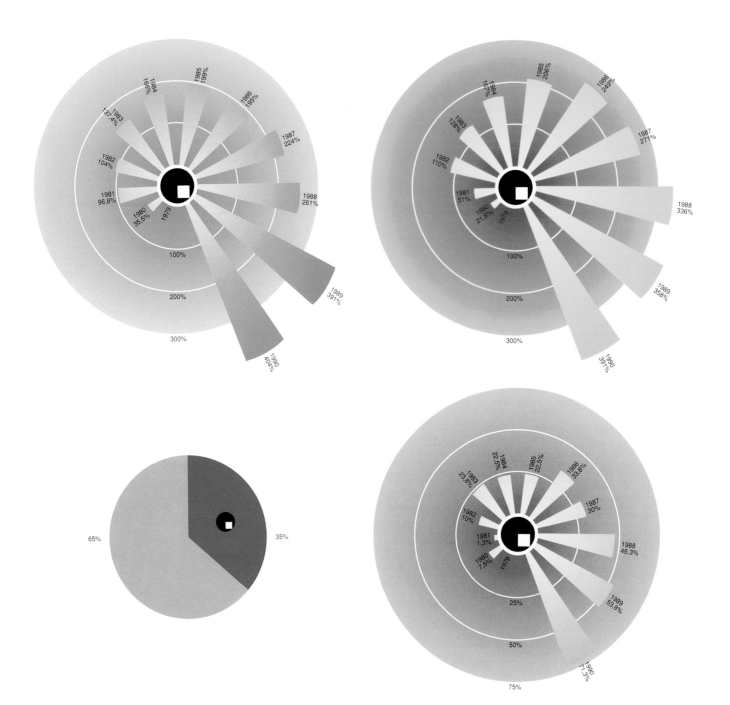

Italy   1994
CD, AD, D, DF: Gianni Bortolotti
CL: MG2 srl

MG2 produces automatic machines for the druggist industry.
The machines have circular movements and a circular shape; the diagrams have the same circular shape.
医薬品販売機器メーカー、MG2の製品（円状に作動する円形の機器）にちなんで、ダイアグラムも円形とした。

会社の業績を示す主な項目が、一見して読み取れるグラフ。総資産の伸びと利用可能な資本、保険契約者の増加、審査請求の結果を示す。

Total Assets
(dollars in millions)
Assets of $1.1 billion
for 1997 set a new
record for the Company.

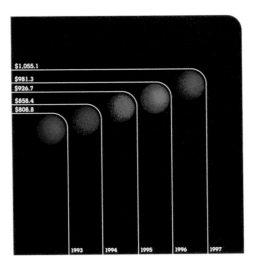

Number of Insureds
As we expand
geographically, our
number of insureds
continues to grow.
In 1997, that number
reached 14,803.

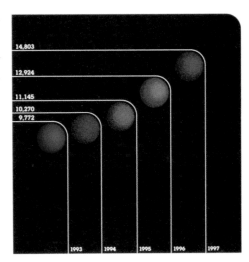

Capital
(dollars in millions)
Our 1997 capital level
of $242.4 million
was further evidence
of our continued
financial soundness.

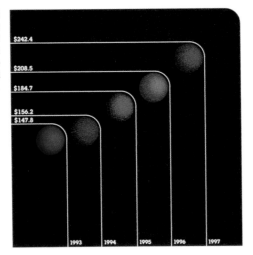

Trial Results
We continued the
tradition of outstanding
protection for our
policyholders, with 97%
of trial results in
their favor in 1997.

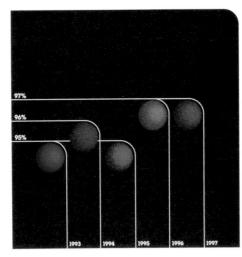

U.S.A. 1998
CD, AD, D: Roger Cook
D: Cathryn Cook
DF: Cook and Shanosky Associates, Inc.
CL: MIIX Group of Companies

*The graphs allow the reader to quickly focus on key elements of the company's performance:
the growth in total assets and available capital, the increased number of policyholders, and the outstanding trial results.
The graphs also allow the reader to visually compare years and see trends in each of these areas.*
会社の業績を示す主な項目が、一見して読み取れるグラフ。総資産の伸びと利用可能な資本、保険契約者の増加、審査請求の結果を示す。
また、年度別の比較もしやすく、各項目の動向を視覚的にとらえることができる。

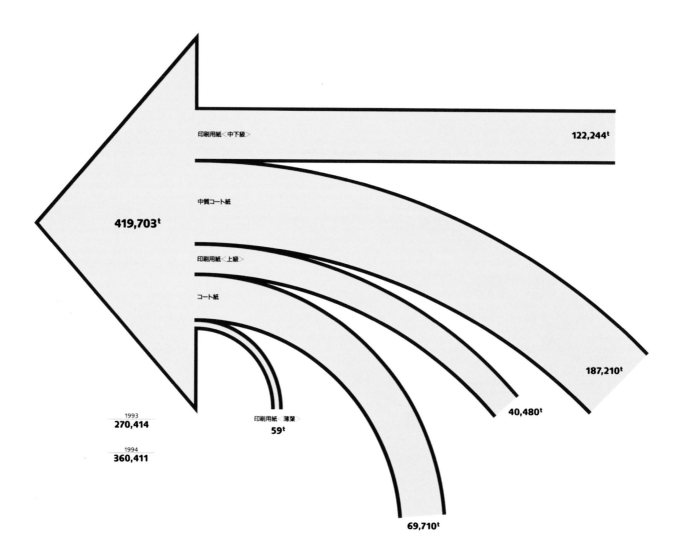

印刷用紙＜中下級＞   122,244ᵗ

中質コート紙

419,703ᵗ

印刷用紙＜上級＞

コート紙

                                                                                187,210ᵗ

                                                                        40,480ᵗ

1993
270,414   印刷用紙＜薄葉＞
                                59ᵗ

1994
360,411

                                        69,710ᵗ

Japan 1995
CD, AD, D: Tetsuya Ohta
CL: Nippon Paper Industries

Imported amounts of various types of paper are shown.
日本製紙の会社案内より。紙の輸入高を表した構成グラフ。

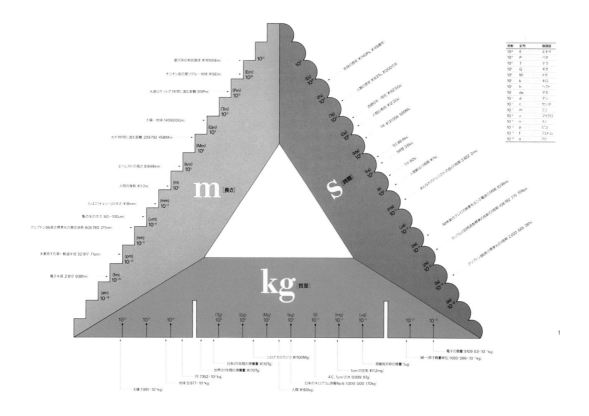

回	1	2	3	4	5	6	7	8	9	10	11	14	15	16	17	18	19	20	21	22	23	24
年	1896	1900	1904	1908	1912	1920	1924	1928	1932	1936	1948	1952	1956	1960	1964	1968	1972	1976	1980	1984	1988
開催地	アテネ	パリ	セントルイス	ロンドン	ストックホルム	アントワープ	パリ	アムステルダム	ロサンゼルス	ベルリン	ロンドン	ヘルシンキ	メルボルン	ローマ	東京	メキシコシティ	ミュンヘン	モントリオール	モスクワ	ロサンゼルス	ソウル
種目数	41	94	95	109	107	162	133	122	124	141	149	152	152	150	163	172	195	198	203	220	241

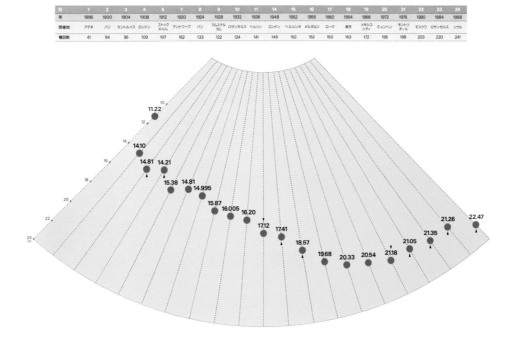

Japan 1991 (2)/1993 (1)
CD, AD, D: Tetsuya Ohta
CL: Visual Message (1)/Japan Coca-Cola (2)

*A comparison graph that illustrates the powers of ten by way of examples,
from micro (radius of an atom) to macro (diameter of the Universe). Examples are given for size, time, and mass.* (1)
雑誌『ビジュアル・メッセージ』より。長さ・時間・質量という世界単位を極小から極大まで同時化した比較図。(1)

*A graph showing the best distance in the Men's Shot Put event, for each Olympic competition.
From a promotional brochure.* (2)
日本コカ・コーラのPR誌より。オリンピックにおける砲丸投げの記録を表したグラフ。(2)

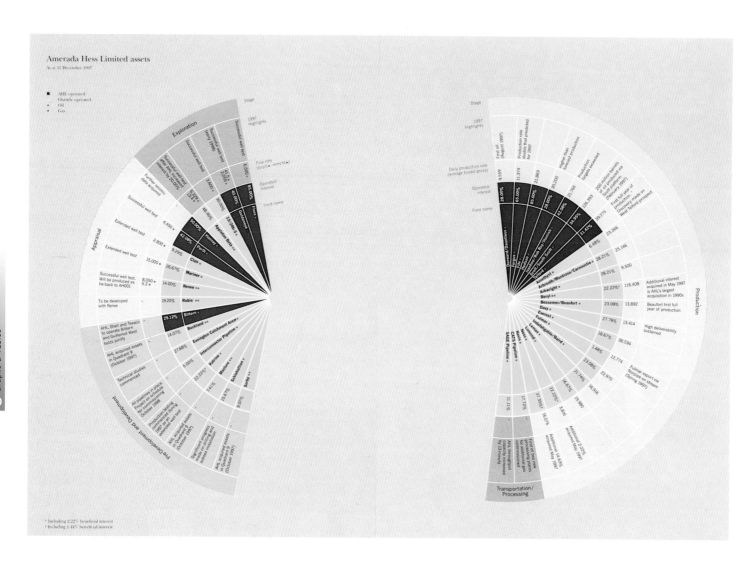

Amerada Hess Limited assets
As at 31 December 1997

U.K. 1998
AD, D: Clifford Hiscock
D: Joanne Wright
DF: Williams and Phoa
CL: Amerada Hess Ltd.

*An at-a-glance pie chart representation of company assets,
broken down into the various production stages and showing much useful information.*
製造過程の詳細やさまざまな有益な情報とともに、会社の資産を示した円グラフ。

ten year financial statistics

1996 financial highlights

EARNINGS AND DIVIDEND PER SHARE (HK$)

Earnings per Share
Dividend per Share

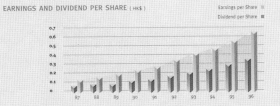

REVENUE PER DOLLAR

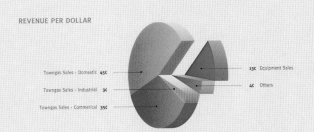

Towngas Sales - Domestic 45¢
Towngas Sales - Industrial 3¢
Towngas Sales - Commerical 35¢

13¢ Equipment Sales
4¢ Others

TOTAL FIXED ASSETS (HK$ million)

Fixed Assets (Cost & Valuation)
Aggregate Depreciation

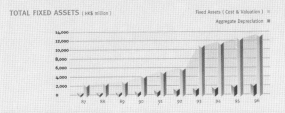

CAPITAL EXPENDITURE (HK$ million)

Capital Expenditure
Depreciation & Amortization

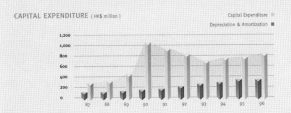

EXPENDITURE PER DOLLAR

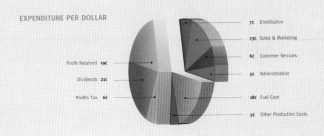

Profit Retained 19¢
Dividends 21¢
Profits Tax 6¢

7¢ Distribution
13¢ Sales & Marketing
6¢ Customer Services
5¢ Administration
18¢ Fuel Cost
5¢ Other Production Costs

Graphs & Tables

101

China 1997
CD, AD: Kan Tai-Keung
AD, D: Eddy Yu Chi Kong
D: Lam Wai Hung
P: Neil Farrin
DF: Kan & Lau Design Consultants
CL: The Hong Kong and China Gas Co., Ltd.

Simple, elegant and straightforward charts designed with lively, cheerful colors, reflecting the company's financial growth in a positive manner.
企業の上向きな成長を、シンプルでエレガントな棒グラフで表した。いきいきと明るい色を使ってデザインしている。

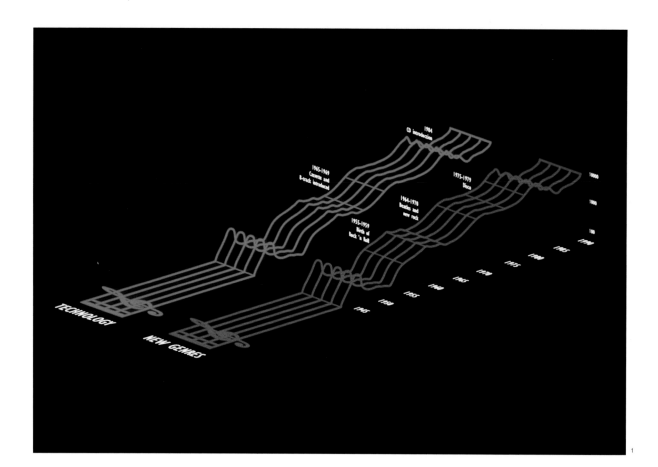

LARGEST LAKES IN AFRICA

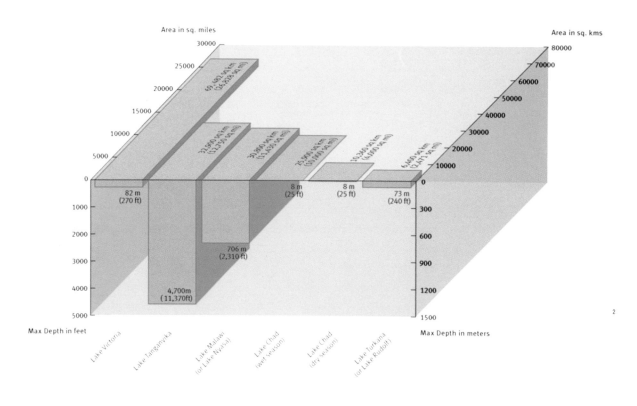

U.K.   1995
CD: Tor Pettersen
CD, AD, D: Jeff Davis
I: David Hunter
DF: Tor Pettersen & Partners Ltd.
CL: EMI Group Plc

The chart shows how new technologies and genres have increased the growth of the music business up to 1990. From an annual report. (1)

新技術と新しいジャンルへの推移が、1990年までの
音楽産業全体をどのように成長させたかを示したグラフ。
アニュアル・リポートより。(1)

U.S.A.   1998
CD: Krzysztof Lenk
D: Chihiro Hosoe
DF: Dynamic Diagrams
CL: Perseus Press

Diagram comparing the largest lakes in Africa in relation to area in square miles (and kilometers) and maximum depth in feet (and meters). (2)

アフリカの大きな湖を、
面積と最大深度で比較した図。(2)

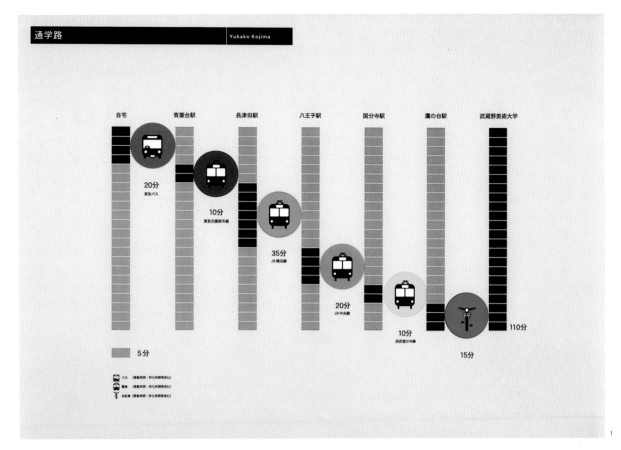

通学路　　　Yukako Kojima

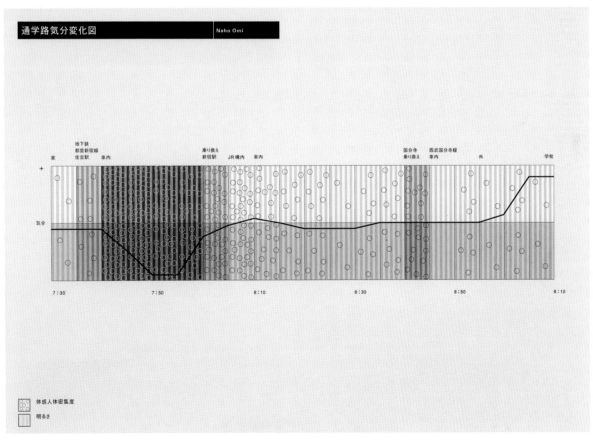

通学路気分変化図　　　Naho Omi

Japan　1999
AD: Tetsuya Ohta
D: Yukako Kojima (1)/Naho Ohmi (2)

Graph shows the different modes of transportation used by a student from home to school, and the amount of time spent on each. (1)
自宅から学校までの通学にかかる時間を、交通手段別に表したグラフ。(1)

Graph that tracks the changes in a student's mood during the morning journey from home to school. (2)
自宅から学校までの通学路において、自分の気分がどのように変化するかを図像で表したグラフ。(2)

Europe by the Number:

Economics

MARKET CAP
Trillions of dollars

$6.9
$3.7 $3.8

Japan   EU   U.S.

GDP GROWTH* ►	U.S.	Germany	France	Britain	Netherlands	Sweden	Italy	Japan	So
1998	3.5%	2.7%	3.1%	2.7%	3.8%	2.8%	1.5%	−2.6%	
1999	1.5%	2.2%	2.4%	0.8%	2.7%	2.2%	2.1%	2.0%	
*Projected.									

EXPORTS ►
As percent of GDP

11.3% 23.6% 23.5% 28.5% 53.3% 40.9% 27.6% 9.4% 33

PER CAPITA ► GNP, in purchasing power	$28,020	$21,110	$21,510	$19,960	$20,850	$18,770	$19,890	$23,420	

E urope is fortunate to be beginning its great single-currency experiment after a strong year. And not-withstanding rumbles from Russia and Latin America, more growth is projected for 1999.

The looming question is this: Why do the major European economies trail America in productivity in nearly every major category, often by a large margin? America uses capital about 15% more efficiently than France or Germany, and 9% more efficiently than Britain. That's an enormous advantage. As is Yankee ingenuity: Americans are far more inventive. Those are imbalances the euro alone cannot resolve.

Productivity

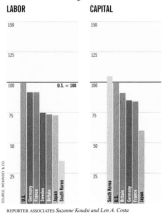

LABOR   **CAPITAL**   **TELECOM**   **AUTOMOBILES**

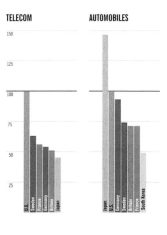

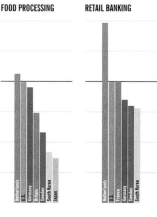

FOOD PROCESSING   **RETAIL BANKING**

SOURCE: MCKINSEY & CO.

REPORTER ASSOCIATES *Suzanne Koudsi and Len A. Costa*

INVENTIONS
Percent of patents issued by U.S.

U.S.
55%
Japan
21%
Germany
6%
France
3%
Britain
2%
South Korea
2%
Sweden
1%
Netherlands
1%
Italy
1%

51 • FORTUNE   December 21, 1998

DIGITAL ILLUSTRATIONS BY ELIOT BERGMAN

U.S.A. 1998
CD: Margery Peters
D, I: Eliot Bergman
CL: Fortune Magazine

Illustrations and charts compare European economies and lifestyles with the U.S.A. and Asian countries.
ヨーロッパの経済、ライフスタイルを、アメリカおよびアジア諸国と比較したイラストとグラフ。

Health

AGING
● Percent over 65   ● In 2010

25
20
15
10
5

S. Korea, U.S., Netherlands, Japan, France, Britain, Germany, Italy, Sweden

POLLUTION
Major pollutants, kg per capita

150
120
90
60
30

U.S., Britain, Germany, Italy, South Korea, Sweden, Netherlands, France, Jpn.

CAR ACCIDENTS
Number injured per 62 million miles driven

U.S.	137
Germany	87
France	36
Britain	72
Netherlands	11
Sweden	33
Italy	63
Japan	129
South Korea	725

OBESITY
Percent overweight

	Men	Women
U.S.	19.9%	24.9%
Germany	18.2%	21.3%
France	8.6%	8.4%
Britain	16.0%	17.0%
Netherlands	8.4%	8.3%
Sweden	5.3%	9.1%
Italy	6.5%	6.3%
Japan	1.8%	2.6%
South Korea	N.A.	N.A.

As a percentage of GDP, the U.S. spends up to twice as much on health care as European countries do. Is that because America has dirtier air, fatter people, and worse drivers? Those are surely contributing factors, but the more important reason has to do with how medical care is delivered—mostly by the private sector in the U.S., mostly by government in Europe. That also helps explain why so many Americans have no coverage at all.

HEALTH-CARE SPENDING
As percent of GDP

14.0% U.S.
10.5% Germany
9.7% France
8.6% Netherlands
7.7% Italy
7.3% Sweden
7.2% Japan
6.9% Britain
4.0% South Korea

CIGARETTE SMOKERS
Percent of population

	South Korea	Japan	France	Netherlands	Italy	Germany	Britain	U.S.	Sweden
Male	61%	57.5%	55.7%	53.2%	39.4%	32%	26%	25.8%	21%
Female	10.8%	14.2%	43.1%	46.8%	28.5%	20%	28%	24.1%	20.7%

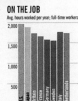

Work

Why do Americans make more money than Europeans? One part of the answer is simple: Americans work more hours and take only ten vacation days a year, the same as the Japanese. Everyone else takes at least 20 days—and the Italians average 26. *La dolce vita* indeed.

ON THE JOB
Avg. hours worked per year; full-time workers

2,000
1,500
1,000
500

U.S., Japan, Britain, France, Germany, Sweden, Italy, Netherlands

TIME OFF
Avg. vacation days per year; full-time workers

30
20
10

U.S., Japan, South Korea, Netherlands, Britain, Germany, France, Sweden, Italy*

*Public sector only.

WOMEN AT WORK
Percent in work force

80%
60%
40%
20%

Sweden, U.S., Britain, Japan, Germany, France, Netherlands, South Korea, Italy

Feeding changing lifestyles

In many of our markets, there are clear demographic and lifestyle changes feeding the growth in demand for food ingredients, petfoods and fast food. In order to meet this growth, we are not only investing in new production facilities in Europe, but also embarking on new product development programmes. Our most important investment is in our people and their expertise. We are developing international managers who are capable of harnessing our technological and product development strengths to take advantage of new market opportunities.

Ideally placed to meet demand

The strategic location of ABC Ingredients' new manufacturing facility in Witstock in northern Germany and PAC's seasonings plant in Muggio, northern Italy provide an invaluable production and distribution network into both western and eastern Europe. This is particularly important when one considers the growing trend in Europe for eating pastas and other mediterranean food.

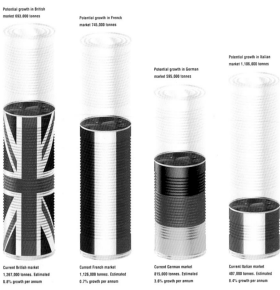

Potential growth in British market 693,000 tonnes

Potential growth in French market 745,000 tonnes

Potential growth in German market 595,000 tonnes

Potential growth in Italian market 1,106,000 tonnes

Current British market 1,267,000 tonnes. Estimated 0.8% growth per annum

Current French market 1,126,000 tonnes. Estimated 0.7% growth per annum

Current German market 815,000 tonnes. Estimated 3.6% growth per annum

Current Italian market 407,000 tonnes. Estimated 8.4% growth per annum

1988-5.9%   1990-8.9%   1992-17.0%   1994-21.2%

Felix, a growing brand

Since 1988 Felix has achieved an increase in UK market share from 6% to over 21%, this performance is doubly impressive considering most other brands remained static or lost market share. There is strong potential for this performance to be repeated in other European markets.

Potential growth in Spanish market 329,000 tonnes

Potential growth in Dutch market 107,000 tonnes

Potential growth in Belgian market 228,000 tonnes

Current Dutch market 207,000 tonnes. Estimated 0.5% growth per annum

Current Spanish market 181,000 tonnes. Estimated 9.3% growth per annum

Current Belgian market 161,000 tonnes. Estimated 3.3% growth per annum

A meaty potential

The market for prepared petfood in continental Europe is currently growing at a rate of 3% per annum. This rate when set against the overall size of the market represents an exciting opportunity for Spillers Petfoods. As a clear number two with a strong portfolio of major brands and a highly developed distribution network, Spillers Petfoods is well placed to capitalise on the growth potential of the European petfood markets.

U.K.   1995
CD: Tor Pettersen
AD, D: David Brown
D: Craig Johnson
I: Daivid Hunter/Julia Wisman
DF: Tor Pettersen & Partners Ltd.
CL: Dalgety

The graphic shows the actual and potential size of the pet food market in each of the seven European countries in which the company operates.
ダルジェティ社の取り扱うヨーロッパ7カ国について、ペットフード市場の現在の規模と、将来の予測規模を示したグラフ。

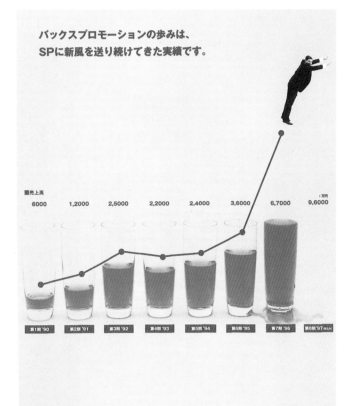

バックスプロモーションの歩みは、
SPに新風を送り続けてきた実績です。

■売上高   (万円)
6000   1,2000   2,5000   2,2000   2,4000   3,6000   6,7000   9,6000

第1期 '90   第2期 '91   第3期 '92   第4期 '93   第5期 '94   第6期 '95   第7期 '96   第8期 '97(見込み)

Japan   1997
AD: Tatsuo Ebina
D: Tetsufumi Saito
P: Tadashi Tomono
CW: Seiichiro Oda
DF: E Co., Ltd.
CL: Backs Promotion Inc.

Graph illustrating a sales increase trend. From a promotion company's informational brochure.
SP会社の会社案内より。売上高の変化を表したグラフ。

A cost effective service

We are at the forefront in the application of advanced technology to control operating costs. As a result, despite significant increases in quality, we remain a low cost operator. Our combined water and sewerage charge per day for the average unmeasured household in 1991/92 is 38p, less than a loaf of bread and considerably lower than a litre of bottled water.

Severn Trent's charge for drinking water is the lowest of the ten privatised companies and much lower than most of the European Community. Cost control initiatives, many of them based on the use of advanced technology, have made this possible.

Power costs have been cut by 5 per cent through our ability to purchase electricity taking advantage of the flexible tariffs of the power companies. Advanced computer systems help us to manage power consumption in our plants. Our large

sewage treatment plants, for example, are virtually self sufficient in power, using methane, a by-product of the treatment processes, to run generators.

Our interlinked drinking water grid permits flexibility in operation and effective distribution of water resources. There were no hosepipe bans in Severn Trent in 1990, despite the hottest and driest summer on record in the Midlands.

A range of operational and administrative systems have resulted in dramatic increases in productivity. DOJM, for example, our work planning system, is linked to our customer bureau to ensure that maintenance works are promptly and efficiently accomplished.

IMPACT, our Image Processing and Customer Transaction System, reduces paperwork and speeds all billing and customer transactions, while CAST (Customer Accounting Severn Trent)

has been implemented to bring real-time facilities to this area.

Computer aided design and expert systems, currently in use or under development, have improved engineering productivity and are helping us to establish the most cost effective design solutions for our capital improvements.

In May 1991 we acquired Stoner Associates, Inc., acknowledged experts in the area of pipeline operational management systems. The "Stoner" System will be implemented during the current year and will be used to target investment for earlier improvements in levels of service to customers.

Process controls, currently in place or under assessment, cost effectively maintain our high quality standards through remote monitoring and control telemetry. New water treatment facilities, for example, require minimum staff intervention and are capable of remote control.

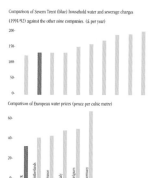

Comparison of Severn Trent (blue) household water and sewerage charges (1991/92) against the other nine companies. (£ per year)

Comparison of European water prices (pence per cubic metre)

Severn Trent's charge for drinking water is the lowest of the ten privatised companies.

£61 per year (Severn Trent) — £66 per year — £66 per year — £66 per year — £67 per year — £80 per year — £81 per year — £83 per year — £94 per year — £104 per year

8

9

U.K.   1994
CD: Tor Pettersen
AD: Jeff Davis
D: Joann Weedon
P: Bob Fyffe
DF: Tor Pettersen & Partners Ltd.
CL: Severn Trent Plc

Simply but with immediate impact, the graph visually reflects the fact that Severn Trent's charges for drinking water is the lowest of the ten major British water companies.
セブン・トレント社は英国の主な飲料水メーカー10社のうち最も料金が安い。グラフはシンプルだが、一見してインパクトを与えるようにデザインされている。

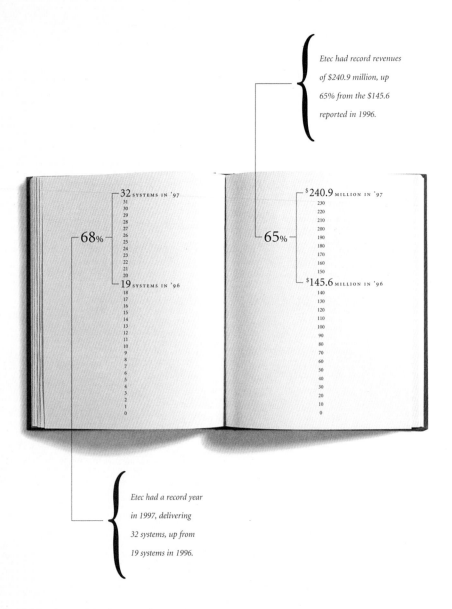

*Etec had record revenues
of $240.9 million, up
65% from the $145.6
reported in 1996.*

32 SYSTEMS IN '97
31
30
29
28
27
26
25
24
23
22
21
20
19 SYSTEMS IN '96
18
17
16
15
14
13
12
11
10
9
8
7
6
5
4
3
2
1
0

68%

$**240.9** MILLION IN '97
230
220
210
200
190
180
170
160
150
$**145.6** MILLION IN '96
140
130
120
110
100
90
80
70
60
50
40
30
20
10
0

65%

*Etec had a record year
in 1997, delivering
32 systems, up from
19 systems in 1996.*

8

U.S.A.   1997
CD, AD: Bill Cahan
D: Lian Ng
P: Fredrik Boden
CW: Etec Systems
DF: Cahan & Associates
CL: Etec Systems

Charts indicating the company's growth rate.
会社の成長率を示したグラフ。

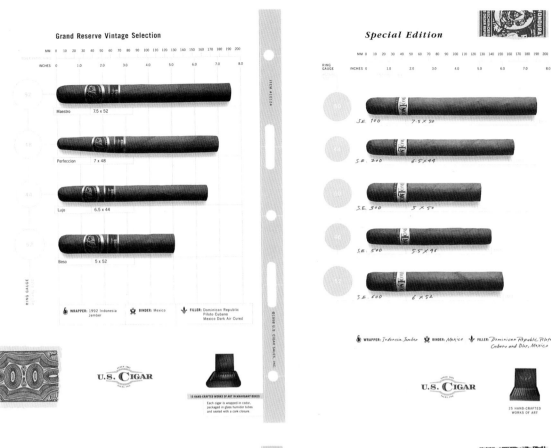

Grand Reserve Vintage Selection

MM 0 10 20 30 40 50 60 70 80 90 100 110 120 130 140 150 160 170 180 190 200
INCHES 0   1.0   2.0   3.0   4.0   5.0   6.0   7.0   8.0

Maestro   7.5 x 52

Perfeccion   7 x 48

Lujo   6.5 x 44

Beso   5 x 52

RING GAUGE

WRAPPER: 1992 Indonesia Jember   **BINDER:** Mexico   **FILLER:** Dominican Republic Piloto Cubano Mexico Dark Air Cured

U.S. CIGAR

15 HAND-CRAFTED WORKS OF ART IN MAHOGANY BOXES
Each cigar is wrapped in cedar, packaged in glass humidor tubes, and sealed with a cork closure.

ITEM #10124

© 1998 U.S. CIGAR SALES, INC.

Special Edition

RING GAUGE
MM 0 10 20 30 40 50 60 70 80 90 100 110 120 130 140 150 160 170 180 190 200
INCHES 0   1.0   2.0   3.0   4.0   5.0   6.0   7.0   8.0

50   S.E. 100   7.5 x 50

44   S.E. 200   6.5 x 44

40   S.E. 300   5 x 50

46   S.E. 500   5.5 x 46

52   S.E. 600   6 x 52

WRAPPER: Indonesia Jember   **BINDER:** Mexico   **FILLER:** Dominican Republic Piloto Cubano and Dlr, Mexico

U.S. CIGAR

25 HAND-CRAFTED WORKS OF ART

ITEM #10223

© 1998 U.S. CIGAR SALES, INC.

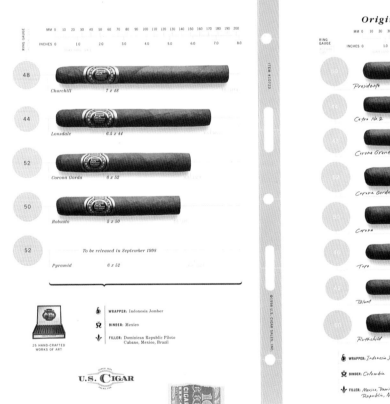

RING GAUGE
MM 0 10 20 30 40 50 60 70 80 90 100 110 120 130 140 150 160 170 180 190 200
INCHES 0   1.0   2.0   3.0   4.0   5.0   6.0   7.0   8.0

48   Churchill   7 x 48

44   Lonsdale   6.5 x 44

52   Corona Gorda   6 x 52

50   Robusto   5 x 50

52   Pyramid   6 x 52   To be released in September 1998

WRAPPER: Indonesia Jember   **BINDER:** Mexico   **FILLER:** Dominican Republic Piloto Cubano, Mexico, Brazil

25 HAND-CRAFTED WORKS OF ART

U.S. CIGAR

ITEM #10223

© 1998 U.S. CIGAR SALES, INC.

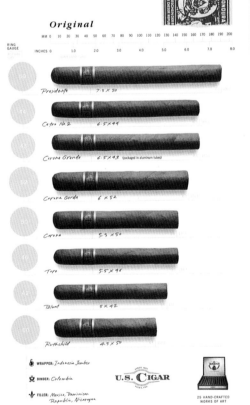

Original

RING GAUGE
MM 0 10 20 30 40 50 60 70 80 90 100 110 120 130 140 150 160 170 180 190 200
INCHES 0   1.0   2.0   3.0   4.0   5.0   6.0   7.0   8.0

Presidente   7.5 x 50

Cetro No 2   6.5 x 44

Corona Grande   6.5 x 43   (packaged in aluminum tubes)

Corona Gorda   6 x 52

Corona   5.5 x 50

Tiro   5.5 x 46

Blunt   5 x 42

Rothchild   4.5 x 50

WRAPPER: Indonesia Jember   **BINDER:** Colombia   **FILLER:** Mexico, Dominican Republic, Nicaragua

U.S. CIGAR

25 HAND-CRAFTED WORKS OF ART

U.S.A. 1998
AD: Jack Anderson
AD, D: Larry Anderson
D: Mary Hermes/Mike Calkins/Michael Brugman
P: David Emmite
I: John Fretz/Jack Unruh/Bill Halinann
CW: John Frazier
DF: Hornall Anderson Design Works, Inc.
CL: U.S. Cigar

These charts, from a U.S. Cigar fact sheet, serve as system indicators of each of the company's brands of cigar. The cigars themselves were employed in the bar chart's measuring scales, which include such data as cigar length, ring gauge, and variety.

U.S. Cigar社の製品情報カタログに使用された、ブランドごとの仕様を表すチャート。
棒グラフに葉巻そのものを使用し、葉巻の長さ、太さ、種類などのデータを示した。

明日の"患者-医師"関係を考える

PHYSIC!AN

No.5
'97 AUTUMN

（医師125人に聞きました）
**Q.あなたは
「口べたで患者さんへの説明が苦手である」
と思いますか?**

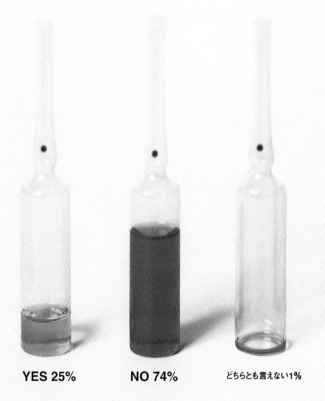

YES 25%　　　　**NO 74%**　　　どちらとも言えない1%

特集
「コミュニケーション・ツール」を考える
—————— 患者と医療者の対話のために

Life Science Publishing

Japan 1996-1998
CD, AD, D: Katsumi Kajiyama
P: Takashi Shima
DF: Integral+
CL: Life Science Publishing

Covers of the medical magazine "Physician," showing results of polls taken of doctors from both large hospitals and smaller clinics.
医療雑誌『PHYSICIAN』の表紙より。勤務医、開業医をアンケート対象者とした意識調査の結果を表すグラフ。

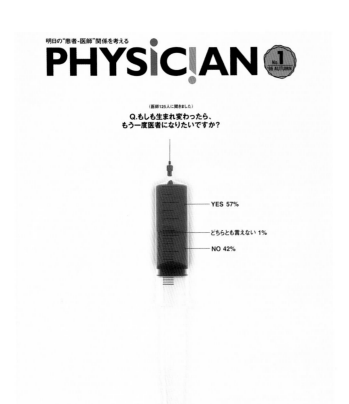

明日の"患者-医師"関係を考える

PHYSICIAN No.1 '96 AUTUMN

（医師125人に聞きました）
**Q.もしも生まれ変わったら、
もう一度医者になりたいですか？**

YES 57%

どちらとも言えない 1%

NO 42%

特集
患者のillness behavior
3000人の実態調査にみる患者の受療行動

Life Science Publishing

明日の"患者-医師"関係を考える

PHYSICIAN No.2 '96 WINTER

（医師125人に聞きました）
**Q.自分の治療が
不安になることがありますか？**

YES 85%

NO 15%

特集
**あなたは患者の"うつ状態"に
どう対応していますか**

Life Science Publishing

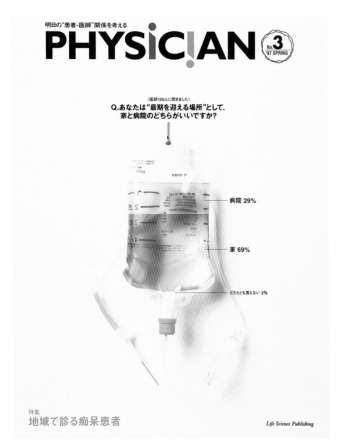

明日の"患者-医師"関係を考える

PHYSICIAN No.3 '97 SPRING

（医師125人に聞きました）
**Q.あなたは"最期を迎える場所"として、
家と病院のどちらがいいですか？**

病院 29%

家 69%

どちらとも言えない 2%

特集
地域で診る痴呆患者

Life Science Publishing

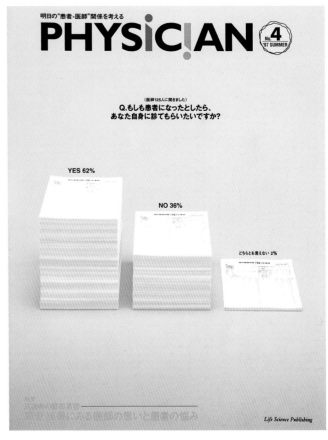

明日の"患者-医師"関係を考える

PHYSICIAN No.4 '97 SUMMER

（医師125人に聞きました）
**Q.もしも患者になったとしたら、
あなた自身に診てもらいたいですか？**

YES 62%

NO 36%

どちらとも言えない 2%

Life Science Publishing

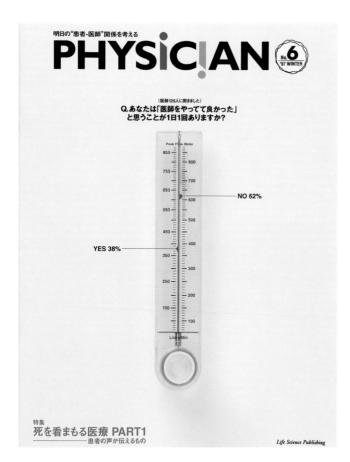

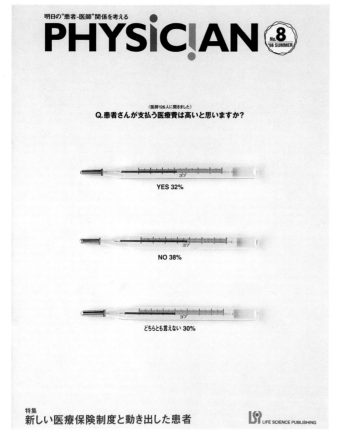

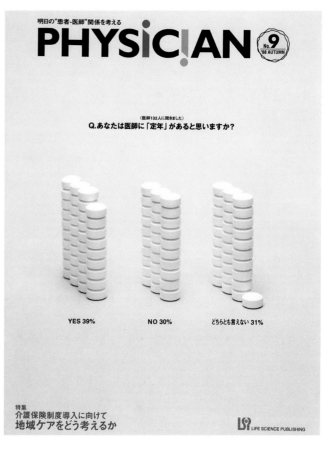

Japan 1996-1998
CD, AD, D: Katsumi Kajiyama
P: Takashi Shima
DF: Integral+
CL: Life Science Publishing

Covers of the medical magazine "Physician," showing results of polls taken of doctors from both large hospitals and smaller clinics.
医療雑誌『PHYSICIAN』の表紙より。勤務医、開業医をアンケート対象者とした意識調査の結果を表すグラフ。

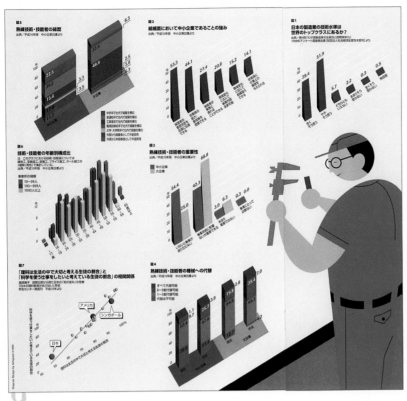

ものづくり 人づくり

財団法人 国際技能振興財団

技能五輪国際大会における日本の順位の推移

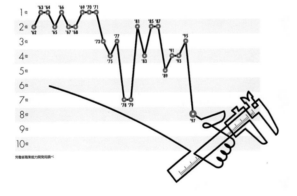

Japan 1999
AD: Kenzo Nakagawa
D: Hiroyasu Nobuyama/
   Satoshi Morikami/Norika Nakayama
DF: NDC Graphics Inc.
CL: The Foundation for the Promotion
    of Crafts and Technology

*Graphs showing Japanese rankings in the International Vocational Training Competition,
and data relating to the skilled Japanese technicians themselves.*
PR誌『ものづくり 人づくり』より。「技能五輪国際大会における日本の順位の推移」ほか、
日本の熟練技術・技能者に関するさまざまなデータをグラフ化した。

あした葉

A s h i t a b a
J a n u a r y
1 9 9 6
N u m b e r 4 7 5

積雪の最深記録

［統計開始年から1993年の春まで｜資料：気象庁 他］

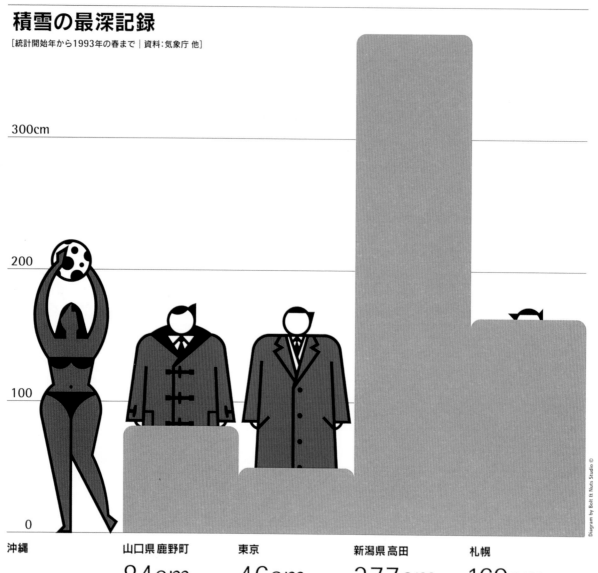

	300cm			
	200			
	100			
	0			

沖縄	山口県 鹿野町	東京	新潟県 高田	札幌
—	**84cm**	**46cm**	**377cm**	**169cm**
	1917年1月9日	1883年2月8日	1945年2月26日	1939年2月13日

Diagram by Bolt & Nuts Studio ©

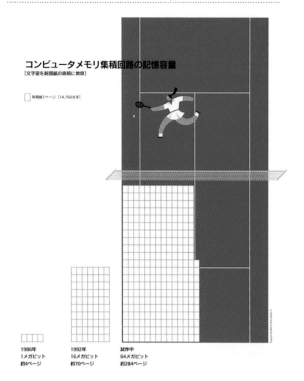

コンピュータメモリ集積回路の記憶容量
[文字量を新聞紙の面積に換算]

□ 新聞紙1ページ [14,760文字]

1986年	1992年	試作中
1メガビット	16メガビット	64メガビット
約4ページ	約70ページ	約284ページ

11.8m

米の1人当たり年間消費量のための作付面積
[資料：農業白書附属統計表／(財)農林統計協会]

139m²

11.8m

日本人が1年間に食べる米の量 [平成4年度]
69.7kg

入浴剤の消費量季節指数
[1995年度／年間消費量の平均を100としたもの／資料：株式会社ツムラ調べ]

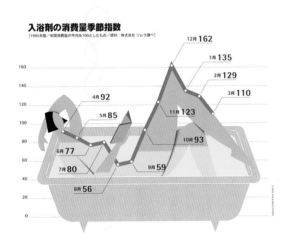

12月162
1月135
2月129
3月110
4月92
11月123
5月85
10月93
6月77
9月59
7月80
8月56

夏をイメージする色
[資料：(社)日本流行色協会編『色のイメージ事典』]

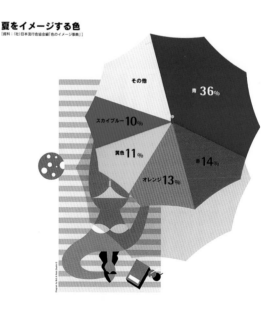

その他
青 36%
スカイブルー 10%
黄色 11%
赤 14%
オレンジ 13%

Japan　1996
AD: Kenzo Nakagawa
D: Hiroyasu Nobuyama/Satoshi Morikami
CW: Chizuko Ishikawa
DF: Bolt Et Nuts Studio
CL: Tokuyama Corp.

Graphs illustrating results of questionnaires pertaining to company products and related matters. From a corporate in-house magazine.

社内報『あした葉』より。自社製品とかかわりのあるさまざまな事象に関するアンケート結果をまとめたグラフ。

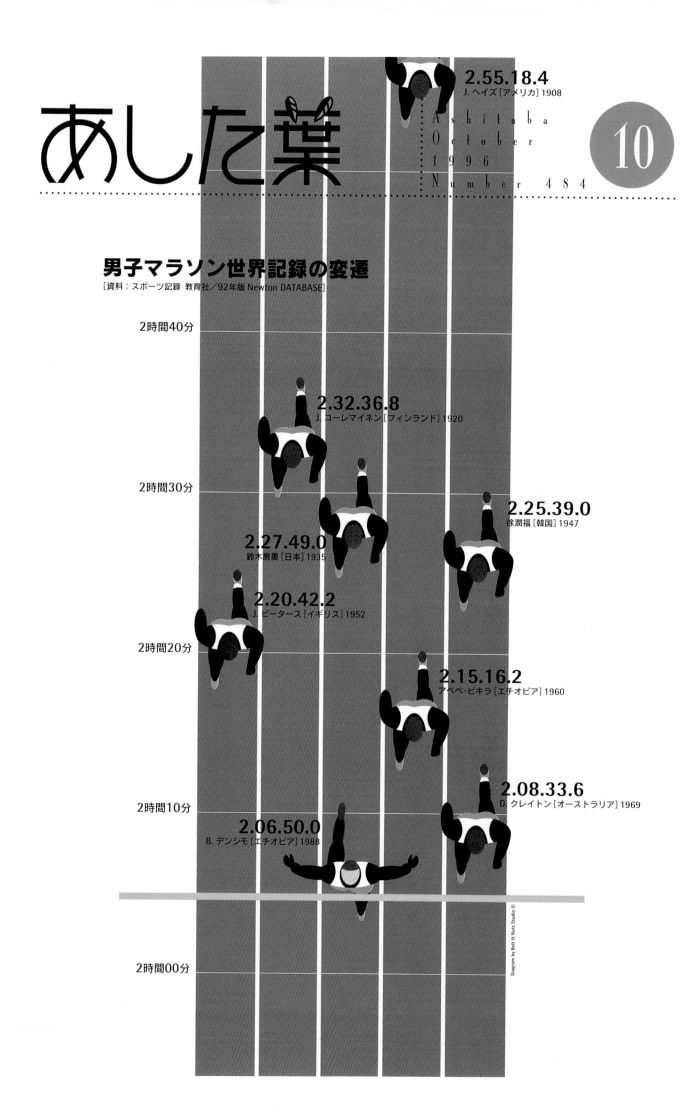

あした葉

A s h i t a b a
O c t o b e r
1 9 9 6
N u m b e r 4 8 4

10

2.55.18.4
J. ヘイズ［アメリカ］1908

男子マラソン世界記録の変遷
［資料：スポーツ記録 教育社／92年版 Newton DATABASE］

2時間40分

2.32.36.8
J. コーレマイネン［フィンランド］1920

2時間30分

2.25.39.0
徐潤福［韓国］1947

2.27.49.0
鈴木房重［日本］1935

2.20.42.2
J. ピータース［イギリス］1952

2時間20分

2.15.16.2
アベベ・ビキラ［エチオピア］1960

2.08.33.6
D. クレイトン［オーストラリア］1969

2時間10分

2.06.50.0
B. デンシモ［エチオピア］1988

2時間00分

Diagram by Bolt & Nuts Studio ©

あした葉

木造と非木造の新設住宅戸数の変化

[資料：建設省建築統計年報]

1984年
1994年

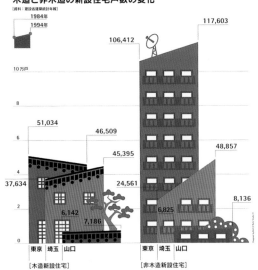

117,603
106,412
51,034
46,509
45,395
48,857
37,634
24,561
8,136
6,142
7,186
6,825

10万戸
8
6
4
2
0

東京　埼玉　山口
[木造新設住宅]
東京　埼玉　山口
[非木造新設住宅]

あした葉

使用灯油量でみる、ガラスとサッシの種類による断熱性能比較

[資料：株式会社トクヤマ調べ]

=100ℓ

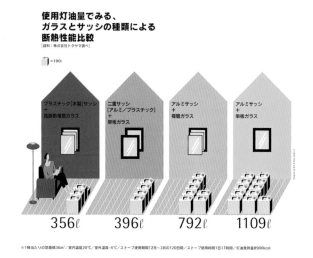

プラスチック[木製]サッシ
＋
高断熱複層ガラス

二重サッシ
[アルミ／プラスチック]
＋
単板ガラス

アルミサッシ
＋
複層ガラス

アルミサッシ
＋
単板ガラス

356ℓ　　396ℓ　　792ℓ　　1109ℓ

※1棟当たりの居面積36㎡／室内温度20℃／室外温度-4℃／ストーブ使用期間12月〜3月の120日間／ストーブ使用時間1日17時間／灯油発熱量8900kcal

あした葉

LPガス事故件数と警報器普及率

[資料：ガス警報器工業会調べ]

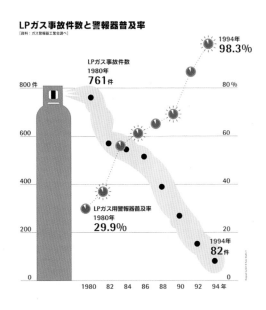

1994年
98.3%

LPガス事故件数
1980年
761件

800件　　　　　　　80%
600　　　　　　　　60
400　　　　　　　　40
200　　　　　　　　20
0　　　　　　　　　0

LPガス用警報器普及率
1980年
29.9%

1994年
82件

1980　82　84　86　88　90　92　94年

あした葉

毎日歯をみがく人

[資料：厚生省[歯科疾患実態調査]]

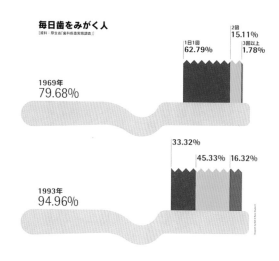

1日1回
62.79%

2回
15.11%

3回以上
1.78%

1969年
79.68%

33.32%　45.33%　16.32%

1993年
94.96%

Japan　1996
AD: Kenzo Nakagawa
D: Hiroyasu Nobuyama/Satoshi Morikami
CW: Chizuko Ishikawa
DF: Bolt Et Nuts Studio
CL: Tokuyama Corp.

Graphs illustrating results of questionnaires pertaining to company products and related matters. From a corporate in-house magazine.

社内報『あした葉』より。自社製品とかかわりのあるさまざまな事象に関するアンケート結果をまとめたグラフ。

Graphs & Tables

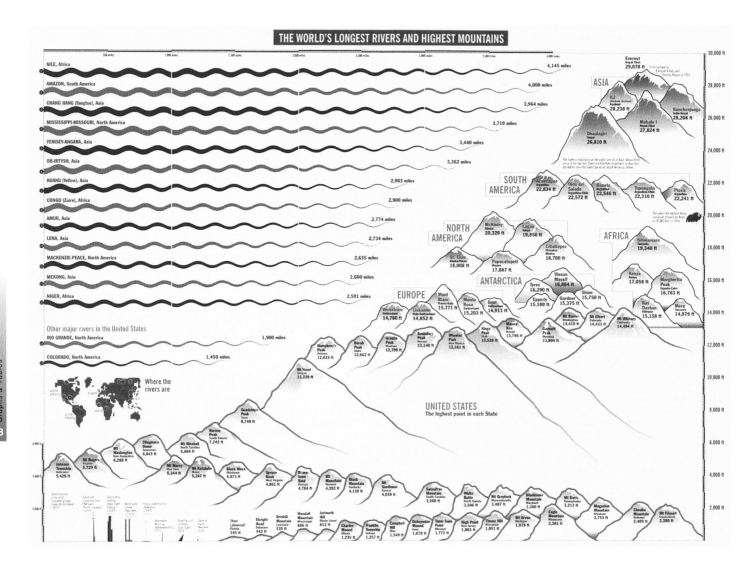

THE WORLD'S LONGEST RIVERS AND HIGHEST MOUNTAINS

U.S.A. 1996
AD, D, I, DF: Nigel Holmes
CL: Time Education Program

Diagram showing the world's longest rivers and highest mountains, all in scale.
世界中の長い川と高い山を正確な縮尺で表した。

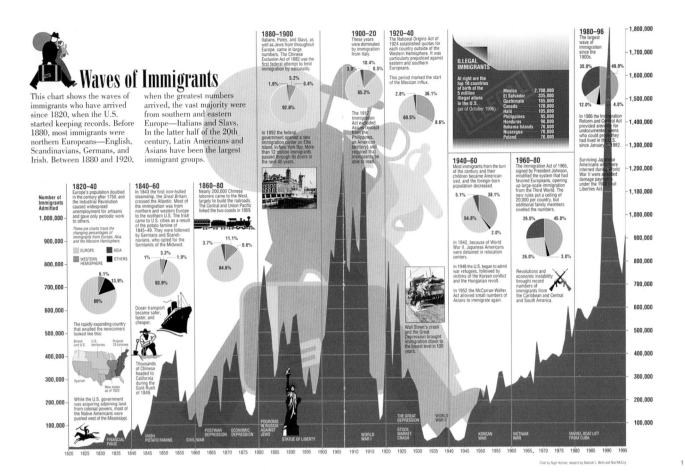

Waves of Immigrants

This chart shows the waves of immigrants who have arrived since 1820, when the U.S. started keeping records. Before 1880, most immigrants were northern Europeans—English, Scandinavians, Germans, and Irish. Between 1880 and 1920,

when the greatest numbers arrived, the vast majority were from southern and eastern Europe—Italians and Slavs. In the latter half of the 20th century, Latin Americans and Asians have been the largest immigrant groups.

Number of Immigrants Admitted

1820–40
Europe's population doubled in the century after 1750, and the Industrial Revolution caused widespread unemployment for artisans and gave only periodic work to others.

These pie charts track the changing percentages of immigrants from Europe, Asia, and the Western Hemisphere.

- EUROPE
- WESTERN HEMISPHERE
- ASIA
- OTHERS

6.1% / 13.9% / 80%

The rapidly expanding country that awaited the newcomers looked like this:

British and U.S. territories / U.S. territories / Original 13 colonies / Spanish / New states as of 1820

While the U.S. government was acquiring adjoining land from colonial powers, most of the Native Americans were pushed west of the Mississippi.

1840–60
In 1843 the first iron-hulled steamship, the *Great Britain*, crossed the Atlantic. Most of the immigration was from northern and western Europe to the northern U.S. The Irish came to U.S. cities as a result of the potato famine of 1845–49. They were followed by Germans and Scandinavians, who opted for the farmlands of the Midwest.

1% / 3.2% / 1.9% / 93.9%

Ocean transport became safer, faster, and cheaper.

Thousands of Chinese headed to California during the Gold Rush of 1849.

1860–80
Nearly 200,000 Chinese laborers came to the West, largely to build the railroads. The Central and Union Pacific linked the two coasts in 1869.

3.7% / 11.1% / 0.6% / 84.6%

1880–1900
Italians, Poles, and Slavs, as well as Jews from throughout Europe, came in large numbers. The Chinese Exclusion Act of 1882 was the first federal attempt to limit immigration by nationality.

1.6% / 5.2% / 0.4% / 92.8%

In 1892 the federal government opened a new immigration center on Ellis Island, in New York Bay. More than 12 million immigrants passed through its doors in the next 40 years.

1900–20
These years were dominated by immigration from Italy.

3.9% / 10.4% / 0.5% / 85.2%

The 1917 Immigration Act excluded Asians (except from the Philippines, an American territory) and required that immigrants be able to read.

1920–40
The National Origins Act of 1924 established quotas for each country outside of the Western Hemisphere. It was particularly prejudiced against eastern and southern Europeans.

This period marked the start of the Mexican influx.

2.8% / 36.1% / 60.5% / 0.6%

ILLEGAL IMMIGRANTS
At right are the top 10 countries of birth of the 5 million illegal aliens in the U.S. (as of October 1996)

Mexico	2,700,000
El Salvador	335,000
Guatemala	165,000
Canada	120,000
Haiti	105,000
Philippines	95,000
Honduras	90,000
Bahama Islands	70,000
Nicaragua	70,000
Poland	70,000

1980–96
The largest wave of immigration since the 1900s.

35.0% / 49.0% / 12.0% / 4.0%

In 1986 the Immigration Reform and Control Act provided amnesty for undocumented aliens who could prove they had lived in the U.S. since January 1, 1982.

Surviving Japanese Americans who were interned during World War II were awarded damage payments under the 1988 Civil Liberties Act.

1940–60
Most immigrants from the turn of the century and their children became American-ized, and the foreign-born population decreased.

5.1% / 38.1% / 54.8% / 2.0%

In 1942, because of World War II, Japanese Americans were detained in relocation centers.

In 1948 the U.S. began to admit war refugees, followed by victims of the Korean conflict and the Hungarian revolt.

In 1952 the McCarran-Walter Act allowed small numbers of Asians to immigrate again.

1960–80
The Immigration Act of 1965, signed by President Johnson, modified the system that had favored Europeans, opening up large-scale immigration from the Third World. The new rules put a ceiling of 20,000 per country, but additional family members swelled the numbers.

26.0% / 45.0% / 26.0% / 3.0%

Revolutions and economic instability brought record numbers of immigrants from the Caribbean and Central and South America.

Wall Street's crash and the Great Depression brought immigration down to the lowest level in 100 years.

FINANCIAL PANIC / IRISH POTATO FAMINE / CIVIL WAR / POSTWAR DEPRESSION / ECONOMIC DEPRESSION / POGROMS IN RUSSIA AGAINST JEWS / STATUE OF LIBERTY / WORLD WAR I / THE GREAT DEPRESSION / STOCK MARKET CRASH / WORLD WAR II / KOREAN WAR / VIETNAM WAR / MARIEL BOAT LIFT FROM CUBA

1820 1825 1830 1835 1840 1845 1850 1855 1860 1865 1870 1875 1880 1885 1890 1895 1900 1905 1910 1915 1920 1925 1930 1935 1940 1945 1950 1955 1960 1965 1970 1975 1980 1985 1990 1995

1,800,000 / 1,700,000 / 1,600,000 / 1,500,000 / 1,400,000 / 1,300,000 / 1,200,000 / 1,100,000 / 1,000,000 / 900,000 / 800,000 / 700,000 / 600,000 / 500,000 / 400,000 / 300,000 / 200,000 / 100,000

Chart by Nigel Holmes, research by Deborah L. Wells and Noel McCoy

1

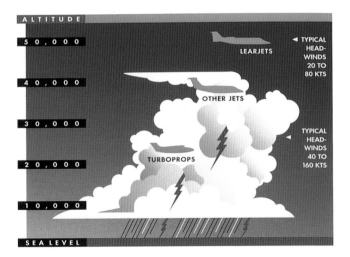

ALTITUDE
50,000 / 40,000 / 30,000 / 20,000 / 10,000 / SEA LEVEL

LEARJETS
◄ TYPICAL HEAD-WINDS 20 TO 80 KTS
OTHER JETS
TYPICAL HEAD-WINDS 40 TO 160 KTS
TURBOPROPS

The Learjet 31A cruises at an altitude of almost 10 miles high, well above the weather—and the competition.

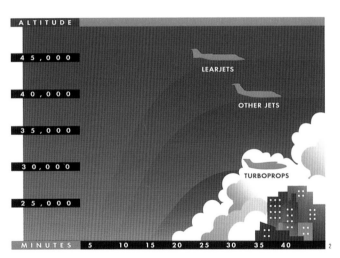

ALTITUDE
45,000 / 40,000 / 35,000 / 30,000 / 25,000
MINUTES 5 10 15 20 25 30 35 40

LEARJETS
OTHER JETS
TURBOPROPS

2

Even at full gross weight, the Learjet 31A can climb direct to 45,000 feet in only 24 minutes.

U.S.A. 1998
AD: Will Hopkins/Mary K. Baumann
D, I, DF: Nigel Holmes
CL: Kids Discover

A graph showing emigration to America from 1820 to 1996. (1)
1820年から1996年における
アメリカへの移住の歴史を説明した図。(1)

U.S.A. 1997
CD, AD: Sonia Greteman
AD, D: James Strange
P: Paul Bowen
CW: Deanna Harms
DF: Greteman Group
CL: Lear Jet

The graphs in this marketing brochure highlight the fact that the jet can fly above the weather, making the trip faster and safer. (2)
リアジェットは、気象の上空を飛ぶことができるため、
より早くより安全な旅ができるという点を強調したグラフ。
マーケティング用ブローシュアより。(2)

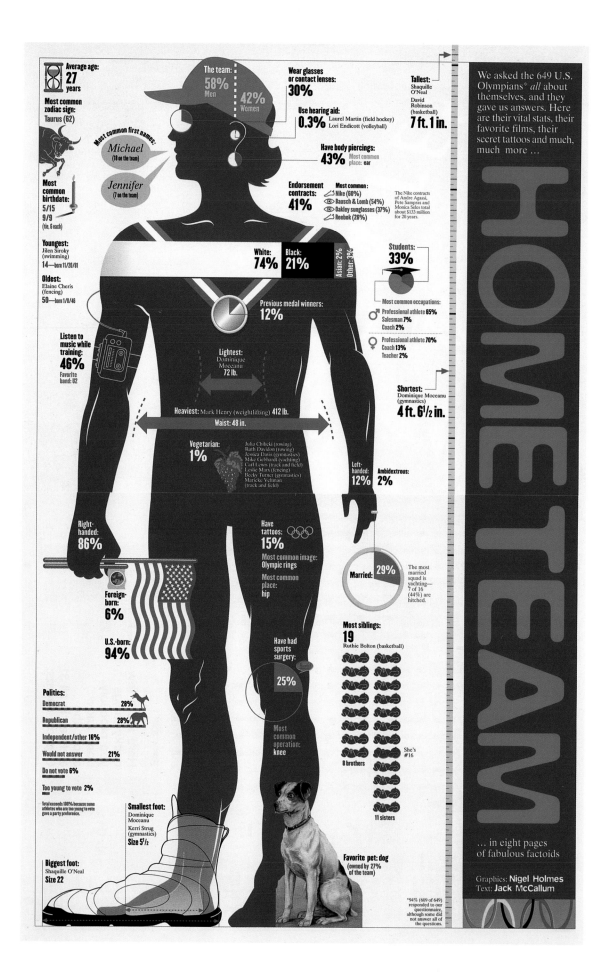

U.S.A. 1996
CD: Steve Hoffman
D, I, DF: Nigel Holmes
CW: Jack McCallum
CL: Sports Illustrated

Personal facts about U.S.A. athletes competing in the 1996 Summer Olympics.
1996年夏のオリンピックに出場した合衆国選手の個人データを集計したもの。

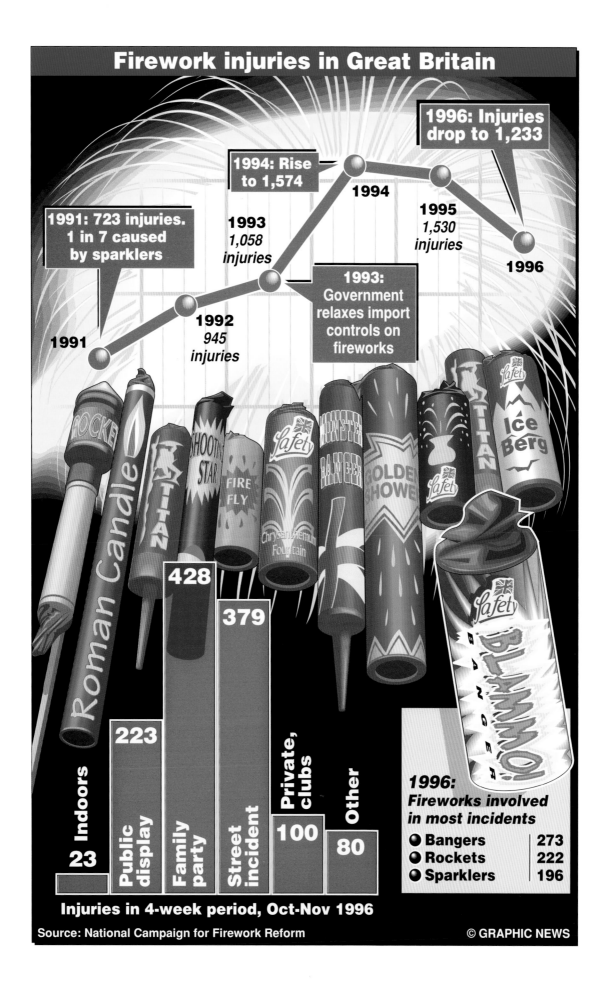

Firework injuries in Great Britain

1996: Injuries drop to 1,233

1994: Rise to 1,574

1991: 723 injuries. 1 in 7 caused by sparklers

1993 *1,058 injuries*

1994

1995 *1,530 injuries*

1996

1993: Government relaxes import controls on fireworks

1991

1992 *945 injuries*

23 Indoors

223 Public display

428 Family party

379 Street incident

100 Private, clubs

80 Other

1996: Fireworks involved in most incidents
- Bangers | 273
- Rockets | 222
- Sparklers | 196

Injuries in 4-week period, Oct-Nov 1996

Source: National Campaign for Firework Reform

© GRAPHIC NEWS

U.K. 1997
AD: Duncan Mil
DF: Graphic News
CL: Subscribing Newspapers

Graphs illustrating the yearly number of fireworks injuries in Great Britain, the most dangerous types of fireworks, and the places where injuries are most likely to occur.
イギリスでの花火によるケガ数の年別統計。最も危険な花火の種類と事故の起こりやすい場所についても示している。

U.K. 1995
CD, AD: Tor Pettersen
CD: Jeff Davis (2)
AD, D: Jeff Davis
D: Nicholas Kendall
I: Anne Magill
DF: Tor Pettersen & Partners Ltd.
CL: Lucas Industries

Pie chart depicting the market share of Lucas Aerospace's engine control systems among aeroengine manufacturers. (1)
ルーカス・エアロスペース社の
エンジン・コントロール・システムの市場シェアを、
他の航空エンジン製造メーカーと比較した円グラフ。(1)

Illustration depicting the market share of Lucas Automotive's diesel and fuel control systems, as represented by the spray of fuel from a fuel injector. (2)
ルーカス・オートモーティブ社のディーゼルと
燃料コントロール・システムの市場シェアを図にしたもの。
噴射装置から噴射される燃料によって表している。(2)

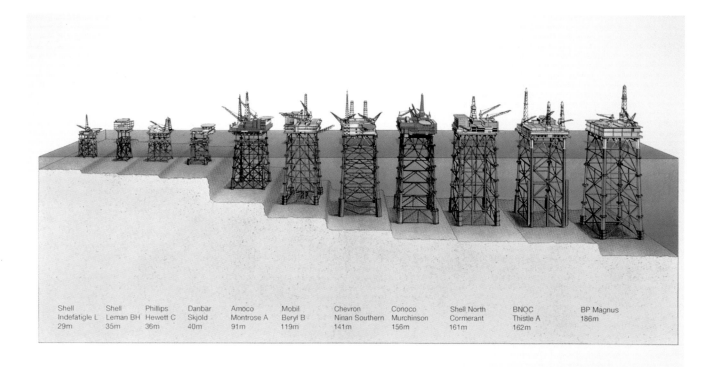

Shell	Shell	Phillips	Danbar	Amoco	Mobil	Chevron	Conoco	Shell North	BNOC	BP Magnus
Indefatigle L	Leman BH	Hewett C	Skjold	Montrose A	Beryl B	Ninan Southern	Murchinson	Cormerant	Thistle A	186m
29m	35m	36m	40m	91m	119m	141m	156m	161m	162m	

1

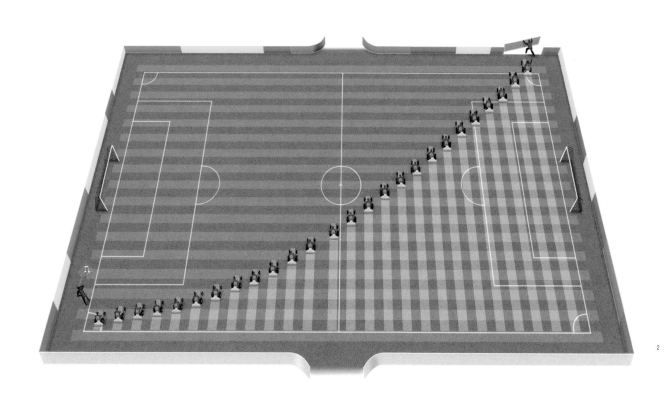

2

U.K. 1994
CD, CW: Tor Pettersen
AD, D: Glen Tutssel
I: Colin Frewin
DF: Tor Pettersen & Partners Ltd.
CL: John Brown Engineering

Increasing sizes of oil rigs emphasize the company's expertise in rig development. From a capability brochure. (1)
掘削装置開発における会社の専門技術を
石油掘削装置の大きさで表した。(1)

The Netherlands 1997
DF: Jean Cloos Art Direction
CL: Nationale Nederlanden

As the client for which this graph was designed is a major sponsor of Dutch soccer, profits paid to its clients are indicated by mowers on a soccer field. (2)
顧客への配当利益をサッカー・コートの
芝刈り機で示したグラフ。この企業は、
オランダ・サッカーの主要スポンサーである。(2)

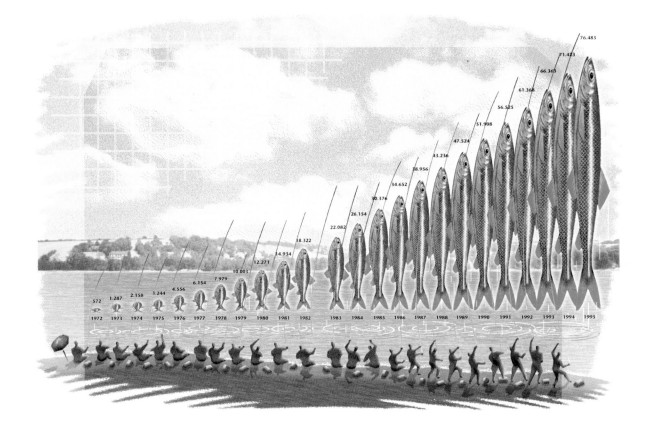

The Netherlands 1995
DF: Jean Cloos Art Direction
CL: Nationale Nederlanden

Profits paid to this life insurance company's clients are symbolized by big fish being pulled out of the water. (1)
生命保険会社の顧客への配当利益を、釣られた魚の大きさで表した。(1)

The Netherlands 1996
DF: Koeweiden-Postma
CL: Postbank

Coconuts represent the profit that can be gained by investing in Postbank funds. (2)
ポストバンクのファンドに投資した場合の利益をココナツの実で表している。(2)

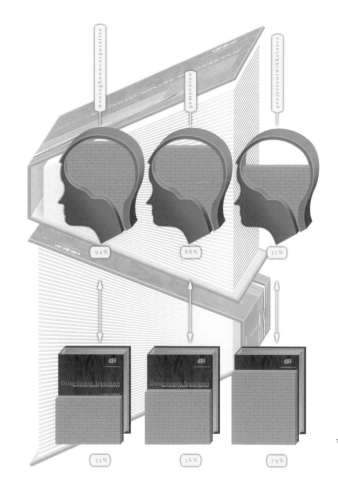

The Netherlands   1998
CL: Ministry of the Environment

Graph showing local civil servants' familiarity with measures of the Ministry of the Environment, and the ways in which these measures are applied. (1)
環境庁の政策・方針に対する地方公務員の習熟度と、これらの方針がどのように適用されたかを示すグラフ。(1)

The Netherlands   1996
DF: Jean Cloos Art Direction
CL: Nationale Nederlanden

Eggs in nests here represent the profits paid to clients. (2)
配当利益を巣の中の卵の数で表した。(2)

NHS: WHAT DOCTORS REALLY THINK

Graphs & Tables

126

Gloomy docs

GPs who expect these to get worse: %

Waiting lists for operations	47%
Waiting lists for specialists	44%
Public satisfaction with NHS	61%
Funding	43%
Overall quality of health care	34%

GPs will have more administration

GPs concerned by this 84%

GPs not concerned by this 6%

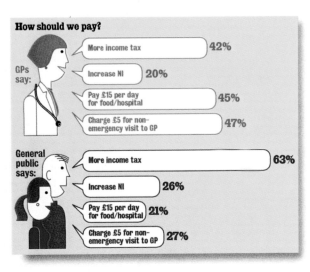

How should we pay?

GPs say:

More income tax	42%
Increase NI	20%
Pay £15 per day for food/hospital	45%
Charge £5 for non-emergency visit to GP	47%

General public says:

More income tax	63%
Increase NI	26%
Pay £15 per day for food/hospital	21%
Charge £5 for non-emergency visit to GP	27%

If I had to choose a career today, I would not become a GP

36% Agree

Health insurance should be tax deductible

Yes 62%

No 29%

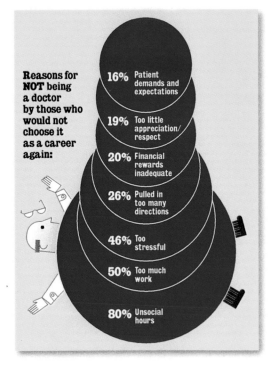

Reasons for NOT being a doctor by those who would not choose it as a career again:

16%	Patient demands and expectations
19%	Too little appreciation/ respect
20%	Financial rewards inadequate
26%	Pulled in too many directions
46%	Too stressful
50%	Too much work
80%	Unsocial hours

U.S.A. 1998
AD: Martin Colyer
D, I, DF: Nigel Holmes
CL: Readers Digest, U.K.

6 charts showing the results of a poll conducted in England about the National Health Service.
イギリスで行われた、国のヘルス・サービスについての調査結果をまとめた6点。

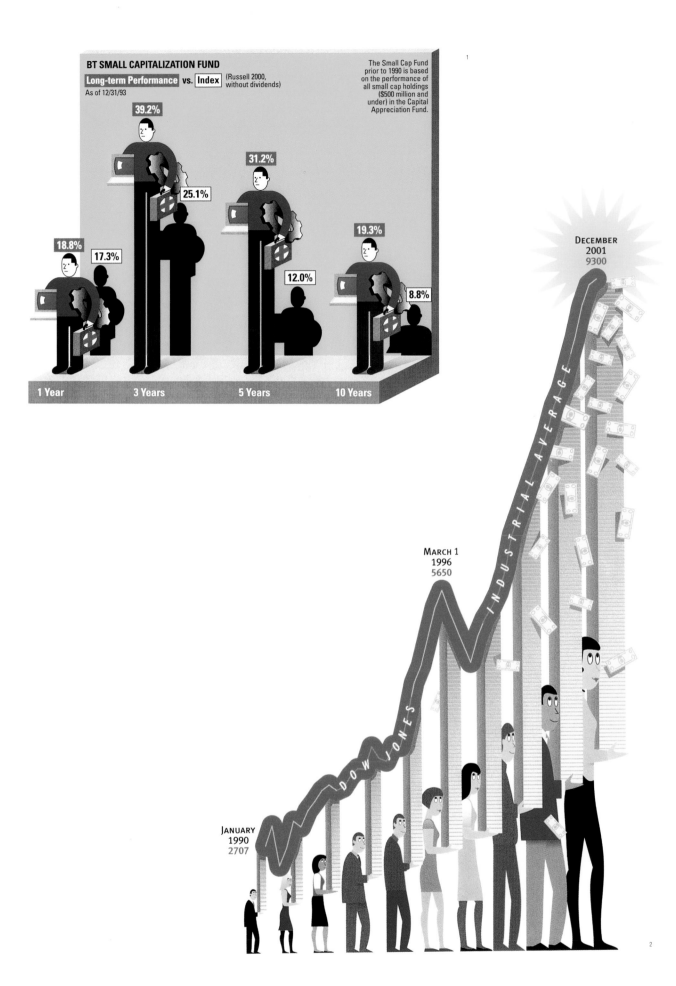

BT SMALL CAPITALIZATION FUND

Long-term Performance vs. **Index** (Russell 2000, without dividends)
As of 12/31/93

The Small Cap Fund prior to 1990 is based on the performance of all small cap holdings ($500 million and under) in the Capital Appreciation Fund.

39.2%

31.2%

25.1%

18.8%   17.3%

19.3%

12.0%

8.8%

1 Year   3 Years   5 Years   10 Years

DECEMBER 2001 9300

INDUSTRIAL AVERAGE

MARCH 1 1996 5650

DOW JONES

JANUARY 1990 2707

U.S.A. 1995
CD: Mellissa Makris
D, I, DF: Nigel Holmes
CL: Bankers Trust

Bar chart illustrates the superior performance of Bankers Trust as compared to another index. (1)
バンカーズ・トラスト社が他の指数裁定取り引きに比べ、優勢であることを示した図。(1)

U.S.A. 1996
AD: Rudy Hoglund
D, I, DF: Nigel Holmes
CL: Money Magazine

Chart that shows how young people's investments are helping to bolster the stock market. (2)
若い世代の株式投資がいかに市場を活性化しているかを表した図。(2)

SNACK ATTACK

Enjoying three square meals a day used to be a nutritional standard to aspire to, but increasingly Americans are opting for fewer meals and more snacks. In the last 10 years the number of Americans who say they eat three meals a day with no between-meal snacks has dropped from 33% to 24%. The younger you are the more likely you are to eschew three squares a day in favor of chewing on a snack or two. Here are some more figures on Americans' on-the-run nutritional habits.

MAKE MINE A LITE
(Percent who say they favor the "light" version of given foods/beverages)

Milk 48%
Soft drinks 24%
Ice cream 20%
Cheese 18%
Salty snacks 17%

MOST POPULAR SNACKS (in decreasing order)

1 Fresh fruit
2 Potato chips/salty snack
3 Cookies
4 Donuts
5 Candy
6 Danish/pastry
7 Crackers
8 Popcorn
9 Bagel
10 Yogurt/nuts (tie)

HOW OFTEN DO YOU SNACK AT WORK?

Not sure 7%
Almost every day 38%
Never 20%
Couple times a week 14%
Occasionally 21%

WHO EATS HOW?
(Age Influences Meals vs. Snacks Behavior)

Ages 18-29: Three meals, no snacks 16% / Three meals, plus snacks 26% / 15% / Other 13% / 31% / Two meals, plus snacks 15%
Ages 30-44: 20% / 23% / 15% / 14% / 28% / Two meals, no snacks 15%
Ages 45-59: 27% / 24% / 15% / 9% / 25% / 15%
Ages 60+: 35% / 26% / 7% / 20% / 12%

Source: Roper Starch Worldwide, 1996
Graphic: MacNeill—Macintosh

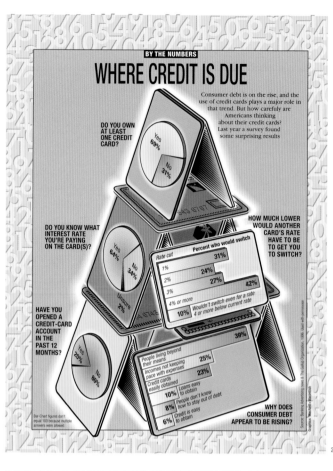

WHERE CREDIT IS DUE

Consumer debt is on the rise, and the use of credit cards plays a major role in that trend. But how carefully are Americans thinking about their credit cards? Last year a survey found some surprising results

DO YOU OWN AT LEAST ONE CREDIT CARD?
Yes 69%
No 31%

DO YOU KNOW WHAT INTEREST RATE YOU'RE PAYING ON THE CARD(S)?
Yes 64%
No 34%
Unsure 2%

HOW MUCH LOWER WOULD ANOTHER CARD'S RATE HAVE TO BE TO GET YOU TO SWITCH?

Rate cut	Percent who would switch
1%	31%
2%	24%
3%	27%
4% or more	42%
Wouldn't switch even for a rate 4 or more below current rate	10%

HAVE YOU OPENED A CREDIT-CARD ACCOUNT IN THE PAST 12 MONTHS?
Yes 20%
No 80%

WHY DOES CONSUMER DEBT APPEAR TO BE RISING?

People living beyond their means 39%
Incomes not keeping pace with expenses 25%
Credit cards easily obtained 23%
Loans easy to obtain 10%
People don't know how to stay out of debt 8%
Credit is easy to obtain 6%

Bar-Chart figures don't equal 100 because multiple answers were allowed.

Source: Banking, Advertising news & The Gallup Organization, 1996. Used with permission
Graphic: MacNeill—Macintosh

HOW AMERICANS VIEW THEIR FINANCES

Have you ever wondered whether other people worry about money the way you do? Or whether your spouse is the best one to control the purse strings? Or whether you should be doing more to plan for your retirement? Below are the results of a survey of more than 2,000 Americans conducted by *Money* magazine. See how you compare.

WHAT ARE YOU DOING TO PREPARE FINANCIALLY FOR RETIREMENT?
(More than one answer possible)

Saving/investing on my own 56%
Using my company's savings plan 45%
Taking steps to cut expenses 28%
Building up my own business 15%
Nothing 10%
Depending on an inheritance 4%

HOW SATISFIED ARE YOU WITH YOUR PERSONAL FINANCIAL SITUATION?
Fairly satisfied 47%
Not too satisfied 29%
Not satisfied at all 15%
Very satisfied 9%

WHO SPENDS MONEY MORE WISELY, MEN OR WOMEN?
Men 30%
Women 37%
Neither 33%

WHO ARE BETTER INVESTORS, MEN OR WOMEN?
Men 50%
Women 18%
Neither 32%

HOW OFTEN DO YOU WORRY ABOUT MONEY?
Very often 22%
Fairly often 36%
Not too often 37%
Never 5%

WHEN YOU RETIRE, DO YOU THINK THE SOCIAL SECURITY ADMINISTRATION WILL BE ABLE TO SEND YOU MONEY REGULARLY?
Yes 37%
No 31%
Don't know 32%

Source: "Americans and Their Money", Money Magazine, 1995.

THERE'S NO PLACE LIKE HOME

It's a beautiful day in the neighborhood: A sidewalk tour of some facts and figures shaping home ownership in the U.S.

TYPES OF HOMES BOUGHT
New houses 20.5%
Condominiums 20.5%
Multi-family dwellings 1.9%
Existing houses 79.5%
Single-family houses 85%

WHY PEOPLE CHOOSE THEIR HOMES
Yard, trees, view 1.4 million
Only one available 1.8 million
Size 2.8 million
Room layout/design 3.5 million
Financial reasons 7 million
Price 16.4 million

Source: Statistical Abstract of the U.S., 1992

MAJOR CHALLENGES FACED BY BUYERS
Credit record 25%
Job security 28%
Monthly Mortgage 44%
Down payment/closing costs 51%

Source: Fannie Mae National Housing Survey, 1992

AMENITIES HOMEOWNERS ENJOY
Functioning fireplaces 42%
Multiple living/recreation rooms 45%
Separate dining rooms 55%
Dishwashers 61%
Garages or carports 74%

CHARTS: MACNEILL•MACINTOSH

U.S.A. 1996 (4)/1997 (1)(3)/1998 (2)
AD: Susan Yousem
D, I: Scott MacNeill
DF: MacNeill & Macintosh
CL: Fidelity Investments

Charts showing the results of surveys of Americans; snack habits, opinions regarding credit card usage, investment plans, and attitudes of home buyers.

「アメリカ人の間食の習慣」「アメリカ人のクレジット・カード利用についての意見」「アメリカ人の投資計画についての調査結果」「アメリカの住宅購入者の傾向」をグラフィックで表したもの。

Maps & Pictograms

Travel and Guide Maps, Distribution Charts, Floor Plans, Pictograms

地域図、分布図、観光地図、道路地図、案内図、ピクトグラム

THE CHANGING FACE OF BRITAIN

The Sunday Telegraph

NEW POLITICAL MAP OF THE BRITISH ISLES

Graphic: Phillip Green

BRITAIN has turned red. The real scale of Labour's victory is shown in Phil Green's unique map which represents each constituency according to the number of voters in it, rather than the number of square miles it covers. The result is astonishing.

It avoids the usual distortion of colouring large areas of the British Isles blue, red or yellow, simply because a single constituency covers a vast area of sparsely populated Scottish Highland or Yorkshire moor. Traditional maps habitually exaggerate the scale of the vote for the minority parties- the Liberal Democrats, the Welsh and Scots Nationalists- who win the big constituencies on the fringes of the UK. They also create a false impression of Conservative domination over most of England, simply because the Tories are strong in the large rural constituencies. They seriously under-represent Labour voters, since those are heavily concentrated in the most densely populated inner city areas.

This map is the first to show the full extent of the Tory rout. There are no Conservatives left in Scotland or Wales. Labour has taken almost complete control of all the major urban areas: instead of a sea of blue interrupted by occasional islands of red, there are swathes of red broken by thin rivulets of blue. The Tories are now penned in the rural South West and the commuter-land of the South East – but even there, there are blotches of unfamiliar red.

"This was a watershed election which took almost all of us pollsters completely by surprise," says David Carlton – as well he might. Up until last week, Carlton, a lecturer in politics at the University of Warwick, was predicting a hung parliament, or maybe even a small Tory majority. It should be remembered that, after Labour's shock defeat in 1992, most pollsters were asserting that Labour could not win another election: the demographic arithmetic simply made it impossible. Their traditional supporters were dwindling, and those that were left were ceasing to vote. The ascendant class of non-manual workers were bound to vote Conservative. Blair's changed that, possibly because he has transformed Labour into a facsimile of the moderate wing of the Conservative Party.

"The Labour landslide means the end of tribal loyalties in British politics," asserts Carlton. "It seems that the class war is over." In the past, when governments have suffered catastrophic defeats, it has been because the government has split, or endured some spectacular humiliation. But the Conservatives have been routed when they have managed the economy well, and when, despite divisions on Europe, there hasn't been a formal fissure in the party. Thanks to the vagaries of the British electoral system, Labour has won a huge majority on a relatively small share of the vote. "Blair took 44 per cent," notes Carlton. "There have been at least three elections since the war when 44 per cent has not been enough to form a majority government."

In 1951, Labour won a larger share of the vote than they have this time – yet lost." There does not seem to be any huge enthusiasm for Labour: the election has been won on the lowest turn-out since the war, with nearly a third of the electorate deciding not to use its vote. But there was a great deal of venomous hostility to the Tories, whom the electorate overwhelmingly wanted to see defeated.

"The essential point seems to be that the transformation of Labour has ended the ideological divide between the two main parties," rationalises Carlton.

The huge majority on a relatively small share of the vote means that a small swing against Labour would cost the party scores of seats. "I think we are entering an era of extreme electoral volatility," predicts Carlton. "I do not think that it will take much to reverse the Labour victory. Electoral choices are no longer based on deeply entrenched socio-economic factors. General elections now seem to manifest the same kind of unpredictability as by-elections. It would be very unwise to say, just because no party until now has ever reversed a 179-seat majority, that it won't happen at the next election. Who knows? The answer is, nobody."

KEY TO NORTHERN IRELAND

- Democratic Unionist
- Sinn Fein
- Social Democrat and Labour (SDLP)
- Ulster Unionist
- United Kingdom Unionist

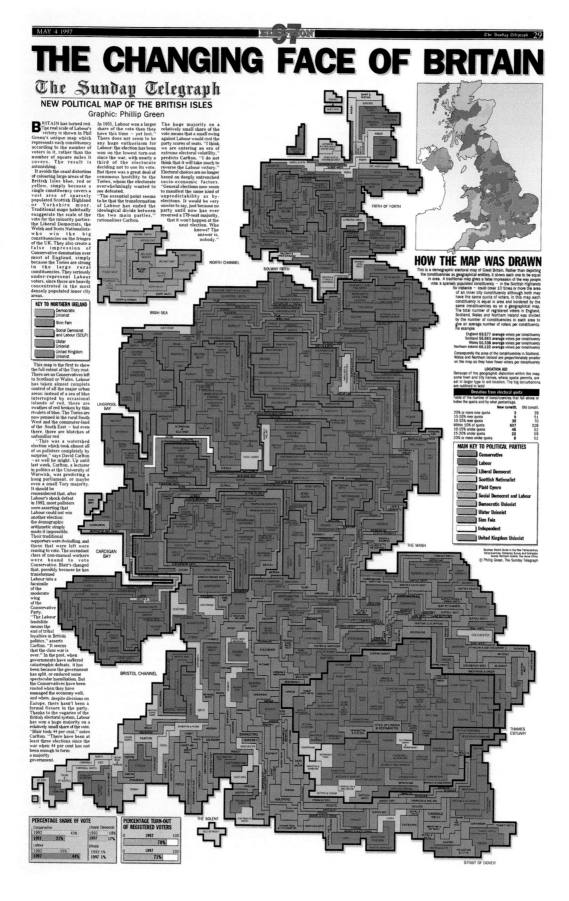

HOW THE MAP WAS DRAWN

This is a demographic electoral map of Great Britain. Rather than depicting the constituencies as geographical entities, it shows each one to be equal in area. A traditional map gives a false impression of the way people vote a sparsely populated constituency – in the Scottish Highlands for instance – could cover 10 times or more the area of an inner city constituency although both may have the same quota of voters. In this map each constituency is equal in area and bordered by the same constituencies as on a geographical map. The total number of registered voters in England, Scotland, Wales and Northern Ireland was divided by the number of constituencies in each area to give an average number of voters per constituency. For example:

England 69,577 average voters per constituency
Scotland 55,563 average voters per constituency
Wales 55,338 average voters per constituency
Northern Ireland 66,122 average voters per constituency

Consequently the sizes of the constituencies in Scotland, Wales and Northern Ireland are proportionately smaller on the map as they have fewer voters per constituency

LOCATION AID
Because of the geographic distortion within the map some town and city names, where space permits, are set in larger type to aid location. The big conurbations are outlined in bold

Deviation from electoral quota
Table of the number of constituencies that fall above or below the quota and by what percentage.

	New constit.	Old constit.
20% and over quota	3	39
15-20% over quota	5	51
10-15% over quota	35	70
Within 10% of quota	537	328
10-15% under quota	46	52
15-20% under quota	22	59
20% or more under quota	8	52

MAIN KEY TO POLITICAL PARTIES

- Conservative
- Labour
- Liberal Democrat
- Scottish Nationalist
- Plaid Cymru
- Social Democrat and Labour
- Democratic Unionist
- Ulster Unionist
- Sinn Fein
- Independent
- United Kingdom Unionist

Sources: Media Guide to the New Parliament by Carol Levinson, Ordnance Survey and Ordnance Survey Northern Ireland, The Home Office

© Phillip Green, The Sunday Telegraph

PERCENTAGE SHARE OF VOTE

Conservative
1992   43%
1997   31%

Labour
1992   35%
1997   44%

Liberal Democrat
1992   18%
1997   17%

Others
1992   1%
1997   1%

PERCENTAGE TURN-OUT OF REGISTERED VOTERS

0		100
1992	78%	
1997	71%	

U.K. 1997
Graphics Editor: Phillip J Green
CL: The Sunday Telegraph

A demographic electoral map that shows where people live and how they voted in Britain's 1997 national elections. The small map (upper right) shows the same results on a traditional geographical constituency map, which shows area rather than voters, giving a distorted view of the political result.

英国の1997年度総選挙における、人々の居住区域と投票の動向を示した選挙結果の統計図。
右上の小地図は、従来の地理的な選挙統計図であるが、有権者の数に関係なく地域ごとの結果を表しているため、
結果について偏った見方を与えている。

Many Were Born in the USA ...

All 649 athletes are shown in the state (or country, below right) where they were born.

The size and shape of each state is determined by the number of athletes born there: California is the birth state of the most U.S. Olympians (138), followed by New York (56) and Pennsylvania (40). Six states have none. Here's the real map in case you get lost finding Atlanta.

One other thing: can you find Izzy, Atlanta's Olympic mascot?

KEY TO THE MAP

MEN WOMEN

OUTDOOR EVENTS

INDOOR EVENTS

WATER EVENTS

OUTDOOR
Archery
Baseball
Beach Volleyball
Cycling
Equestrian
Field Hockey
Modern Pentathlon
Mountain Biking
Shooting
Soccer
Softball
Tennis
Track and Field

INDOOR
Badminton
Basketball
Boxing
Fencing
Gymnastics
Handball
Judo
Table Tennis
Volleyball
Weightlifting
Wrestling

WATER
Canoeing/Kayaking
Diving
Rowing
Swimming
Synchronized Swimming
Water Polo
Yachting

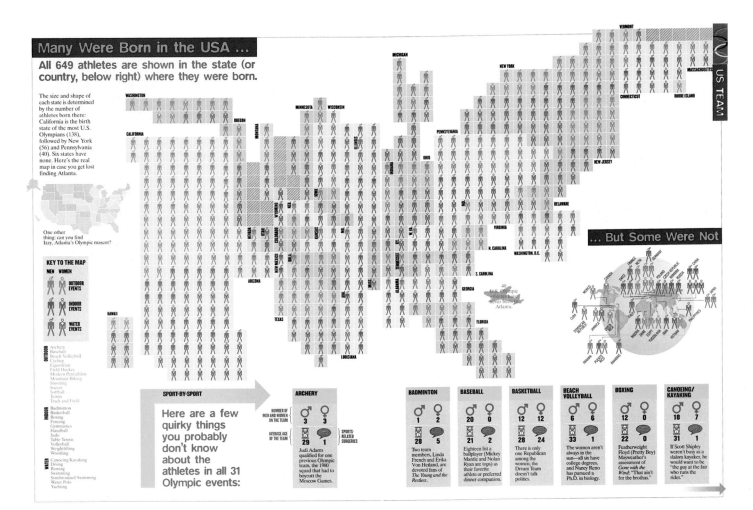

... But Some Were Not

40 U.S. Olympic athletes have never been to Atlanta.

US TEAM

SPORT-BY-SPORT

Here are a few quirky things you probably don't know about the athletes in all 31 Olympic events:

ARCHERY

NUMBER OF MEN AND WOMEN ON THE TEAM
♂ 3 ♀ 3

AVERAGE AGE OF THE TEAM
29 1 — SPORTS-RELATED SURGERIES

Judi Adams qualified for one previous Olympic team, the 1980 squad that had to boycott the Moscow Games.

BADMINTON
♂ 1 ♀ 2
28 5

Two team members, Linda French and Erika Von Heiland, are devoted fans of *The Young and the Restless*.

BASEBALL
♂ 20 ♀ 0
21 2

Eighteen list a ballplayer (Mickey Mantle and Nolan Ryan are tops) as their favorite dinner companion.

BASKETBALL
♂ 12 ♀ 12
28 24

There is only one Republican among the women; the Dream Team doesn't talk politics.

BEACH VOLLEYBALL
♂ 6 ♀ 6
33 1

The women aren't always in the sun—all six have college degrees, and Nancy Reno has pursued a Ph.D. in biology.

BOXING
♂ 12 ♀ 0
22 0

Featherweight Floyd (Pretty Boy) Mayweather's assessment of *Gone with the Wind*: "That ain't for the brothas."

CANOEING/ KAYAKING
♂ 18 ♀ 7
31 1

If Scott Shipley weren't busy as a slalom kayaker, he would want to be "the guy at the fair who runs the rides."

U.S.A. 1996
CD: Steve Hoffman
D, I, DF: Nigel Holmes
CW: Jack McCallum
CL: Sports Illustrated

Map indicating the birthplaces of US athletes competing in the 1996 Summer Olympics.
1996年夏のオリンピックに出場した合衆国選手の出生地を示した地図。

FROM HERE TO THERE

Ever wonder about the distance America's daily licorice intake would cover if you stretched it all out? No? Well, we couldn't resist sinking our teeth into the subject anyway. So...here's a marathon of meandering goods.

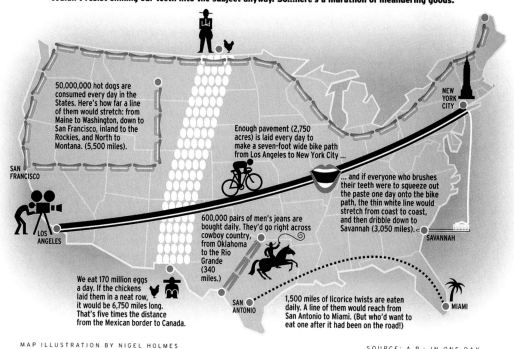

50,000,000 hot dogs are consumed every day in the States. Here's how far a line of them would stretch: from Maine to Washington, down to San Francisco, inland to the Rockies, and North to Montana. (5,500 miles).

Enough pavement (2,750 acres) is laid every day to make a seven-foot wide bike path from Los Angeles to New York City ...

... and if everyone who brushes their teeth were to squeeze out the paste one day onto the bike path, the thin white line would stretch from coast to coast, and then dribble down to Savannah (3,050 miles).

600,000 pairs of men's jeans are bought daily. They'd go right across cowboy country, from Oklahoma to the Rio Grande (340 miles.)

We eat 170 million eggs a day. If the chickens laid them in a neat row, it would be 6,750 miles long. That's five times the distance from the Mexican border to Canada.

1,500 miles of licorice twists are eaten daily. A line of them would reach from San Antonio to Miami. (But who'd want to eat one after it had been on the road!)

MAP ILLUSTRATION BY NIGEL HOLMES

SOURCE: A.P.: *IN ONE DAY*

WHERE THE KING IS STILL REALLY KING

Elvis Presley still swings in the East, according to marketing surveys. Out West, well, there are Presley pockets. But if you're a major fan, don't step in the map's blue suede areas.

PLACES WHERE PEOPLE THINK ELVIS IS GOLDEN

PLACES WHERE PEOPLE THINK ELVIS IS TRASH

MAP ILLUSTRATION BY NIGEL HOLMES

SOURCE: AMERICAN DEMOGRAPHICS

U.S.A. 1998
AD: Susan Bogle
D, I, DF: Nigel Holmes
CL: Navigator

2 of a series: Daily quantities of food & jeans translated to distances; Elvis lovers & haters.
2作シリーズ。食物とジーンズが1日に利用される量を距離で表したもの。エルビス・プレスリーを好きな人、嫌いな人の分布。

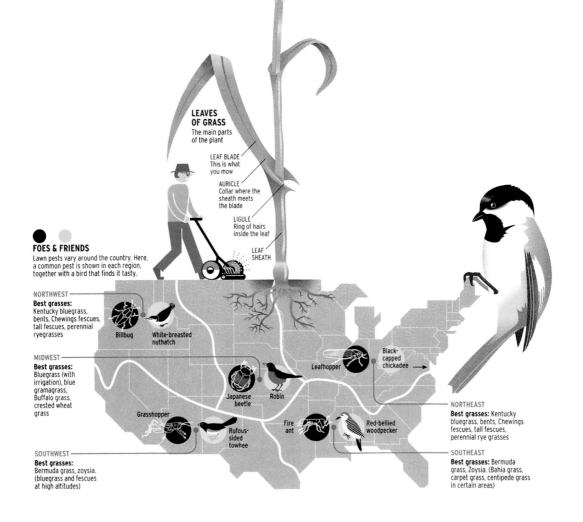

LEAVES OF GRASS
The main parts of the plant

LEAF BLADE
This is what you mow

AURICLE
Collar where the sheath meets the blade

LIGULE
Ring of hairs inside the leaf

LEAF SHEATH

FOES & FRIENDS
Lawn pests vary around the country. Here, a common pest is shown in each region, together with a bird that finds it tasty.

NORTHWEST
Best grasses: Kentucky bluegrass, bents, Chewings fescues, tall fescues, perennial ryegrasses

Billbug
White-breasted nuthatch

MIDWEST
Best grasses: Bluegrass (with irrigation), blue gramagrass, Buffalo grass, crested wheat grass

Japanese beetle
Robin

Grasshopper
Rufous-sided towhee

Leafhopper

Black-capped chickadee

Fire ant
Red-bellied woodpecker

SOUTHWEST
Best grasses: Bermuda grass, zoysia. (bluegrass and fescues at high altitudes)

NORTHEAST
Best grasses: Kentucky bluegrass, bents, Chewings fescues, tall fescues, perennial rye grasses

SOUTHEAST
Best grasses: Bermuda grass, Zoysia. (Bahia grass, carpet grass, centipede grass in certain areas)

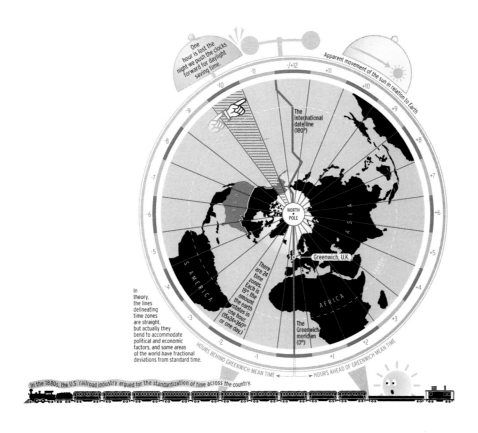

One hour is lost the night we push the clocks forward for daylight saving time.

Apparent movement of the sun in relation to Earth

-11 -/+12 +11

-10 +10

-9 +9

-8 +8

The international date line (180°)

-7 +7

-6 +6

NORTH POLE

ASIA

-5 +5

Greenwich, U.K.

S. AMERICA

There are 24 time zones, each is 15° the amount the earth rotates in one hour. (15x24=360° or one day.)

-4 +4

AFRICA

In theory, the lines delineating time zones are straight, but actually they bend to accommodate political and economic factors, and some areas of the world have fractional deviations from standard time.

-3 +3

The Greenwich meridian (0°)

-2 +2

HOURS BEHIND GREENWICH MEAN TIME

-1 +1

HOURS AHEAD OF GREENWICH MEAN TIME

In the 1880s, the U.S. railroad industry argued for the standardization of time across the country.

U.S.A. 1998
AD: Paul Carstensen
D, I, DF: Nigel Holmes
CL: Attaché

Series of diagrams explaining everyday processes: Map detailing different types of lawns in the U.S.A., and a diagram explaining time zones.
日常的なテーマを取り上げたシリーズより。アメリカのさまざまなタイプの芝生の分布図と、タイム・ゾーンについて。

welcome to twin town

ようこそ、ツイン・タウンへ

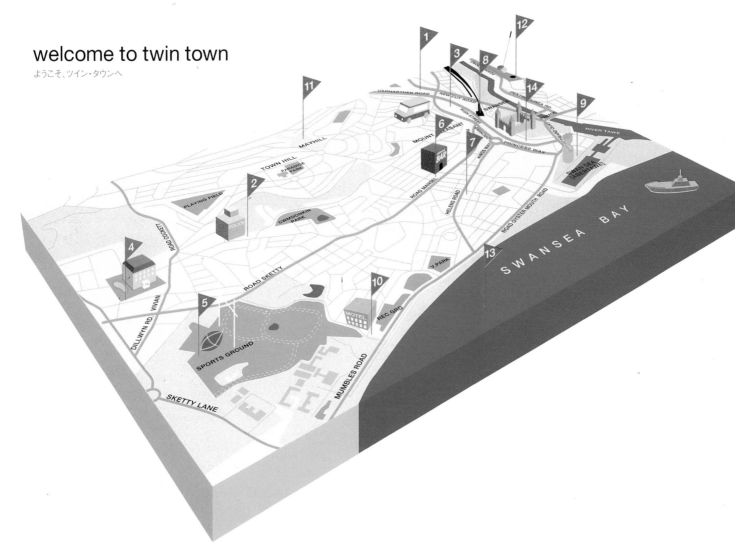

1. ツインズ一家とその愛犬カントナが長年暮らすトレーラーハウス
2. テリーとグレヨの汚職刑事ふたりが勤めるスウォンジー西署
3. エディが勤めるピンクなマッサージ・パーラー。但し、従業員はオバサンばかり
4. 町の実力者ブリンが住む豪邸。プールとスロット・カー専用ルーム付き
5. ブリンがオーナーを務めるラグビー・クラブのグラウンド。緑の芝生が美しい
6. 週末には町中の老若男女がオシャレして集う、大人気のカラオケ・バー、バロンズ
7. インド料理店。マスターは愛想がよいが、実はウェールズ人にはシニカル
8. ディラン・トーマスの詩を駅前に刻む町の玄関口、スウォンジー駅

9. ボブ・ディランも敬愛するスウォンジーの誇り、ディラン・トーマス像
10. 刑事グレヨとエディのいきつけのモーテル
11. "カラオケ・キング"ダイと、ブリンの娘ボニーが密会する丘
12. ゴルフ場。ツインズが深夜にラウンドすることもある
13. スウォンジー湾
14. スウォンジー城

※おことわり　本マップは実在する町ウェールズ、スウォンジーとはちょっとしか関係ありません。

Japan　1998
DF: Groovisions
CL: Asmik Ace Entertainment Inc.

A map of Swansea, a provincial town in Wales that was the setting for the movie "Twin Town."
映画『ツイン・タウン』の舞台となったウェールズの田舎町スウォンジーの地図。

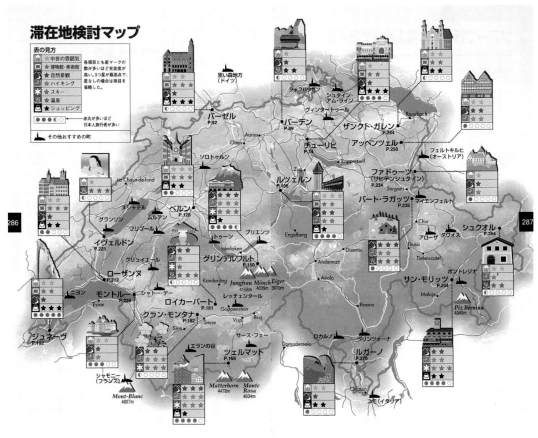

Japan　1997 (1) /1998 (2)
CD: Hiroyuki Kimura
D: Sachiko Hagiwara
DF: Tube Graphics
Original Map: Sensyusha (1)
CL: Jitsugyo No Nihon Sha Ltd.

From "Wagamama Aruki (Going Your Own Way): San Francisco."
This bird's-eye-view guide map of the city of hills includes tourist spots and cable car routes. (1)

旅行ガイドブック『わがまま歩き　サンフランシスコ』より。
サンフランシスコの観光ポイントと、ケーブルカーの路線ルートをふかん図上に展開し、坂の町の「らしさ」を出した。(1)

From "Wagamama Aruki: Switzerland." Recommended tourist destinations are identified by labels,
such as "Scenic Nature" and "From the Middle Ages." Famous buildings are incorporated within regional icons. (2)

旅行ガイドブック『わがまま歩き　スイス』より。主要観光地のおすすめ度を、「自然景観」「中世の雰囲気」など、
いくつかの項目に分けて採点表示。各地のアイコンには、その地域を代表する建築物を使用した。(2)

ローマわがまま歩きマップ

グラフィック・マップ

見どころがたくさんあるローマ。歩くには広すぎるけど、地下鉄やバスを使いこなすのは難しい。そこでわがまま歩き流に市内を7つのエリアに分け、エリアの個性と便利な交通手段を解説。その日の気分と体力に相談して、ひと味違う街歩きを楽しもう!

Japan 1998
CD: Hiroyuki Kimura
D: Naomi Sugita
DF: Tube Graphics
Original Map: Sensyusha
CL: Jitsugyo No Nihon Sha Ltd.

*From "Wagamama Aruki: Italy." This map divides Rome into seven areas,
identifying special features of each area and detailing convenient means of transportation.*

旅行ガイドブック『わがまま歩き イタリア』より。ローマを7つのエリアに分け、
それぞれのエリアの個性と行動するのに便利な交通手段を図解したマップ。

Japan 1998
CD: Hiroyuki Kimura
D: Naomi Sugita (1)/Nozomi Hatakeyama (2)
DF: Tube Graphics
Original Map: Sensyusha
CL: Jitsugyo No Nihon Sha Ltd.

From "Wagamama Aruki: Italy." A map of secret tourist spots far from the major Italian cities. Characteristics of the cities, and "must see" locations, are indicated by the size of the accompanying icon. (1)

旅行ガイドブック『わがまま歩き　イタリア』より。大都市から離れた隠れた観光スポットを紹介したマップ。それぞれの町の個性と必見度をアイコンの大きさで表示した。(1)

From "Wagamama Aruki: New York."
This guide map identifies ethnic neighborhoods and food stall areas located in Manhattan. (2)

旅行ガイドブック『わがまま歩き　ニューヨーク』より。マンハッタン島内で商売をする屋台の出没エリアと、エスニックエリアを紹介したガイドマップ。(2)

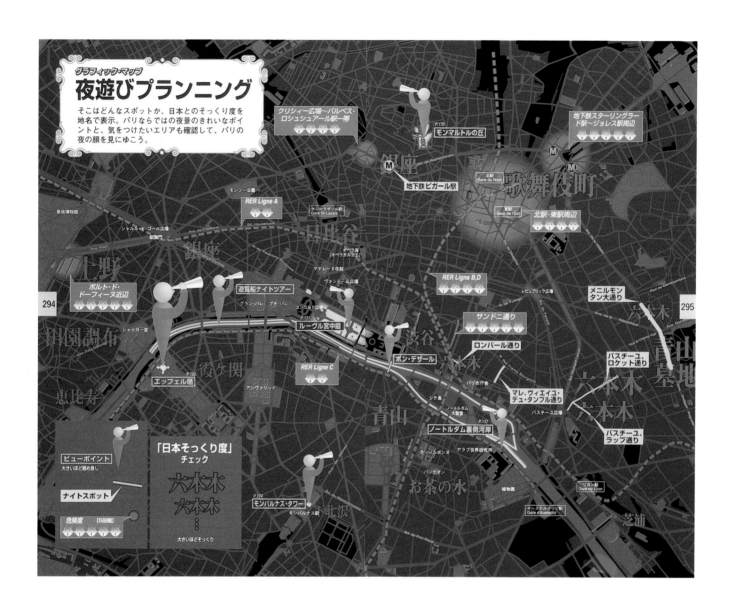

Japan 1997
CD: Hiroyuki Kimura
D: Naomi Sugita
DF: Tube Graphics
Original Map: Sensyusha
CL: Jitsugyo No Nihon Sha Ltd.

From the travel guide book, "Wagamama Aruki: Paris."
Nightlife guide map indicates relative levels of danger of various areas of nighttime Paris.
旅行ガイドブック『わがまま歩き　パリ』より。夜のパリで危険とされている地域のそれぞれの危険度を示した夜遊び用マップ。

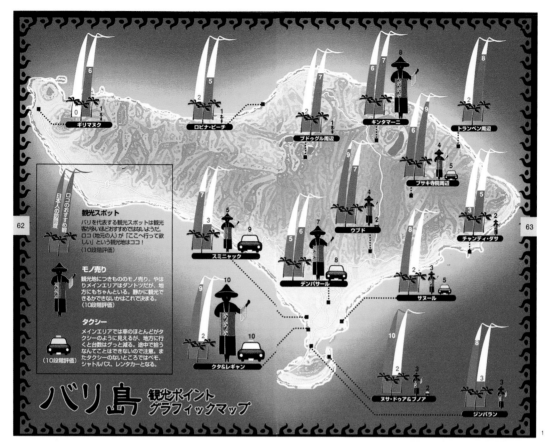

Japan 1998
CD: Hiroyuki Kimura
D: Hiroko Enomoto (1) /Sachiko Hagiwara (2)
DF: Tube Graphics
Original Map: Sensyusha (1)
CL: Jitsugyo No Nihon Sha Ltd.

*From "Wagamama Aruki: Bali." Recommended areas popular with Japanese tourists are shown,
with locations of street vendors and taxi frequency also indicated.* (1)

旅行ガイドブック『わがまま歩き　バリ』より。バリ島内の観光ポイントのおすすめ度と日本人の訪問度、
そしてそこにいるモノ売りたちやタクシーの出没度を表示したマップ。(1)

*From "Wagamama Aruki: Canada." With a view stretching to the Arctic,
this bird's-eye map introduces specialties and temperature ranges of each area of Canada.* (2)

旅行ガイドブック『わがまま歩き　カナダ』より。北極圏を望む広大なカナダ全土をふかん図で表し、各地の特産物と気温をチャートで紹介。(2)

U.S.A. 1999
CD, AD, I: Stephan Van Dam
D: Gerry Krieg/Mt Gunther Vollath
P: André Grossmann
DF: In-house

Comprehensive dining, shopping, arts and entertainment maps & guides to New York City.
The patented origami map is fun to use, and has been copyrighted as a kinetic sculpture.
ニューヨーク市のレストラン、ショッピング、エンタテインメントのガイドマップ。
ヴァンダム社特許の折り紙マップになっており、キネティック（動く）彫刻として著作権を保有している。

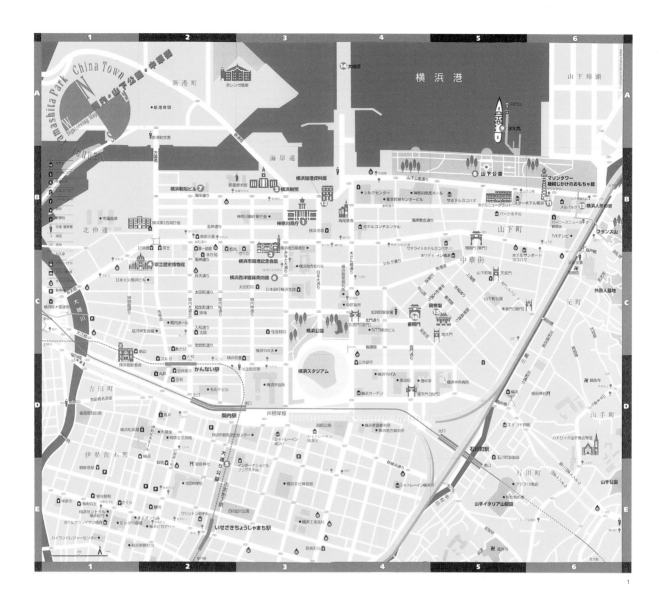

nightclubbing in
ROPPONGI /
AZABU-JUBAN

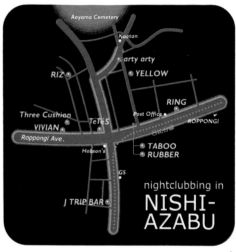

nightclubbing in
NISHI-
AZABU

Japan　1998
AD: Kenzo Nakagawa
D: Satoshi Morikami/Hiromi Maekawa/
　Hiroyuki Inda/Norika Nakayama/
　Akira Shimizu
I: Hiroyasu Nobuyama
CW: Maki Nakatsuka
DF: NDC Graphics Inc.
CL: Yokohama-shi

*A tourist guide map of the City of Yokohama.
From the National Athletic Meet guidebook.* (1)
神奈川国体横浜市総合ガイドブックより。
横浜市の観光案内図。(1)

Japan　1998
CD: Hiroyuki Kimura
D: Ryu Sato
DF: Tube Graphics
CL: Magazine House Ltd.

*A map from the "Night Play" issue
of Popeye, a youth-oriented fashion
magazine, showing the locations of the
businesses featured in the article.* (2)
若者向けのファッション誌『POPEYE』の
「夜遊び特集」に掲載されたマップ。
特集内で紹介されているショップの
位置関係を表している。(2)

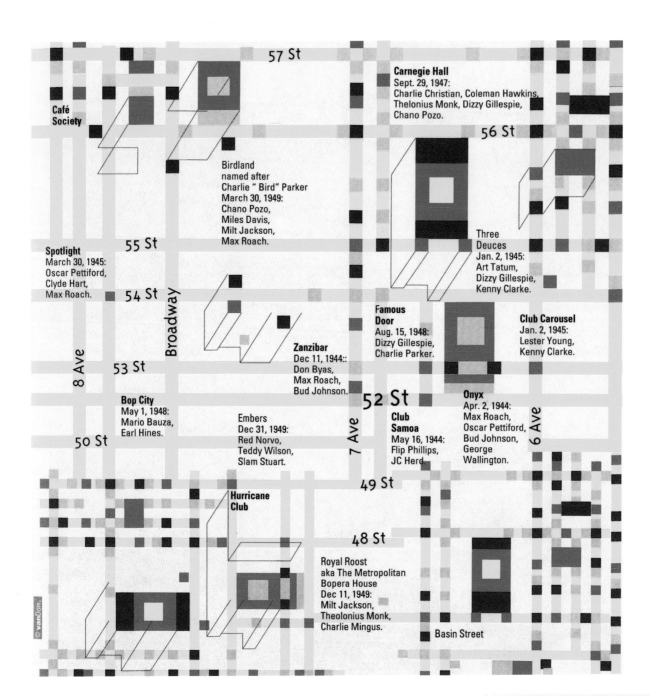

57 St

Café Society

Carnegie Hall
Sept. 29, 1947:
Charlie Christian, Coleman Hawkins,
Thelonius Monk, Dizzy Gillespie,
Chano Pozo.

56 St

Birdland
named after
Charlie " Bird" Parker
March 30, 1949:
Chano Pozo,
Miles Davis,
Milt Jackson,
Max Roach.

**Three
Deuces**
Jan. 2, 1945:
Art Tatum,
Dizzy Gillespie,
Kenny Clarke.

55 St

Spotlight
March 30, 1945:
Oscar Pettiford,
Clyde Hart,
Max Roach.

Broadway

54 St

**Famous
Door**
Aug. 15, 1948:
Dizzy Gillespie,
Charlie Parker.

Club Carousel
Jan. 2, 1945:
Lester Young,
Kenny Clarke.

8 Ave

53 St

Zanzibar
Dec 11, 1944::
Don Byas,
Max Roach,
Bud Johnson.

Bop City
May 1, 1948:
Mario Bauza,
Earl Hines.

Embers
Dec 31, 1949:
Red Norvo,
Teddy Wilson,
Slam Stuart.

52 St

7 Ave

**Club
Samoa**
May 16, 1944:
Flip Phillips,
JC Herd

Onyx
Apr. 2, 1944:
Max Roach,
Oscar Pettiford,
Bud Johnson,
George
Wallington.

6 Ave

50 St

49 St

**Hurricane
Club**

48 St

Royal Roost
aka The Metropolitan
Bopera House
Dec 11, 1949:
Milt Jackson,
Theolonius Monk,
Charlie Mingus.

Basin Street

© vanDam.

Stephan Van Dam

NY@tlas

Praise for VanDam
"The map to NYC
...a sophisticated
resource..."
New York Times

$10.95

**The Complete Five Boro
City Street Guide in**
* **3-D Super Scale**
* **Top Attractions**
Museums * Shops
Nightlife * Nature
Dining * Hotels
plus a cultural
history of NYC
in the 20th
Century.

vanDam. ☎ 800-UNFOLDS 80 cities worldwide

U.S.A. 1998
CD, AD, I, CW: Stephan Van Dam
D: Gerry Krieg/Mt Gunther Vollath
P: André Grossmann
I: Mirko Illis/Alex Reandou
DF: Van Dam, Inc.

4A comprehensive, easy-to-use NYC atlas.
This complete walking guide includes 10 haiku histories explaining how NYC has shaped 20th Century pop culture.
詳細で使いやすいニューヨーク市の地図。
ニューヨークが20世紀のポップ・カルチャーをどう形作ってきたかという歴史を、10点の俳句によって紹介している。

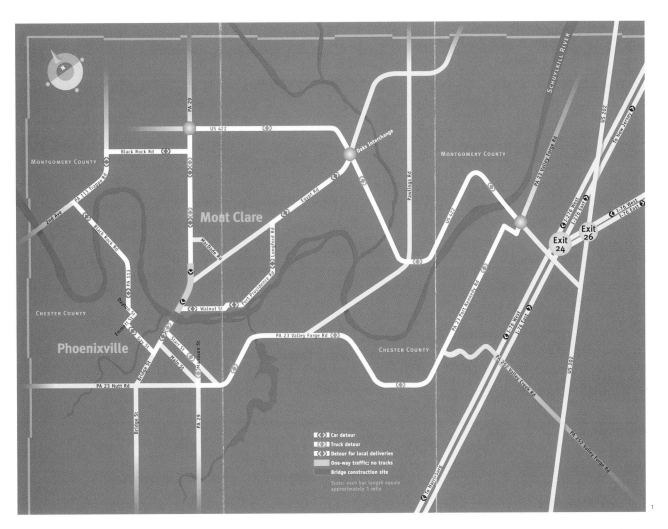

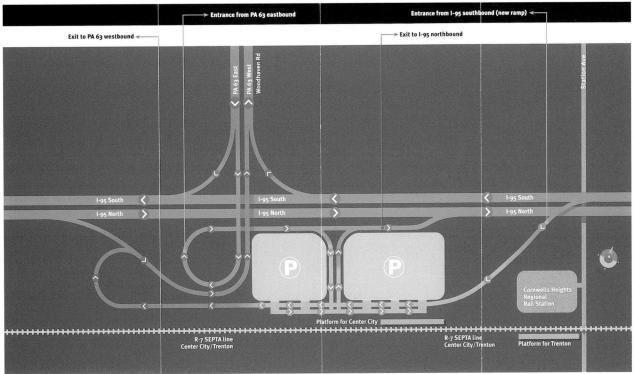

U.S.A. 1996 (1)/1997 (2)
CD, D, P: Joel Katz
D, I: David Weinberger (1)
I: David Schpok (2)
CW: Eugene Blaum (Penn DOT)
DF: Joel Katz Design Associates
CL: Penn DOT

Simplified diagrammatic maps intended to make complex road patterns clearly understandable.
For the Pennsylvania Department of Transportation.
複雑な道路地図を簡略化し、わかりやすくした図。ペンシルバニア州交通局のためのもの。

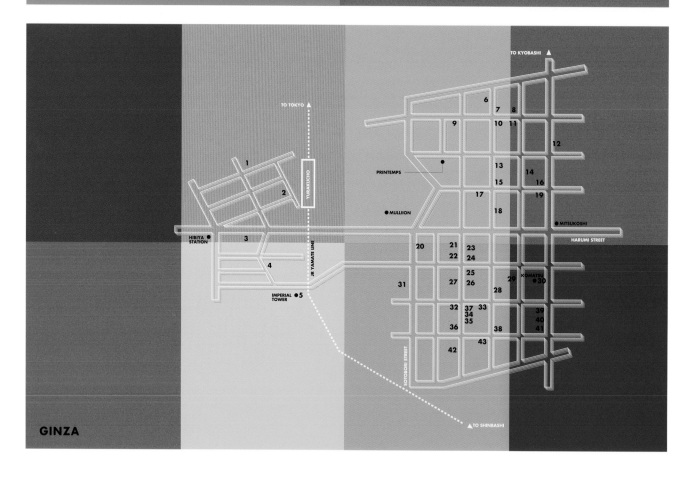

AOYAMA

GINZA

Japan 1999
AD: Yasushi Fujimoto
D: Youichi Iwamoto/Noriteru Minezaki
I: Kenji Oguro
DF: Cap
CL: Infas

Maps showing fashion boutiques that have recently opened in four areas of Tokyo.
雑誌『流行通信』より。東京の4つのエリアに、新しくオープンしたファッション系のショップを紹介したマップ。

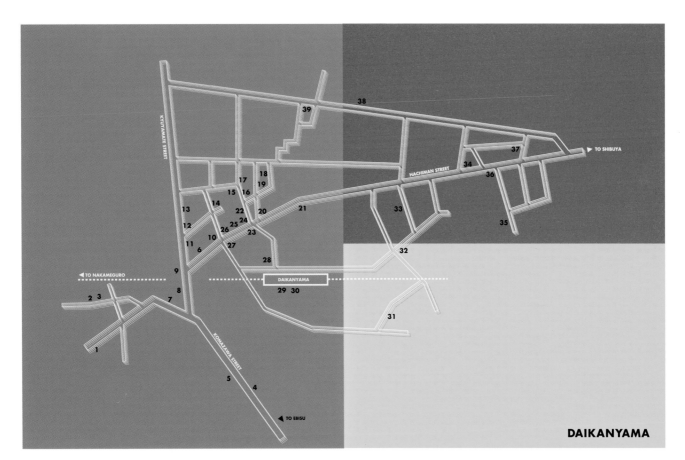

DAIKANYAMA

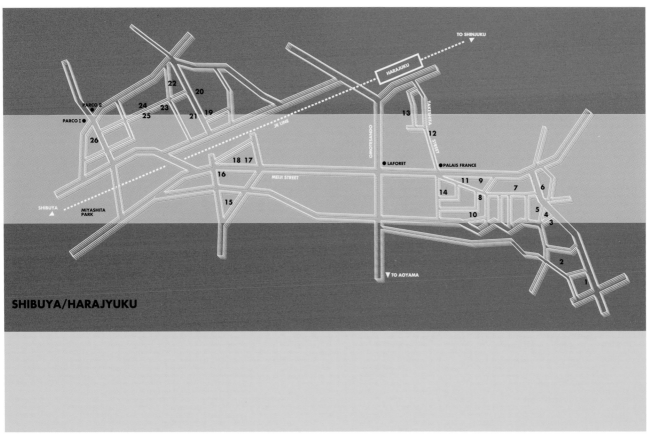

SHIBUYA/HARAJYUKU

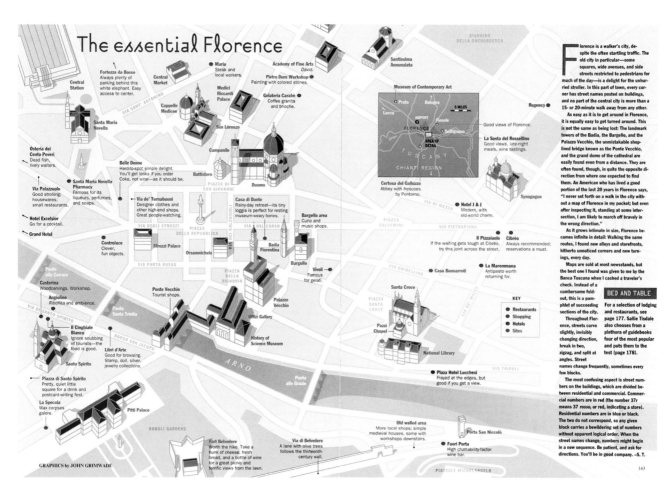

U.S.A.   1997
AD: Robert Best
D: Carla Frank
I: John Grimwade
CL: Condé Nast Traveler

Map showing landmarks in
Florence, Italy, and the writer's selection
of restaurants, shopping, and hotels.
イタリア、フィレンツェのランドマークと
著者の選んだレストラン、ショップ、ホテルを
示した地図。

U.S.A.   1998
AD, D, I: Robin Ghelerter O'Connell/
Cindy Vance
DF: Robin Ghelerter O'Connell
CL: Bayside District Co.

This map provides points of interest
and information for visitors to
Santa Monica's downtown area.
The frame of reference to the ocean helps
to orient tourists to their surroundings.
The brightly-colored universal icons
create a fun look.
サンタモニカのダウンタウン・エリアガイド。
海を臨むレイアウトは、旅行者にとって
使いやすいようにしたもの。
普遍的だが、明るい色のアイコンが楽しい。

WALK THIS WAY

Your guide to navigating the new Grand Central

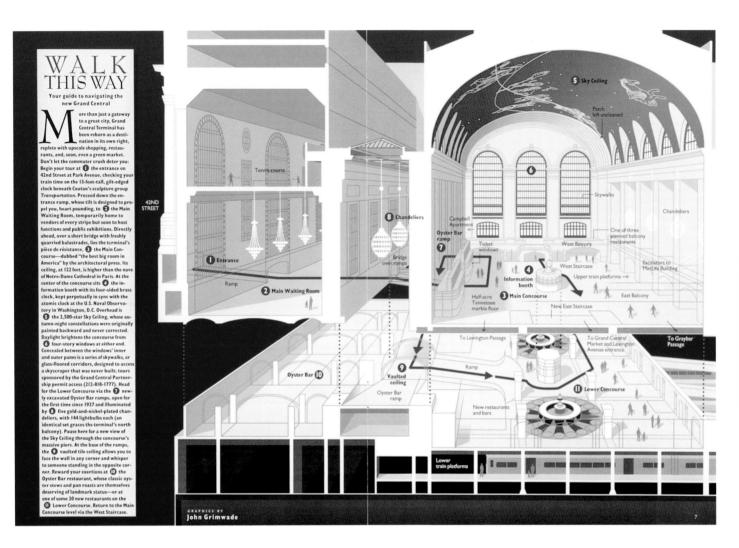

More than just a gateway to a great city, Grand Central Terminal has been reborn as a destination in its own right, replete with upscale shopping, restaurants, and, soon, even a green market. Don't let the commuter crush deter you: Begin your tour at ❶ the entrance on 42nd Street at Park Avenue, checking your train time on the 13-foot-tall, gilt-edged clock beneath Coutan's sculpture group *Transportation*. Proceed down the entrance ramp, whose tilt is designed to propel you, heart pounding, to ❷ the Main Waiting Room, temporarily home to vendors of every stripe but soon to host functions and public exhibitions. Directly ahead, over a short bridge with freshly quarried balustrades, lies the terminal's pièce de résistance, ❸ the Main Concourse—dubbed "the best big room in America" by the architectural press. Its ceiling, at 122 feet, is higher than the nave of Notre-Dame Cathedral in Paris. At the center of the concourse sits ❹ the information booth with its four-sided brass clock, kept perpetually in sync with the atomic clock at the U.S. Naval Observatory in Washington, D.C. Overhead is ❺ the 2,500-star Sky Ceiling, whose autumn-night constellations were originally painted backward and never corrected. Daylight brightens the concourse from ❻ four-story windows at either end. Concealed between the windows' inner and outer panes is a series of skywalks, or glass-floored corridors, designed to access a skyscraper that was never built; tours sponsored by the Grand Central Partnership permit access (212-818-1777). Head for the Lower Concourse via the ❼ newly excavated Oyster Bar ramps, open for the first time since 1927 and illuminated by ❽ five gold-and-nickel-plated chandeliers, with 144 lightbulbs each (an identical set graces the terminal's north balcony). Pause here for a new view of the Sky Ceiling through the concourse's massive piers. At the base of the ramps, the ❾ vaulted tile ceiling allows you to face the wall in any corner and whisper to someone standing in the opposite corner. Reward your exertions at ❿ the Oyster Bar restaurant, whose classic oyster stews and pan roasts are themselves deserving of landmark status—or at one of some 20 new restaurants on the ⓫ Lower Concourse. Return to the Main Concourse level via the West Staircase.

GRAPHICS BY John Grimwade

U.S.A. 1998
AD: Robert Best
I: John Grimwade/John Tomanio
CL: Condé Nast Traveler

A guide to the restored Grand Central Terminal in New York City.
ニューヨークのグランド・セントラル・ターミナル（修復後）のガイド。

HITLER'S BUNKER: BERLIN 1945

BERLIN
Russian front line
1 May 1945
Reichstag
Brandenburg Gate
Tiergarten
Spree
Chancellery
Hitler's Bunker
1 mile

Underground emergency exit in Foreign Office garden

Air raid shelters and connecting tunnels
Reich Chancellery buildings
250 FEET
Hitler's underground city
VIEW OF MAIN DRAWING OF BUNKERS
Pool
Gardens

1. Führerbunker. 2. Vorbunker. 3. Exit to chancellery garden. 4. Observation tower. 5. Exit to Foreign Office garden. 6. Tunnel to ministries. 7. Tunnel to Propaganda ministry. 8,9. Aides and military staff. 10,12,13. Civilian staff. 11. Field hospital. 14. Canteen. 15,16. Garage. 17. Drivers. 18. Garage. 19. Above ground bomb-proof garages with fuel reserve. 20-24. Emergency exits. 25. Vehicle lift.

Shallow underground tunnel linking the Führerbunker with other underground facilities

DIPLOMATS' HALL

Old Chancellery garden wall

VORBUNKER. Constructed 1936

FÜHRERBUNKER. Construction begins in the winter of 1943-44

Ventilation tower

The Chancellery garden was strewn with building materials and equipment of the unfinished bunker

Emergency exit with gas tight armoured door

Unfinished pillbox

INSIDE THE BUNKERS

1, Tunnel from the Reich Chancellery to the Vor (front)bunker. 2, Corridor of the Vorbunker; doors on left lead to the kitchens, pantry, refrigerators and wine cellar, doors on right to communal mess and servant's rooms. 3, Rooms occupied by Goebbels family. 4, Connecting stairs. 5, Passage with armoured door to Führerbunker. 6, Corridor of the Führerbunker. 7, Machinery room with diesel powered plant for air-conditioning 8, Dr Morrel's room. 9, Communications room. 10, Social room. 11, Hitlers valet and orderly officers room. 12, Wash rooms, here Hitler's Alsatian Blondi was kept and 13 toilets. 14, Second corridor/reception room. 15, Situation conference room. 16, 17, 18, Hitler's apartment. 19, Hitler and Eva Braun's bathroom. 20, Eva Braun's bedroom. 21, Air-lock corridor to exits. 22, Exit to observation tower. 23, Exit to chancellery garden.

Vorbunker
Hitler's first air raid shelter was constructed in 1936 below the Diplomats' Hall to the rear of the old Reichs Chancellery

Führerbunker
In the winter of 1943-44 Allied bombing of Berlin intensified. Hitler ordered a second bunker, 50ft below ground, with a roof 10ft thick to be built alongside the Vorbunker. As a command centre the Führerbunker had major drawbacks. Communications were dependent on a small, one-man telephone switchboard with a scrambler and a medium and long range radio transmitter.
There was no direct line from the bunker to Armed Forces High Command communications centre 15 miles south of Berlin. The ventilation was also poor. The noise of the diesel motor which ran the ventilation and water pumping systems was such that Hitler ordered it turned off during conferences. The bunker would then become stuffy and the conference participants would complain of headaches.

3.35pm, 30 April 1945 Adolf and Eva Hitler commit suicide in the Führer's apartment

Graphic: Phil Green

Adolf Hitler　**Eva Braun**

THE LAST DAYS

HITLER and his mistress, Eva Braun, entered the bunker on April 15, as the Russians opened their offensive to seize the Reich capital. Albert Speer called the concrete city, below the old Chancellery "the Island of the Departed."

Its airless-claustrophobia, as night merged into day in the baleful glare of electric lights, emphasised the artificiality and isolation of Hitler's existence.

He would rise at noon, and the last military conference would end just before dawn. In darkness he would emerge to exercise his dog, Blondi.

The Fuhrer was broken and visibly ageing, his hair almost white, his head stooped, his hands palsied. But under the influence of drugs he could still rant at his Generals - demanding why armies, which existed only in his imagination, had not come to the rescue.

On April 26 came the news of Himmler's attempted peace negotiations, relayed gleefully by Goebbels. Hitler was white with rage. Even the SS had betrayed him. The German people had betrayed him. It was the signal for the end.

Just after midnight on April 29 he married Eva Braun. The next day he held one last military conference and in a fetid corridor bade farewell to his secretaries, staff, Goebbels and Nazi Party secretary, Martin Bormann.

Around 3.35 pm, sitting facing her husband, Eva Hitler bit a cyanide capsule. Hitler shot himself through the mouth. Their bodies were doused in petrol and set alight. Next morning Goebbels gave poison to his six children - and was shot with his wife, Magda, by the SS guards.

In 1945 Hugh Trevor-Roper, then a young intelligence officer, assembled these facts but he admitted later Hitler's bones might have survived. Earlier this year the Russians opened their files, confirming Trevor-Roper's findings and completed the story. The bones indeed survived, buried at Magdeburg in East Germany. In 1970 they were finally incinerated. Thus expired the Third Reich.

Hitler's Bunker: Berlin 1945
30 April 1995
Phil Green
The Sunday Telegraph
Freehand3
473k

U.K.　1995
Graphics Editor: Phillip J Green
CL: The Sunday Telegraph

Cutaway graphic of Hitler's bunker in the last days of WWII, published on the 50th anniversary of the end of the war in Europe.
第二次世界大戦の末期におけるヒトラーの隠れ家の切断図。ヨーロッパの戦後50周年を記念して出版された。

Metrô começa a sair do buraco

PAULO SÉRGIO MARQUEIRO

Há vida debaixo da terra. Depois de uma interrupção de cerca de seis anos, recomeçam no próximo dia 4 as escavações do túnel que levará o Metrô até Copacabana. Segundo a Secretaria estadual de Transportes, as obras, que estão a cargo da construtora Andrade Gutierrez, serão iniciadas com dinheiro do Tesouro do estado, já que os R$ 55 milhões prometidos pela Prefeitura ainda não foram liberados. A expansão até a Praça Cardeal Arcoverde, em Copacabana, porém, não é o único alento de um sistema de transporte que parecia ter perdido o bondé da História.

Na quinta-feira passada, o estado retomou a construção do rabicho da Tijuca, que servirá de pátio de manobras, garagem de trens e estacionamento de veículos. A obra, sob responsabilidade da construtora Mendes Júnior, custará cerca de R$ 12 milhões e permitirá a redução do intervalo entre os trens, que hoje é de 3 minutos e 45 segundos, para um minuto e meio. Enfim, o Metrô do Rio começa a deixar para trás a estação do abandono.

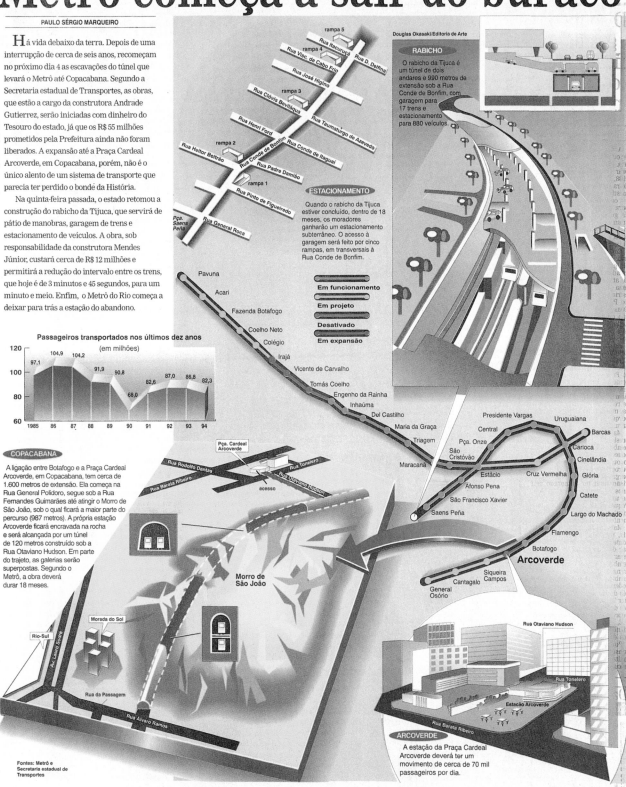

Passageiros transportados nos últimos dez anos
(em milhões)

120 — 104,9 104,2
97,1 — 91,9 90,8 — 87,0 86,8 — 82,3
100 — 82,6
80 — 68,0
60
1985 86 87 88 89 90 91 92 93 94

RABICHO
O rabicho da Tijuca é um túnel de dois andares e 990 metros de extensão sob a Rua Conde de Bonfim, com garagem para 17 trens e estacionamento para 880 veículos.

Douglas Okasaki/Editoria de Arte

rampa 5
rampa 4
Rua Itacuruçá
Rua D. Delfina
Rua Visc. de Cabo Frio
Rua José Higino
rampa 3
Rua Clóvis Bevilácqua
Rua Henri Ford
Rua Taumaturgo de Azevedo
Rua Heitor Beltrão
Rua Conde de Bonfim
Rua Conde de Itaguaí
Rua Padre Damião
rampa 2
rampa 1
Rua Pinto de Figueiredo
Rua General Roca
Pça. Saens Peña

ESTACIONAMENTO
Quando o rabicho da Tijuca estiver concluído, dentro de 18 meses, os moradores ganharão um estacionamento subterrâneo. O acesso à garagem será feito por cinco rampas, em transversais à Rua Conde de Bonfim.

- Em funcionamento
- Em projeto
- Desativado
- Em expansão

Pavuna
Acari
Fazenda Botafogo
Coelho Neto
Colégio
Irajá
Vicente de Carvalho
Tomás Coelho
Engenho da Rainha
Inhaúma
Del Castilho
Maria da Graça
Triagem
Maracanã
Saens Peña

Presidente Vargas
Central
Uruguaiana
Barcas
Carioca
Cinelândia
Glória
Catete
Largo do Machado
Flamengo
Botafogo
Pça. Onze
São Cristóvão
Estácio
Cruz Vermelha
Afonso Pena
São Francisco Xavier
Arcoverde
Siqueira Campos
Cantagalo
General Osório

COPACABANA
A ligação entre Botafogo e a Praça Cardeal Arcoverde, em Copacabana, tem cerca de 1.600 metros de extensão. Ela começa na Rua General Polidoro, segue sob a Rua Fernandes Guimarães até atingir o Morro de São João, sob o qual ficará a maior parte do percurso (987 metros). A própria estação Arcoverde ficará encravada na rocha e será alcançada por um túnel de 120 metros construído sob a Rua Otaviano Hudson. Em parte do trajeto, as galerias serão superpostas. Segundo o Metrô, a obra deverá durar 18 meses.

Pça. Cardeal Arcoverde
Rua Rodolfo Dantas
Rua Tonelero
Rua Barata Ribeiro
Rua Otaviano Hudson
acesso
Morro de São João
Morada do Sol
Rio-Sul
Av. Lauro Sodré
Rua da Passagem
Rua Álvaro Ramos

Rua Otaviano Hudson
Rua Tonelero
Estação Arcoverde
Rua Barata Ribeiro

ARCOVERDE
A estação da Praça Cardeal Arcoverde deverá ter um movimento de cerca de 70 mil passageiros por dia.

Fontes: Metrô e Secretaria estadual de Transportes

Brazil 1995
AD: Leo Tavjansky
D: Douglas Okasaki
CW: Paulo Sergio Marouelro
CL: O Globo Newspaper

Rio de Janeiro's subway system: Plans to reform some stations and construct new ones.
リオデジャネイロの地下鉄システム。リフォームと新駅建設の計画。

The Netherlands 1999
CD, AD, D, CW: Kristian Kieft
P: Tan Zonneveld
DF: KKFT

*The map shows the route of the Whitbread Round The World Race;
the illustration at lower right details the dimensions of the W-60, the standard race yacht.*
ホイットブレッド世界周遊レースのルートを示した地図。右下は、標準的なレースヨットであるホイットブレッド60を図解したもの。

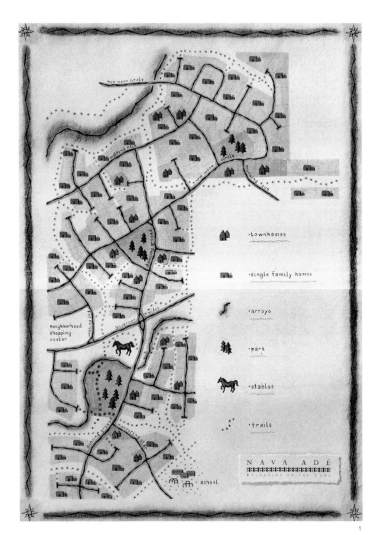

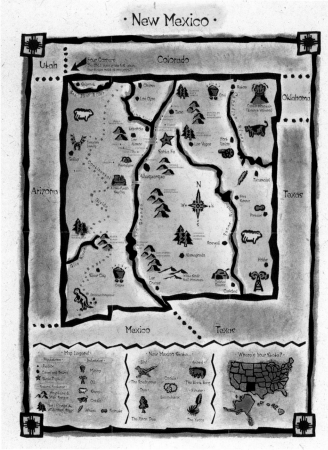

Canada 1996
CD: Marjorie Reichman
D, I: Vivian Harder
DF: Reichman+Hall Design
CL: Auerbach Southwest

A map intended to give potential buyers
an accurate schematic of housing plots for sale.
A welcoming comforting style emphasizes
the preservation and appreciation
of the natural environment of the Southwest. (1)
見込み客向けに販売住宅の位置を示した概略地図。
心地よい、見やすいスタイルのイラストによって、
サウスウエスト社の環境自然保護に対する姿勢を強調している。(1)

Canada 1995
AD: Steve Wedeen
I: Vivian Harder
DF: Vaughn Wedeen Creative, Inc.
CL: Juniper Learning

An educational map
of New Mexico included
in a learning kit used by teachers
to illustrate to young children
general facts about the state. (2)
ニューメキシコ州について総合的に
理解を深めるための、教師用の低学年向け
学習教材セットに使用された州地図。(2)

Flight 800's Fatal Plunge

Bound for Paris, Flight 800 made it only 50 miles from New York City when something went terribly wrong. Days of search and rescue found only corpses and twisted shards of metal. Now investigators will try to piece together what happened.

BOEING 747 PLANE SPECIFICATIONS

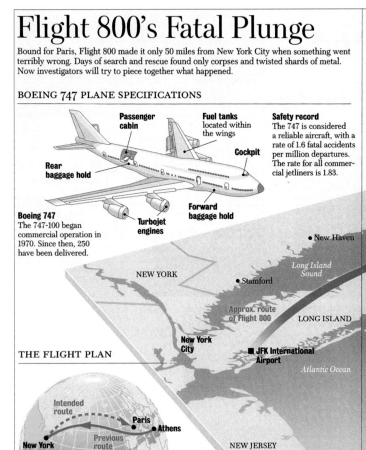

Passenger cabin

Fuel tanks located within the wings

Cockpit

Rear baggage hold

Turbojet engines

Forward baggage hold

Safety record
The 747 is considered a reliable aircraft, with a rate of 1.6 fatal accidents per million departures. The rate for all commercial jetliners is 1.83.

Boeing 747
The 747-100 began commercial operation in 1970. Since then, 250 have been delivered.

THE FLIGHT PLAN

Intended route

Paris

Athens

New York

Previous route

SOURCES: U.S. COAST GUARD, NTSB, JANE'S FIGHTING SHIPS, JANE'S ALL THE WORLD'S AIRCRAFT, MACMILLAN VISUAL DICTIONARY. RESEARCH BY DANTE CHINNI. DRAWINGS BY STANFORD KAY, DIXON ROHR—NEWSWEEK.

THE SEARCH FOR CLUES

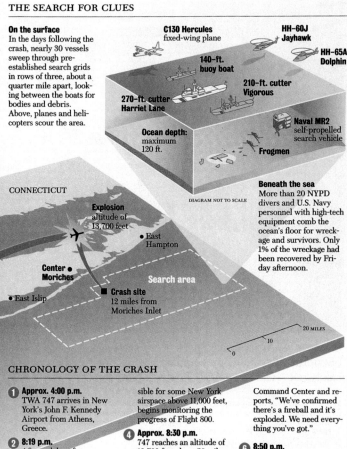

On the surface
In the days following the crash, nearly 30 vessels sweep through pre-established search grids in rows of three, about a quarter mile apart, looking between the boats for bodies and debris. Above, planes and helicopters scour the area.

C130 Hercules fixed-wing plane

HH-60J Jayhawk

HH-65A Dolphin

140-ft. buoy boat

210-ft. cutter Vigorous

270-ft. cutter Harriet Lane

Ocean depth: maximum 120 ft.

Naval MR2 self-propelled search vehicle

Frogmen

DIAGRAM NOT TO SCALE

Beneath the sea
More than 20 NYPD divers and U.S. Navy personnel with high-tech equipment comb the ocean's floor for wreckage and survivors. Only 1% of the wreckage had been recovered by Friday afternoon.

CONNECTICUT

Explosion altitude of 13,700 feet

New Haven

East Hampton

Center Moriches

Search area

East Islip

Crash site 12 miles from Moriches Inlet

NEW YORK

Stamford

Long Island Sound

Approx. route of Flight 800

LONG ISLAND

New York City

JFK International Airport

Atlantic Ocean

NEW JERSEY

20 MILES / 10 / 0

CHRONOLOGY OF THE CRASH

1 Approx. 4:00 p.m.
TWA 747 arrives in New York's John F. Kennedy Airport from Athens, Greece.

2 8:19 p.m.
After a delay of more than an hour, Flight 800 takes off from JFK bound for Paris.

3 Approx. 8:25 p.m.
Boston Air Route Traffic Control Center, respon-sible for some New York airspace above 11,000 feet, begins monitoring the progress of Flight 800.

4 Approx. 8:30 p.m.
747 reaches an altitude of 13,700 feet about 50 miles away from JFK and dis-appears from radar.

5 8:39 p.m.
Boston Air Route Traffic Control Center calls Boston Coast Guard

Command Center and re-ports, "We've confirmed there's a fireball and it's exploded. We need every-thing you've got."

6 8:50 p.m.
Within 10 minutes, nine cutters, four helicopters and one Falcon jet are on their way to the scene. Coast Guard cutter Adak, an 82-foot patrol boat, is the first at the scene.

U.S.A. 1996
Design Director: Lynn Staley
Graphics Director, D: Bonnie Scranton
I: Stanford Kay/Dixon Rohr
CW: Dante Chinni
CL: Newsweek Magazine

This graphic details the crash of Flight 800, and the rescue efforts undertaken.
800便の事故の詳細と救助活動についてグラフィック化したもの。

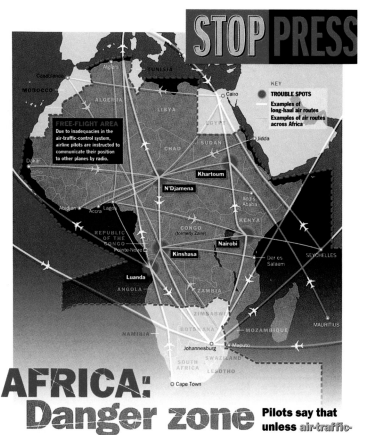

STOP PRESS

AFRICA:
Danger zone

Pilots say that unless air-traffic-control improves, a catastrophe is all but inevitable

INTERNATIONAL AIRLINE PILOTS HAVE DECLARED the air corridors over Africa dangerous and a threat to passenger safety. They have warned African governments and inter-

By Frank Barrett and Sam Kiley national airline associations that unless immediate action is taken to improve air-traffic-control procedures, "a catastrophic accident" is in the offing.

A number of near misses over this past year—one involving the U.S. ambassador to the United Nations, Bill Richardson,

(see "How the U.S. Marines saved their man")—and the fatal collision last September of a U.S. Air Force transport plane and a German military aircraft in Namibian airspace have confirmed pilots' fears. According to Peter Quaintmere, the London-based technical director of the International Federation of Air Line Pilots' Associations (IFALPA), the Namibia collision "was an accident we've

GRAPHICS BY JOHN GRIMWADE

43

U.S.A. 1997
AD: Robert Best
D: Linda Root
I: John Grimwade
CL: Condé Nast Traveler

A map indicating African air routes, for a magazine article on traffic problems in the African skies.
アフリカ上空の交通課題についての記事に使用された、アフリカの航空路線図。

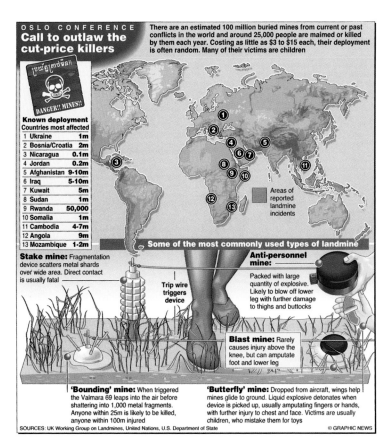

U.K. 1997
AD: Duncan Mil
DF: Graphic News
CL: Subscribing Newspapers

Maps and illustrations showing various types of land mines, and the countries that are most affected by their implementation.
さまざまな地雷の種類を図解し、地雷の敷設によって最も影響を受けた国々を地図上に示した。

THE EARTH'S ICE CROWN

Both are realms of ice, but the earth's two poles are environmental opposites: The South Pole is on a continent that is surrounded by oceans, while the North Pole is in an ocean that's surrounded by continents.

A frozen membrane of "pack ice" covers the Arctic Ocean like a layer of frosting. The polar ice cap is fractured into ice fields and floes that spread in winter and shrink in summer, but on average they combine to cover four million square miles—an area as big as Canada, with Alaska thrown in.

The ice cap is permanent, but it is not stable. Variable conditions of wind, cold, ocean current, and snowfall cause the ice fields to melt and form anew and to develop cracks and "pres-

sure ridges." As a result of this instability, at least ten percent of the Arctic Ocean is open water year-round, but even so, icebreakers such as the *Yamal* attempt the Pole only in summer, when the pack ice is in retreat and at its thinnest.

Icebergs are not a factor in navigating the Arctic Basin, because the ice cap is virtually devoid of them: Icebergs are formed on land, of which the North Pole has none. They are, however, a factor in getting to the Arctic Ocean. The glaciers of Greenland alone launch about 10,000 icebergs a year, ranging from the size of sofas (called "growlers"), to small

houses ("bergy bits"), to the largest known Arctic iceberg, recorded in 1882 as being 7 miles long and 3.7 miles wide. (Antarctica, in contrast, holds more than 90 percent of the world's glacial ice and launches individual icebergs as large as 90 miles in length.)

Going to extremes

Obviously, midsummer is the time to break ice and break out the champagne at the North Pole. QUARK EXPEDI-

TIONS' 1995 sailing aboard the *Yamal* departs Murmansk July 5 and returns July 21. For most of the voyage the sun shines 24 hours a day, revealing Arctic islands, polar bears, walrus, and how much the Russians love to party on the ice (800-356-5699; $16,900, plus airfare to Murmansk).

If you can't quite shake the image of Chernobyl afloat, there are also nonnuclear, hull-hardened ships that crunch all the way to the Pole, then at least

close enough to put you in the realm of polar bears and eternal daylight.

Quark is not the only choice for an Arctic cruise. Last year, for SEVEN SEAS CRUISE LINE, the *Hanseatic* crossed the Northwest Passage—a route that has been successfully completed only four times by passenger ships. This year's itinerary will include a sail through a portion of the Passage, without crossing it com-

pletely (800-285-1835). The *World Discoverer* cruises the Bering Sea for SOCIETY EXPE-DITIONS (800-548-8669). Finally, both the *Polish Star* and the *Nordbrise* cruise above the eightieth parallel for EURO CRUISES (212-691-2099 or 800-688-3876).

Of course, icebreakers aren't the only way to get to the Pole. For women who are ready to risk developing a culinary interest in dogmeat to get to the

North Pole, the NORTHWEST PASSAGE's all-female dogsled-ding expedition is led by the first woman to make it overland by skis to both poles, Ann Bancroft. Participants fly from Resolute Bay, Canada, to within 150 miles of the Pole—a distance team members then mush over the ice. To

qualify, candidates do a week-long winter shakedown in Ely, Minnesota (800-732-7328; qualification, Jan. 9–15; expedition, April 25–May 11; $23,500, plus airfares to Ely and Resolute Bay). —B. P.

THE LIST
CRUISE LINES

Today's passenger ships ply waters from pole to pole. Our guide to 25 of the best cruise lines begins on page 170.

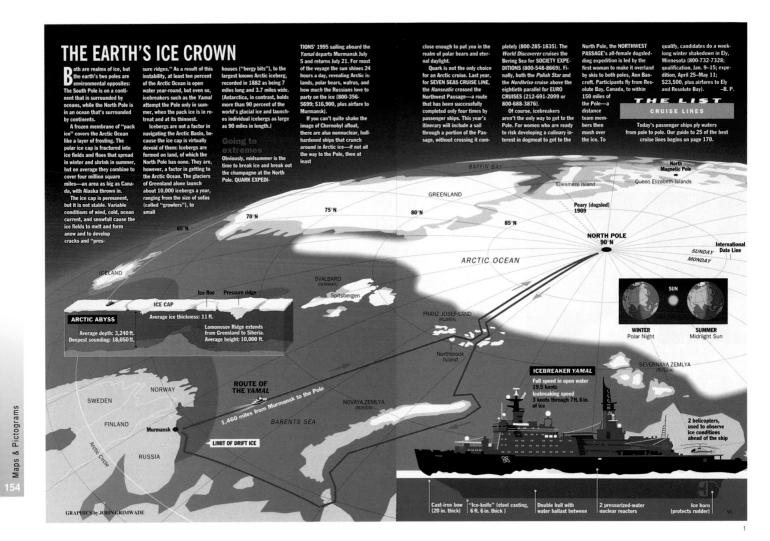

GRAPHICS by JOHN GRIMWADE

91

1

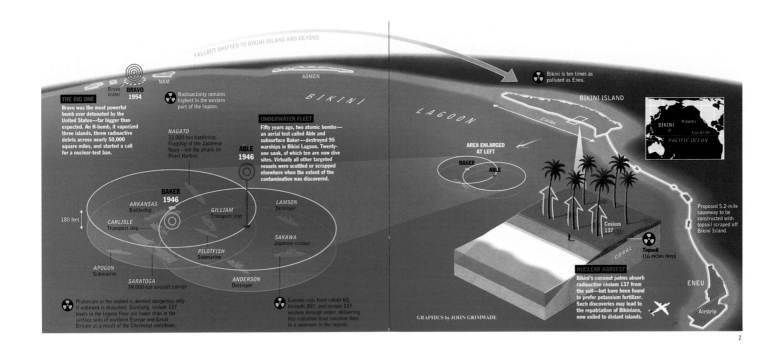

GRAPHICS by JOHN GRIMWADE

2

JUST TO THE EAST OF THE RED BASIN OF Sichuan, the Yangtze River forces its way through a huge barrier of limestone ridges: This is the famous Three Gorges, a series of deep and mysterious cliff-bound defiles whose beauty and majesty have lured and inspired poets and artists for centuries, and which for the last hundred years have attracted legions of amazed foreign travelers. Since 1919 they have beckoned also to scores of equally enthusiastic hydraulic engineers. In 1956 Mao had dreamed of what they might do there, as he explained in his poem "Swimming":

Walls of stone will stand upstream to the west
To hold back Wushan's clouds and rain
Till a smooth lake rises in the narrow gorges.
The mountain goddess if she is still there
Will marvel at a world so changed.

Will weep, more likely. For this is an utterly precious part of the world, matchless in the canon, a place that does not wish to be changed, and whose centuries of admirers have set special store by its sheer changelessness. Even the more obvious short-comings caused by fifty years of Communist husbandry—the choking gray pollution, the irredeemably ugly architecture, the chaos of riverbank industry—cannot diminish the awe that any traveler feels upon first seeing the gorges. The combination they present—of formidable river, unsurpassable geology—and with the leavening brush of China's ancient civilization everywhere, exerts a strange and perpetual magnetism. Once seen, the Yangtze Gorges are never to be forgotten.

THE DAY SPENT SAILING DOWN-stream from where the boats gather in Chongqing offers some preparation. Dozens of pagodas, temples built either as sentinels, spirit-guardians, or tombs, are perched high on the rising hills. Orange groves tumble down the hillsides, and in the spring the fields are pink with peach blossoms. You see towns where locals make the thick bamboo hawsers that trackers once used to haul junks up the rapids, and other towns that turn out fans, or shipyards that build small sampans. There is another town, more macabre, where the museums are filled with old torture equipment and whose tombs are devoted to ghosts. At one point there is an ancient water gauge, the flood levels marked by the eyes of carp that were carved in stone two thousand years ago. And at a temple in a place called White Emperor City, where monkeys scamper among the altars, there is a marble plate with a long poem written on petrified bamboo leaves.

And then the boat turns a corner, and for everyone aboard who sees, the heart suddenly misses a beat. For although it seems that the river might be about to end in the solid wall of vertical rock ahead, its speed suddenly picks up and it rushes and foams toward cliffs that rise half a mile into the sky and are

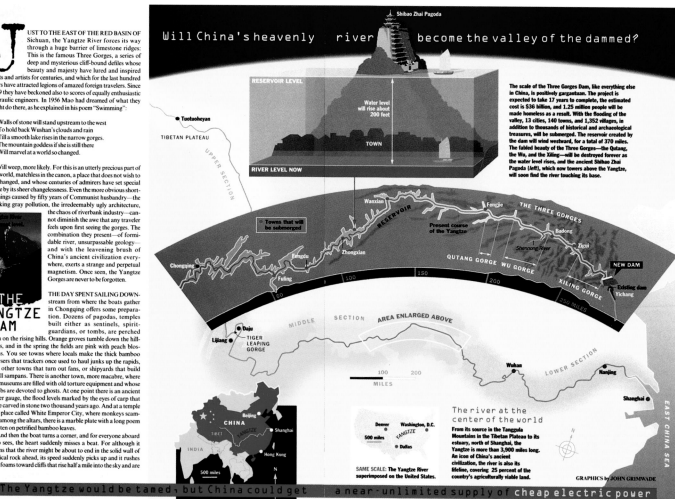

Will China's heavenly river become the valley of the dammed?

Shibao Zhai Pagoda

RESERVOIR LEVEL
Water level will rise about 200 feet
TOWN
RIVER LEVEL NOW

TIBETAN PLATEAU
Tuotuoheyan
UPPER SECTION

The scale of the Three Gorges Dam, like everything else in China, is positively gargantuan. The project is expected to take 17 years to complete, the estimated cost is $36 billion, and 1.25 million people will be made homeless as a result. With the flooding of the valley, 13 cities, 140 towns, and 1,352 villages, in addition to thousands of historical and archaeological treasures, will be submerged. The reservoir created by the dam will wind westward, for a total of 370 miles. The fabled beauty of the Three Gorges—the Qutang, the Wu, and the Xiling—will be destroyed forever as the water level rises, and the ancient Shibao Zhai Pagoda (*left*), which now towers above the Yangtze, will soon find the river touching its base.

Wanxian
Fengjie   THE THREE GORGES
Present course of the Yangtze
Badong
Towns that will be submerged
RESERVOIR
Zhongxian   Shennong River   Zigui
Chongqing   Fengdu   QUTANG GORGE   WU GORGE   NEW DAM
Fuling   XILING GORGE   Existing dam   Yichang
50   100   150   200   250 MILES

MIDDLE   SECTION   AREA ENLARGED ABOVE

Daju
Lijiang   TIGER LEAPING GORGE
Wuhan   LOWER SECTION   Nanjing
100   200   MILES
Shanghai

CHINA
Beijing
TIBET   YANGTZE   Shanghai
INDIA   Hong Kong
500 miles
N

Denver   Washington, D.C.
500 miles   YANGTZE
Dallas
SAME SCALE: The Yangtze River superimposed on the United States.

The river at the center of the world
From its source in the Tanggula Mountains in the Tibetan Plateau to its estuary, north of Shanghai, the Yangtze is more than 3,900 miles long. An icon of China's ancient civilization, the river is also its lifeline, covering 25 percent of the country's agriculturally viable land.

GRAPHICS by JOHN GRIMWADE

EAST CHINA SEA

The Yangtze would be tamed, but China could get a near-unlimited supply of cheap electric power

THE YANGTZE DAM

U.S.A. 1995 (1)/1996 (2)(3)
AD: Diana Laguardia (1)/Robert Best (2)(3)
D: Stephen Orr (1)
I: John Grimwade
CL: Condé Nast Traveler

Traveling to the North Pole by icebreaker. (1)
砕氷船による北極への旅のコースを示した案内図。(1)

A map of the Bikini Atoll, site of atomic tests fifty years ago that has been reopened for tourism. (2)
50年前の原水爆実験場であったビキニ環礁の地図。観光スポットとして近年再公開された。(2)

Map showing the extent of the new Yangtze reservoir.
Inset shows a typical town that will become submerged when the dam is completed. (3)
揚子江の新ダム建設による貯水路を表した地図。上の図は、ダムが完成した際に水没することになる町について説明している。(3)

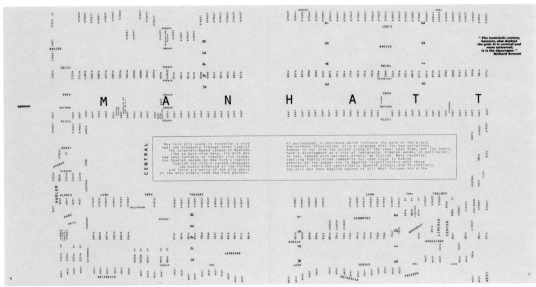

Germany 1997
CD, AD, D, P, CW, DF: Antonia Henschel
CL: Antonia Henschel

*Cityscapes is an experimental magazine that investigates four different cities.
The magazine's structure is based on maps as subjective diagrams.*
Cityscapesは、4つの都市を探索する実験マガジン。主観的にデザインされた地図によって構成されている。

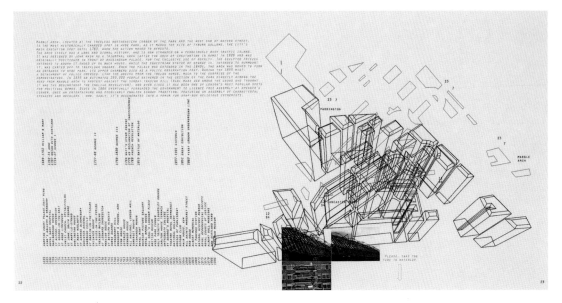

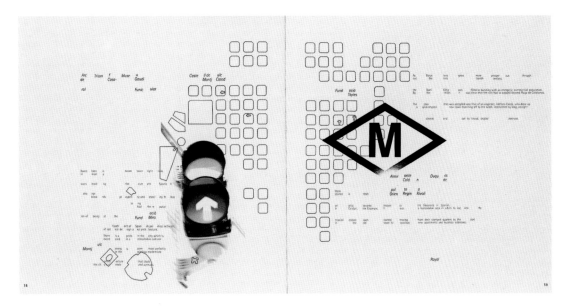

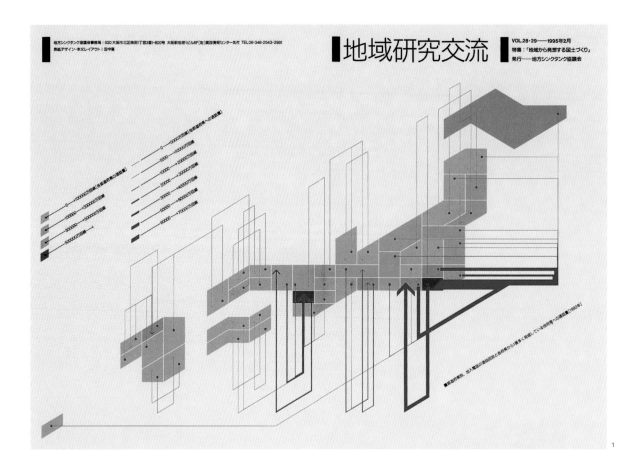

地方シンクタンク協議会事務局｜530 大阪市北区梅田1丁目3番1-800号　大阪駅前第1ビル6F［財］関西情報センター気付 TEL06-346-2543-2981
表紙デザイン・本文レイアウト｜田中晋

■地域研究交流　VOL.28・29──1995年2月
特集：「地域から発想する国土づくり」
発行──地方シンクタンク協議会

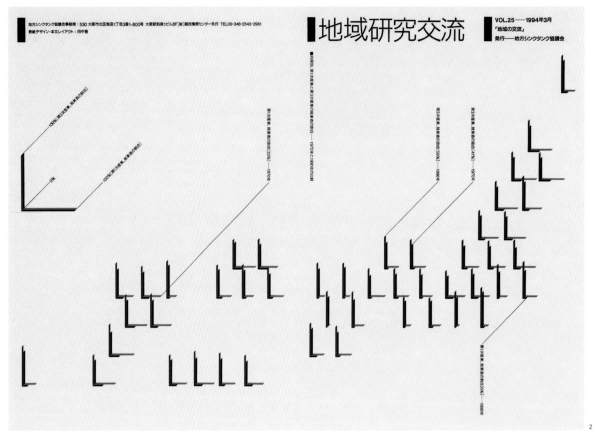

地方シンクタンク協議会事務局｜530 大阪市北区梅田1丁目3番1-800号　大阪駅前第1ビル6F［財］関西情報センター気付 TEL06-346-2543-2981
表紙デザイン・本文レイアウト｜田中晋

■地域研究交流　VOL.25──1994年3月
「地域の交流」
発行──地方シンクタンク協議会

Japan　1994（2）/1995（1）
AD: Shin Tanaka
D: Hiroaki Yazaki
DF: Shin Tanaka Design Room

Frequency of calls made in 1992, and the prefecture to which most calls were made, in each of Japan's prefectures. (1)
都道府県別に調査した1992年の全国加入電話の通話回数と、各都道府県からいちばん多く発信されている他都道府県への通話量を表した地図。(1)

Map of Japan indicates, by prefecture, the percentages of workers in primary and tertiary industry sectors, comparing 1970 and 1990 figures. (2)
都道府県別に調査した1990年の第1次産業および第3次産業の就業者の割合を、1970年のデータと比較している。(2)

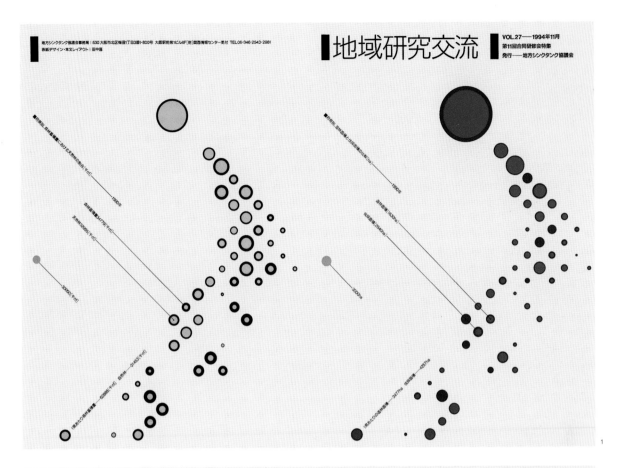

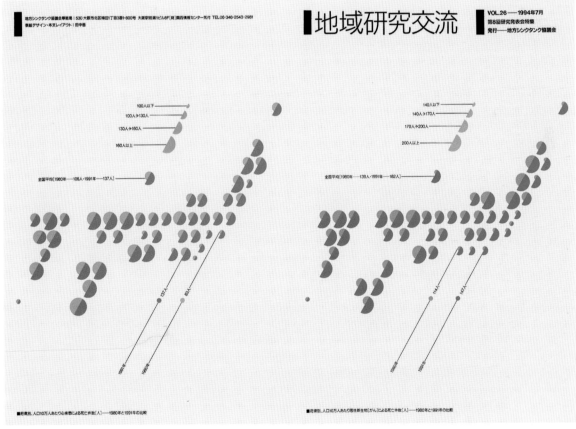

Japan   1994
AD: Shin Tanaka
D: Hiroaki Yazaki
DF: Shin Tanaka Design Room

*Maps of Japan showing 1990 amounts of afforested and deforested areas,
as well as the percent of forest area that is original growth, by prefecture.* (1)

都道府県別に調査した1990年の造林面積と伐採面積の比較および森林蓄積量における天然林の割合を示した地図。(1)

*Graphs showing numbers of deaths in Japan per 100,000 from cancer and heart disease.
1991 and 1980 figures are compared, by prefecture.* (2)

都道府県別に調査した1991年の人口10万人あたりのガンおよび心疾患による死亡件数を、1980年のデータと比較している。(2)

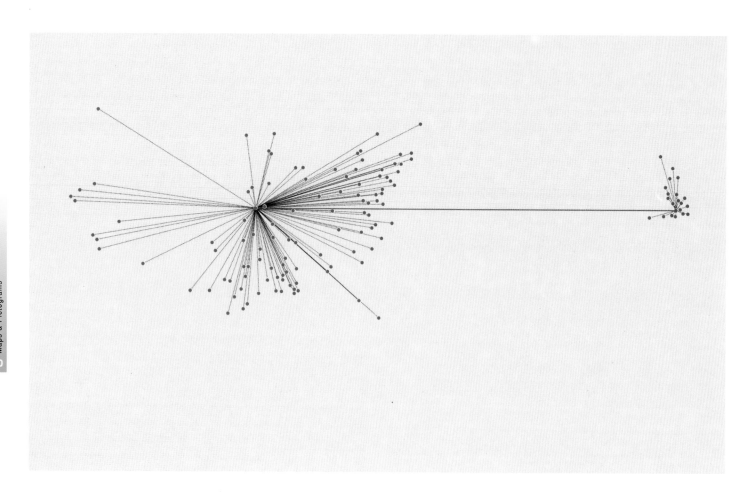

U.K.   1996
CD, D: Tor Pettersen
AD, D: Jeff Davis
D: Nicholas Kendall
I: David Baker
DF: Tor Pettersen & Partners Ltd.
CL: Cable & Wireless Plc

The map plots precisely the Exxon offices in the U.S.A. and Esso offices in the U.K.,
and illustrates the Global Virtual Private Network provided by Cable & Wireless Business Networks that links all the offices.
アメリカのエクソン社とイギリスのエッソ社のオフィスを図に示し、それらをリンクするケーブル＆ワイヤレス・ビジネス・ネットワーク社の
グローバル・バーチャル・プライベート・ネットワークを表したもの。

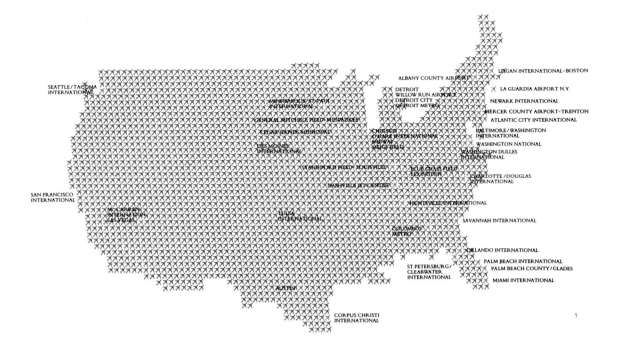

SEATTLE / TACOMA
INTERNATIONAL

SAN FRANCISCO
INTERNATIONAL

MINNEAPOLIS / ST. PAUL
INTERNATIONAL

GENERAL MITCHELL FIELD-MILWAUKEE

CEDAR RAPIDS MUNICIPAL

DES MOINES
INTERNATIONAL

STANDIFORD FIELD-LOUISVILLE

NASHVILLE JET CENTER

MCCARRAN
INTERNATIONAL
LAS VEGAS

TULSA
INTERNATIONAL

COLUMBUS
METRO

AUSTIN

CORPUS CHRISTI
INTERNATIONAL

ALBANY COUNTY AIRPORT

LOGAN INTERNATIONAL-BOSTON

LA GUARDIA AIRPORT N.Y.

DETROIT
WILLOW RUN AIRPORT
DETROIT CITY
DETROIT METRO

NEWARK INTERNATIONAL

MERCER COUNTY AIRPORT-TRENTON

ATLANTIC CITY INTERNATIONAL

CHICAGO
O'HARE INTERNATIONAL
MIDWAY
MEIGS FIELD

BALTIMORE / WASHINGTON
INTERNATIONAL

WASHINGTON NATIONAL

WASHINGTON DULLES
INTERNATIONAL

BLUE GRASS FIELD
LEXINGTON

CHARLOTTE / DOUGLAS
INTERNATIONAL

HUNTSVILLE INTERNATIONAL

SAVANNAH INTERNATIONAL

ORLANDO INTERNATIONAL

ST. PETERSBURG /
CLEARWATER
INTERNATIONAL

PALM BEACH INTERNATIONAL
PALM BEACH COUNTY / GLADES

MIAMI INTERNATIONAL

1

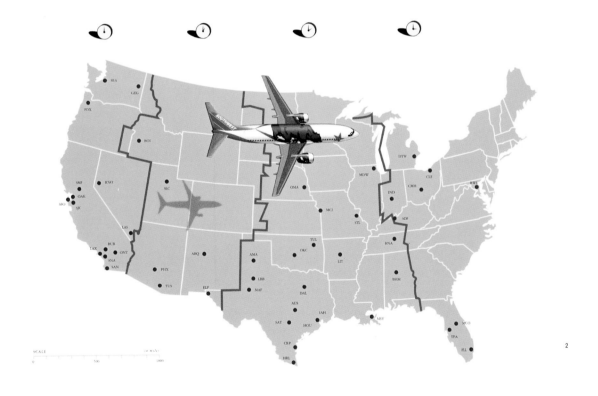

SCALE   (in miles)
0   500   1000

2

U.K. 1994
CD: Tor Pettersen
AD, D: Nicholas Kendall
I: David Baker
DF: Tor Pettersen & Partners Ltd.
CL: BBA Group Plc

*The map shows the enlarged network
of aviation service centres
in the U.S.A. owned by Signature Flight Support,
one of the world's largest networks
for general aviation services.* (1)
世界でも最大の総合航空サービス・ネットワークである
シグナチャー・フライト・サポート社が所有する、
アメリカ国内におけるサービス・センターの拡大ネットワーク。(1)

U.S.A. 1996
CD: Time McClure/
    GSD&M Advertising
AD, D: Rex Peteet
D: K. C. Teis/Matt Heck
I: Peter Kramer
DF: Sibley/Peteet Design
CL: Southwest Airlines

*This chart illustrates destinations
to which Southwest Airlines flies
in the continental U.S.A.
The plane flying overhead represents
the company's newest plane.* (2)
サウスウエスト航空の北米大陸における路線図。
上空の航空機は同社の最新型のものである。(2)

U.K. 1994
CD, AD: Tor Pettersen
D: David Freeman
I: Peter Hill
DF: Tor Pettersen & Partners Ltd.
CL: British Telecom

Illustration from BT's Mediat brochure.
A net theme helps emphasise
such benefits as security,
nationwide coverage and perfomance. (1)
ブリティッシュ・テレコム社のブローシュアより。
網を広げた図はセキュリティ、全国規模の
サービス基盤と実績を強調している。(1)

U.K. 1994
CD: Tor Pettersen
AD, D: David Freeman/Colleen Crim
DF: Tor Pettersen & Partners Ltd.
CL: International Leisure/Air Europe

The map, which is made up
as lines drawn in the sand,
shows the airline's destinations
in Europe. (2)
ヨーロッパにおけるエア・ヨーロッパの
航空路線図を砂に描いた線で表したもの。(2)

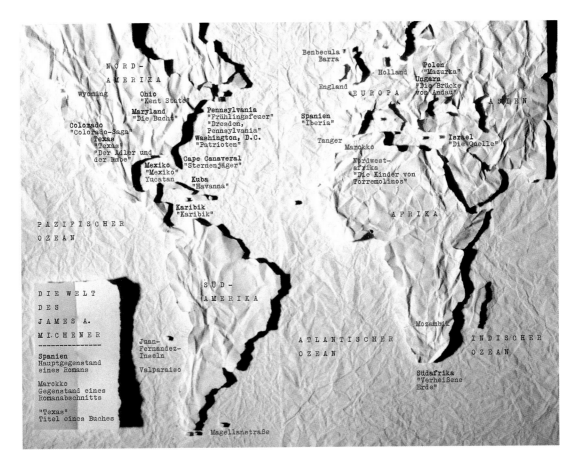

DIE WELT

DES

JAMES A.

MICHENER

Spanien
Hauptgegenstand
eines Romans

Marokko
Gegenstand eines
Romanabschnitts

"Texas"
Titel eines Buches

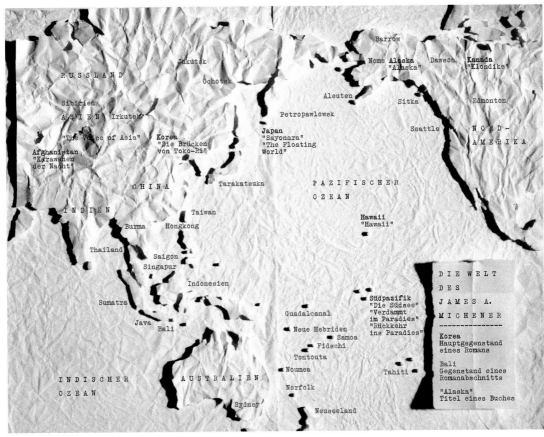

DIE WELT

DES

JAMES A.

MICHENER

Korea
Hauptgegenstand
eines Romans

Bali
Gegenstand eines
Romanabschnitts

"Alaska"
Titel eines Buches

Germany 1995
AD, I: Achim Frederic Kiel
P: Lutz Pape
DF: Pencil Corporate Art
CL: Gustav Luebbe Verlag

*Each endpaper shows one of the two halves of the world of James A.
Michener, who always used a mechanical typewriter to produce his manuscripts.
Blue text indicates the site of a novel; red, the site of a section of a novel; black, the title of a book.*

見返し部分に、ジェームス・A・ミチェナーの世界を二等分して示したもの。彼は原稿作成に常にタイプライターを使用していた。
青字は小説の舞台となった場所、赤字は小説の中に登場した場所、黒字は本のタイトルとなった場所を指す。

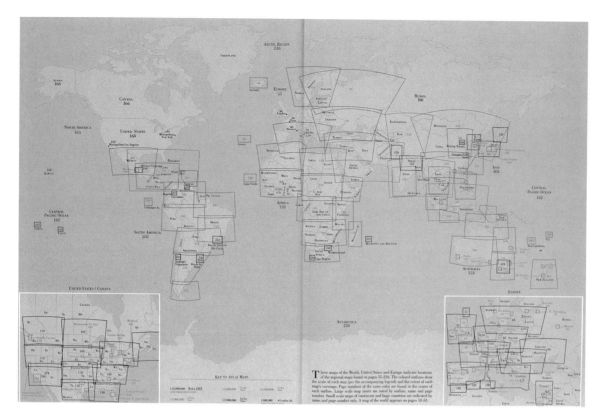

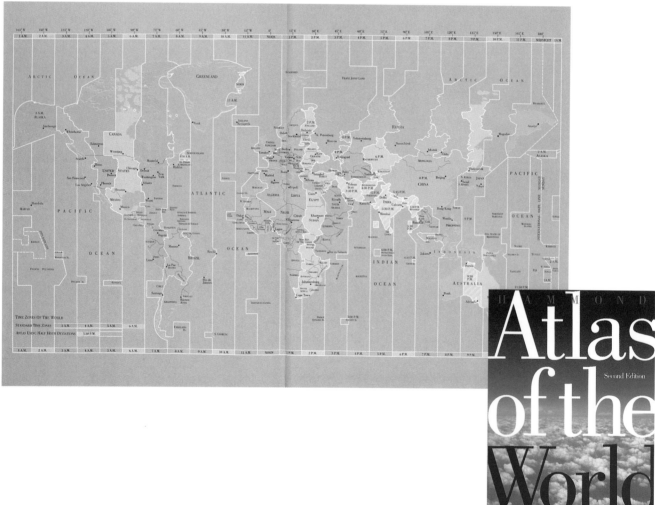

U.S.A.   1998
AD: Michael Gericke
D: Su Mathews
DF: Pentagram Design
CL: Hammond, Inc.

Maps showing the world divided into sections, and into world time zones.
世界の区分地図と、タイムゾーンを表した地図。

DESIGNS ON ANGKOR

AS CAMBODIA SELLS OUT ITS GLORIOUS ANCIENT CITY TO FOREIGN DEVELOPERS, THE WORLD COMMUNITY PRESSES TO PROTECT A POOR NATION'S MOST SACRED SITE

Cambodia has been called a one-asset country, and that asset is on the block: the great city of Angkor, capital of the Khmer empire when it extended from southwestern China to Thailand. At one hundred square miles, it is the largest temple complex in the world—hundreds of monuments, built a thousand years ago as a dwelling place for the gods near the inland sea, Tonle Sap.

Money has already changed hands: A Malaysian developer owns a ninety-nine-year lease on 2,700 adjacent acres, and more bids have been invited. This newborn worship of tourist dollars may even involve limiting the access of Cambodians to engage in more traditional forms of worship at Angkor's temples. At press time, no building had yet begun and protests were mounting, led by experts who suspect more greed than need in a government's decision to sell off its nation's past in a rush toward the future.

GRAPHICS BY JOHN GRIMWADE

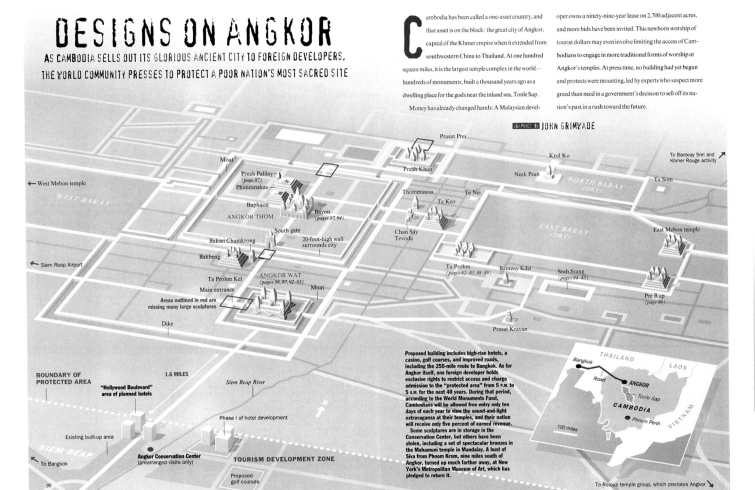

Proposed building includes high-rise hotels, a casino, golf courses, and improved roads, including the 250-mile route to Bangkok. As for Angkor itself, one foreign developer holds exclusive rights to restrict access and charge admission to the "protected area" from 5 P.M. to 5 A.M. for the next 40 years. During that period, according to the World Monuments Fund, Cambodians will be allowed free entry only ten days of each year to view the sound-and-light extravaganza at their temples, and their nation will receive only five percent of earned revenue.

Some sculptures are in storage in the Conservation Center, but others have been stolen, including a set of spectacular bronzes in the Mahamuni temple in Mandalay. A bust of Siva from Phnom Krom, nine miles south of Angkor, turned up much farther away, at New York's Metropolitan Museum of Art, which has pledged to return it.

U.S.A. 1997
AD: Robert Best
I: John Grimwade
CL: Condé Nast Traveler

Map of Angkor Wat, Cambodia.
カンボジアのアンコールワットの地図。

Stuyves

Queensboro Bridge   **Sutton**   **Turtle Bay**   **Kips Bay**

East River Bikew

U.S.A. 1998
CD, AD, D, P, I, CW: Nigel Walker
CW: Mark Allen
DF: That's Nice L.L.C.
CL: NYC Economic Development Corporation

A diagramatic signage system for an East River waterfront development project,
which will include a Bikeway and Esplanade.
自転車専用道路、遊歩道など、イースト・リバーのウォーターフロント開発プロジェクトにおける案内表示システム。

East River Park

The Sheds

Williamsburg Bridge

Between
the Bridges

Manhattan Bridge

The East River Docks

Brooklyn Bridge

The Battery

and Esplanade

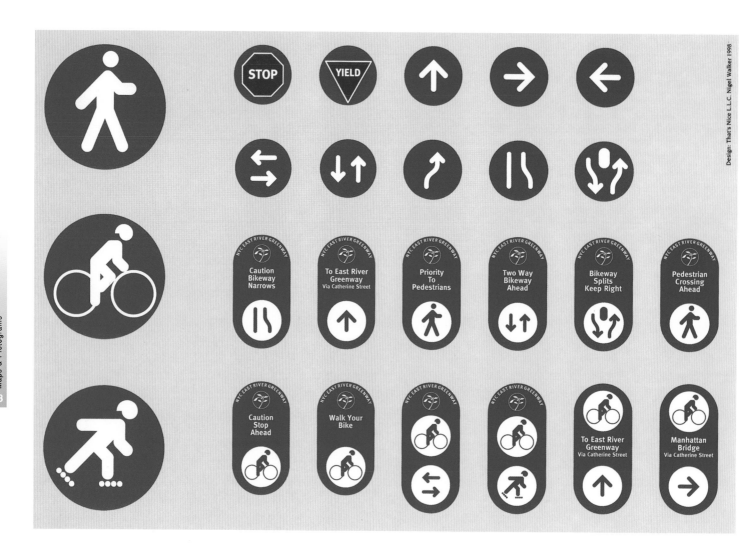

Design: That's Nice L.L.C. Nigel Walker 1998

自転車専用道路、遊歩道など、イースト・リバーのウォーターフロント開発プロジェクトにおける案内表示システム。

U.S.A. 1998
CD, AD, D, P, I, CW: Nigel Walker
CW: Mark Allen
DF: That's Nice L.L.C.
CL: NYC Economic Development Corporation

A diagramatic signage system for an East River waterfront development project,
which will include a Bikeway and Esplanade.
自転車専用道路、遊歩道など、イースト・リバーのウォーターフロント開発プロジェクトにおける案内表示システム。

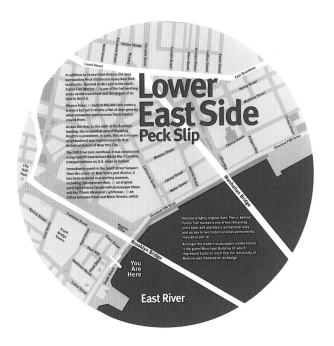

Lower East Side
Peck Slip

In addition to its maritime history, the area surrounding *Peck Slip* boasts many New York landmarks. Opened in 1812 just to the south, *Fulton Fish Market* is one of the last working areas on the waterfront and the largest of its kind in the U.S.

Meyers Hotel, built in the late 19th century, is now a bar but it retains a feel of days gone by when renowned markswoman Annie Oakley stayed there.

Across the river, to the right of the Brooklyn landing, the residential area of Brooklyn Heights is prominent. In 1965, this picturesque neighborhood was registered as the first historical district of New York City.

The *FDR Drive* runs overhead. It was constructed using landfill from blitzed World War II London, transported here on U.S. ships as ballast.

Immediately south is the *South Street Seaport*. Once the center of New York's port district, it has been restored as a working museum, including *Schermerhorn Row*, an original early 19th century facade with picturesque shops and the *Titanic Memorial Lighthouse*, on Fulton between Pearl and Water Streets, which

features a highly original clock, *Pier 17*, behind Fulton Fish Market is one of few remaining piers here, and provides a recreational area and access to two historical ships permanently moored at pier 16.

Amongst the modern skyscrapers visible inland is the grand *Municipal Building* which impressed Stalin so much that the University of Moscow was modeled on its design.

East River

Lower East Side
1767

This reach of the East River, from here to *Rutgers Slip* is rich in maritime history. Peck Slip was one of last and most important of New York harbor's slips. The burgeoning population of European immigrants reclaimed new land from the East River to expand their thriving harbor community in the late 18th and early 19th centuries. The shoreline was extended east from *Pearl Street*.

The Dutch were the first settlers in this waterfront district. Later Irish, German and English immigrants worked in the maritime industry that dominated this area — shipyards, ironworks, docks and ferries. These would be found along the shoreline and at the nearby slips and piers.

More recently, many Italians and European Jews also settled on the "Lower East Side", creating one of the first "melting pot" communities in the city.

As river traffic and the size of vessels increased, slips were gradually replaced with piers. Peck Slip, a bustling center for maritime industry, remained longer than most other slips. Now, even the piers are gone, except for a handful south of Fulton Street. To sample the atmosphere of thriving maritime New York, visit the Fulton Fish market early in the morning or the South Street Historic District.

Walton House was built in 1752 at 326–328 Pearl Street, next to Peck Slip, by William Walton. For 30 years it was New York's most handsome residence and his lavish entertainment prior to the revolution encouraged the British government to raise taxes.

Pier numbering as of 1840

East River

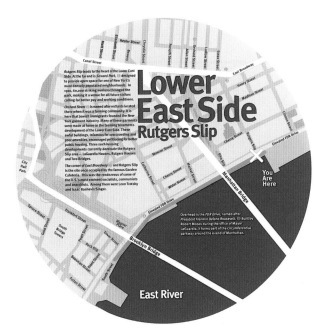

Lower East Side
Rutgers Slip

Rutgers Slip leads to the heart of the Lower East Side. At the far end is *Seward Park*, designed to provide open space for one of New York's most densely populated neighborhoods. In 1910, 60,000 striking workers thronged the park, making it a venue for all future strikes calling for better pay and working conditions.

Orchard Street is named after orchards located there when it was a farming community. It is here that Jewish immigrants founded the New York garment industry. Many of these garments were made at home in the teeming tenements developments of the Lower East Side. These awful buildings, infamous for overcrowding and poor amenities, encouraged petitioning for better public housing. Three such housing developments currently dominate the Rutgers Slip area — LaGuardia Houses, Rutgers Houses and Two Bridges.

The corner of *East Broadway* and Rutgers Slip is the site once occupied by the famous Garden Cafeteria. This was the rendezvous of some of the U.S.'s most eminent socialists, communists and anarchists. Among them were Leon Trotsky and Isaac Bashevis Singer.

Overhead is the *FDR Drive*, named after *President Franklin Delano Roosevelt*. Built by Robert Moses during the office of Mayor LaGuardia, it forms part of the circumferential parkway around the island of Manhattan.

You Are Here

East River

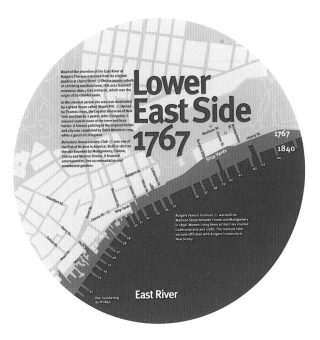

Lower East Side
1767

Much of the shoreline of the East River at Rutgers Slip was extended from its original position at *Cherry Street*. Once a country suburb of a thriving maritime town, this area featured extensive cherry tree orchards, which was the origin of its colorful name.

In the colonial period, the area was dominated by a grand house called *Mount Pitt*. Owned by Thomas Jones, the Loyalist Historian of New York and then by a patriot, John Livingston, it enjoyed superb views of the town and busy harbor. A famous painting of the original harbor and city was completed by Saint Memin in 1794, while a guest of Livingston.

Belvedere House Country Club was one of the first of its kind in America. Built in 1872 on the site bounded by Montgomery, Clinton, Cherry and Monroe Streets, it boasted entertainment, fine accommodation and ornamental gardens.

Rutgers Female Institute was built on Madison Street between Clinton and Montgomery in 1838. Women living there at that time studied traditional arts and crafts. The Institute later became affiliated with Rutgers University in New Jersey.

Pier numbering as of 1840

East River

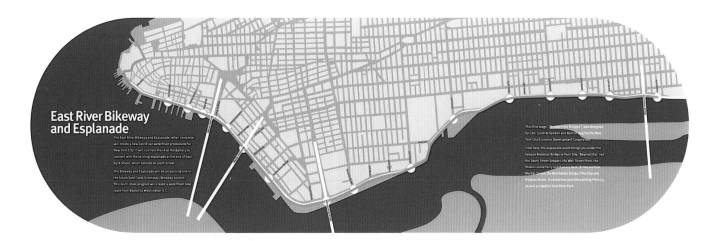

East River Bikeway and Esplanade

The East River Bikeway and Esplanade, when complete, will create a new East River waterfront promenade for New York City. It will run from Pier A at the Battery to connect with the existing esplanade at the end of East 63rd Street, which extends to 125th Street.

The Bikeway and Esplanade will be an exciting link in the future East Coast Greenway/Bikeway system. This multi-state program will create a waterfront bike route from Boston to Washington D.C.

This first stage, "Between the Bridges", was designed by Carr, Lynch & Sandell and built in 1997 by the New York City Economic Development Corporation.

From here, the esplanade south brings you under the famous Brooklyn Bridge to Peck Slip. Beyond that, lies the South Street Seaport, the Wall Street Piers, the Staten Island Ferry and Battery Park. To the north lies Market Street, the Manhattan Bridge, Pike Slip and Rutgers Street. A connection past the existing Piers 35, 36 and 42 leads to East River Park.

SNOW HARP
スノーハープのご案内 女子15kmクラシカル
Ladies' 15km Classical

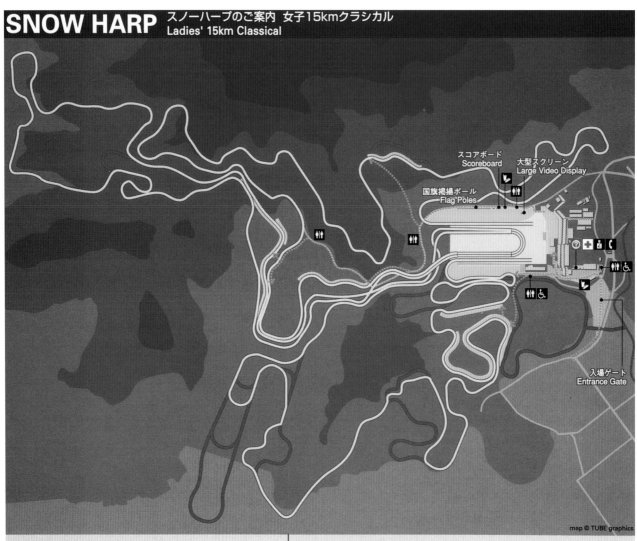

スコアボード
Scoreboard

大型スクリーン
Large Video Display

国旗掲揚ポール
Flag Poles

入場ゲート
Entrance Gate

map © TUBE graphics

すべて立見・自由席です。会場内では
図中オレンジ色の点線 ⋯⋯⋯ に沿って
移動し、競技中のコース内には絶対に
入らないでください

The standing gallery is non-reserved. Please keep to the path indicated in orange on the map and do not enter the course.

インフォメーション Information	公衆電話 Telephone	観客エリア Spectator Area
救護室 First Aid Station	売店 Kiosk	競技エリア Competition Area
トイレ Toilet	警察事務室 Police Office	
車イス用トイレ Toilet		

禁止されている行為 Matters prohibited within the Venues

■ 会場内での喫煙・宣伝・広告物の掲示、印刷物やビラの配布および散布
Smoking, placing of publicity materials/advertisements, and the distribution or scattering of printed matter.

■ 競技会場内への物の投げ込み、競技観戦中のフラッシュ撮影、観客席での携帯電話・PHS・ポケットベル等の使用
Throwing objects into the competitions area, usage of flashes, and the use of portable phones, PHS, and beepers in the spectators' seats.

お客様へのお願い Request for your cooperation

■ ゴミの持ち帰りにご協力願います
Please take home your own garbage and cooperate in keeping the venue clean.

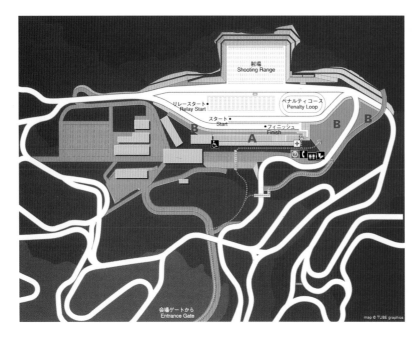

射場
Shooting Range

リレースタート
Relay Start

ペナルティコース
Penalty Loop

スタート
Start

フィニッシュ
Finish

会場ゲートから
Entrance Gate

map © TUBE graphics

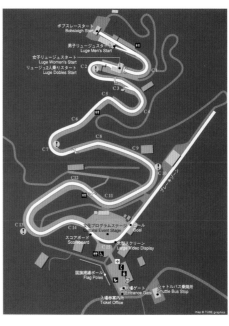

ボブスレースタート
Bobsleigh Start

男子リュージュスタート
Luge Men's Start

女子リュージュスタート
Luge Women's Start
リュージュ2人乗りスタート
Luge Dobles Start

C2
C3
C5
C6
C7
C8
C9
C12
C11
C13
C14
C15

文化プログラムステージ
Cultural Event Stage

ゴール
Goal

スコアボード
Scoreboard

大型スクリーン
Large Video Display

国旗掲揚ポール
Flag Poles

入場ゲート
Entrance Gate

シャトルバス乗降所
Shuttle Bus Stop

入場券案内所
Ticket Office

map © TUBE graphics

1

WHITE RING ホワイトリングのご案内

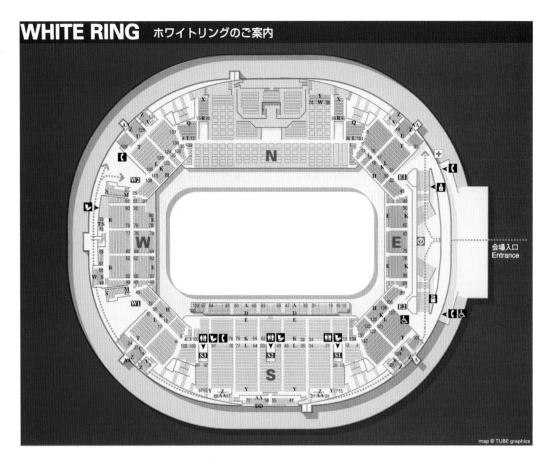

長野冬季オリンピックのデイリープログラムより。

map © TUBE graphics

AQUA WING アクアウイングのご案内

長野冬季オリンピックのデイリープログラムより。

map © TUBE graphics 2

Japan 1998
CD: Hiroyuki Kimura
D: Hiroko Enomoto/Sachiko Hagiwara/
   Naomi Sugita/Nozomi Hatakeyama/
   Ryu Sato
DF: Tube Graphics
CL: NAOC/Panasonic

*From the Daily Program of
the Nagano Winter Olympics.
Maps of venues, courses,
and surrounding facilities.* (1)
長野冬季オリンピックのデイリープログラムより。
競技場と併設されている施設の位置を表したマップ。(1)

Japan 1998
CD: Hiroyuki Kimura
D: Hiroko Enomoto/Sachiko Hagiwara/
   Naomi Sugita/Nozomi Hatakeyama/
   Ryu Sato
DF: Tube Graphics
CL: NAOC/Panasonic

*From the Daily Program of
the Nagano Winter Olympics.
Floor plan of two of
the indoor venues.* (2)
長野冬季オリンピックの
デイリープログラムより。
屋内競技場内の見取り図。(2)

LONDON

ROMA

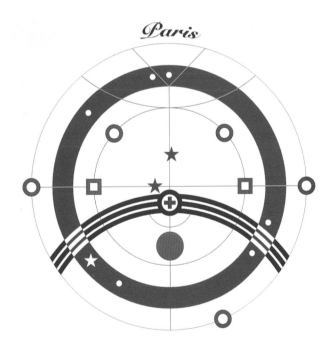

Paris

PHILADELPHIA

U.S.A.   1995
CD, D: Joel Katz

A personal project to "redesign" great cities of the world with circles, re-aligning key elements and articulating otherwise obscured relationships.
円を用いて大都市を「再デザイン」しようという個人プロジェクト。主な要素を再配置し、隠された関係を探る。

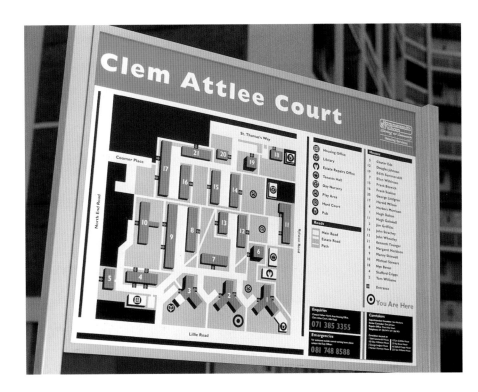

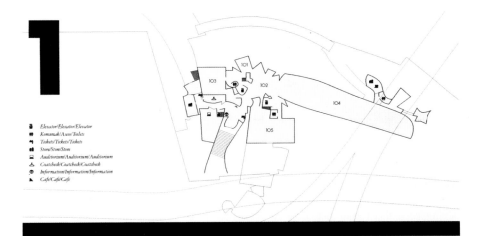

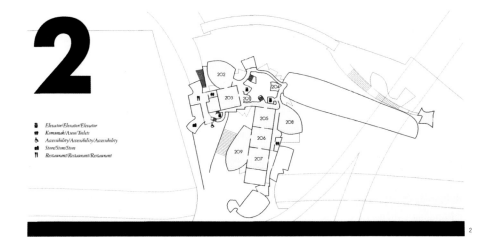

U.K. 1995
CD, D, I: Peter Grundy
AD: Tilly Northedge
DF: Grundy & Northedge
CL: H+F Council

*Pictograms for an area information sign,
one of 15 similar signs in London.* (1)
ロンドン市内に15カ所設置された
エリア案内板のためのピクトグラム。(1)

U.S.A. 1997
AD: Massimo Vignelli
D, I: J. Graham Hanson
DF: Vignelli Associates
CL: Guggenheim Museum Bilbao

*Maps drawn for sign and print directories
of the Guggenheim Museum Bilbao, Spain,
designed to effectively guide visitors
through the museum's complex layout.* (2)
スペインのグッゲンハイム・ミュージアム・ビルバオ
の案内板とパンフレットに使われた地図。
ビジターを効果的にガイドするため、ミュージアムの
複雑なレイアウトをシンプルに表現したもの。(2)

LEVEL 6 - DEPARTURES BOARDING LEVEL
WEST HALL AND SOUTHWEST CONCOURSE

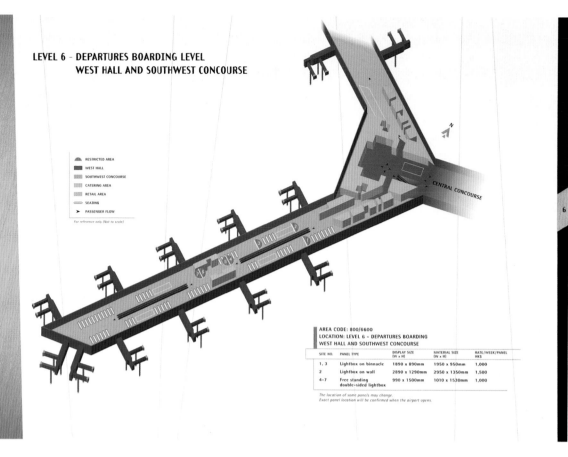

RESTRICTED AREA
WEST HALL
SOUTHWEST CONCOURSE
CATERING AREA
RETAIL AREA
SEATING
PASSENGER FLOW

For reference only (Not to scale)

AREA CODE: 800/6600
LOCATION: LEVEL 6 - DEPARTURES BOARDING
WEST HALL AND SOUTHWEST CONCOURSE

SITE NO.	PANEL TYPE	DISPLAY SIZE (W x H)	MATERIAL SIZE (W x H)	RATE/WEEK/PANEL HK$
1, 3	Lightbox on binnacle	1890 x 890mm	1950 x 950mm	1,000
2	Lightbox on wall	2890 x 1290mm	2950 x 1350mm	1,500
4-7	Free standing double-sided lightbox	990 x 1500mm	1010 x 1530mm	1,000

The location of some panels may change.
Exact panel location will be confirmed when the airport opens.

LEVEL 5 - ARRIVALS LEVEL
BAGGAGE RECLAIM HALL AND
CUSTOMS

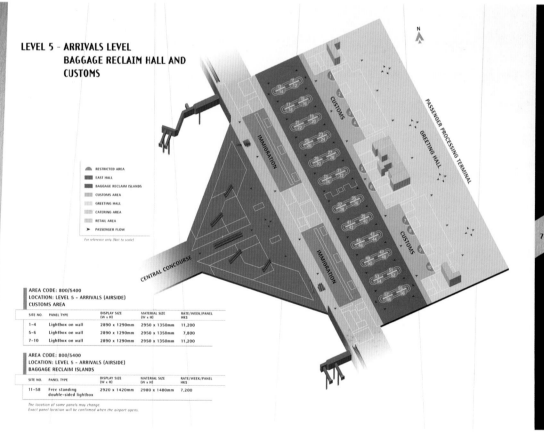

RESTRICTED AREA
EAST HALL
BAGGAGE RECLAIM ISLANDS
CUSTOMS AREA
GREETING HALL
CATERING AREA
RETAIL AREA
PASSENGER FLOW

For reference only (Not to scale)

AREA CODE: 800/5400
LOCATION: LEVEL 5 - ARRIVALS (AIRSIDE)
CUSTOMS AREA

SITE NO.	PANEL TYPE	DISPLAY SIZE (W x H)	MATERIAL SIZE (W x H)	RATE/WEEK/PANEL HK$
1-4	Lightbox on wall	2890 x 1290mm	2950 x 1350mm	11,200
5-6	Lightbox on wall	2890 x 1290mm	2950 x 1350mm	7,800
7-10	Lightbox on wall	2890 x 1290mm	2950 x 1350mm	11,200

AREA CODE: 800/5400
LOCATION: LEVEL 5 - ARRIVALS (AIRSIDE)
BAGGAGE RECLAIM ISLANDS

SITE NO.	PANEL TYPE	DISPLAY SIZE (W x H)	MATERIAL SIZE (W x H)	RATE/WEEK/PANEL HK$
11-58	Free standing double-sided lightbox	2920 x 1420mm	2980 x 1480mm	7,200

The location of some panels may change.
Exact panel location will be confirmed when the airport opens.

China 1997
CD, AD: Eric Chan
D, I: Kanic Wong
DF: Eric Chan Design Co., Ltd.
CL: Pearl & Dean

Floor plan of the new airport in Hong Kong. Terminal building, Departures/Boarding level: West Hall and Southwest Concourse, and the Baggage Claim Hall and Customs Arrivals level.
香港新空港の平面図。ターミナル・ビルの出発／搭乗階、西ホールと南西コンコース、
そしてバゲージ・クレーム・ホールと税関／到着階の案内マップ。

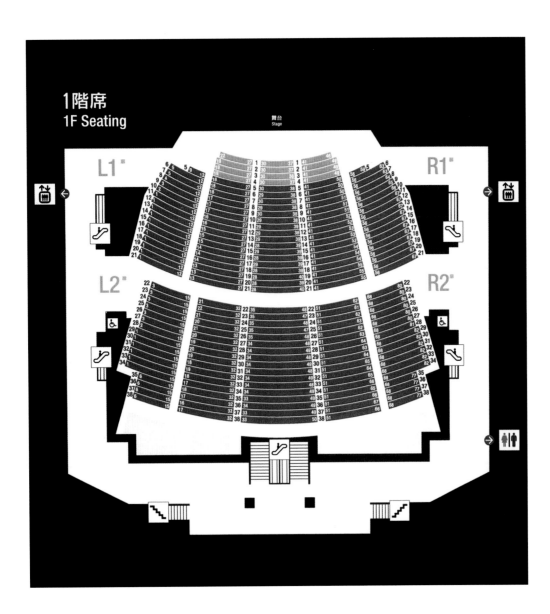

Japan 1996
AD, D: Kei Miyazaki
D: Yuko Nakayama
P: Kenji Kobayashi
DF: Plants Associates Inc.
Product Design, Architect: Rafael Viñoly
CL: City of Tokyo

Facility guides and pictograms for trash containers at the Tokyo International Forum,
a public facility whose purpose is international cultural exchange .
日本国内外の文化情報交流を目的とした大規模公共施設「東京国際フォーラム」の施設案内図と、ゴミ分別ピクトグラム。

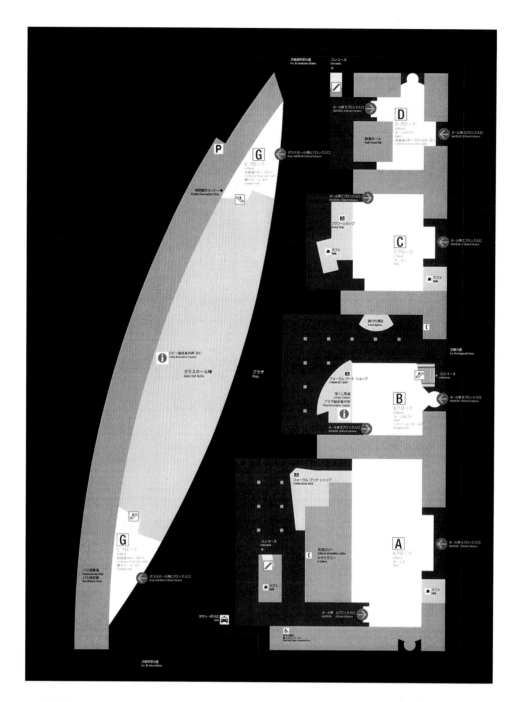

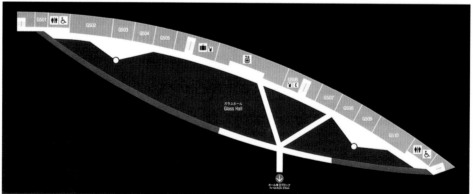

Japan   1996
AD, D: Kei Miyazaki
D: Yuko Nakayama
P: Kenji Kobayashi
DF: Plants Associates Inc.
Architect: Rafael Viñoly
CL: City of Tokyo

Facility guides for the Tokyo International Forum. Guides are designed specifically for each area.
日本国内外の文化情報交流を目的とした大規模公共施設「東京国際フォーラム」の施設案内図。それぞれの地点での情報を中心に表現。

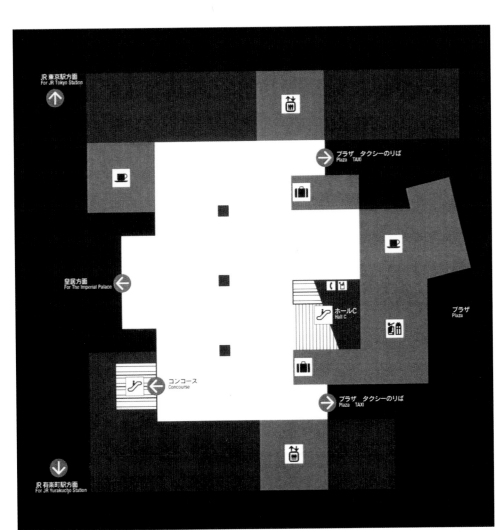

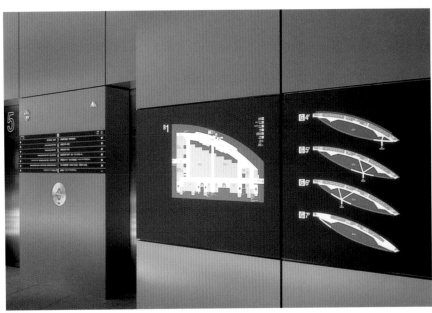

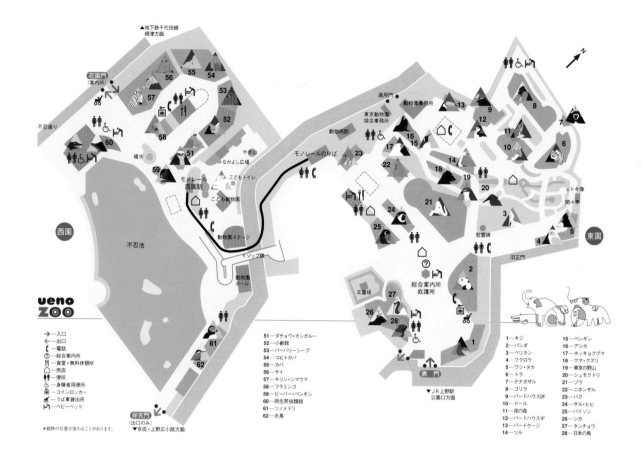

Japan 1996
AD, D: Tomoyuki Hasumi
D: Eriko Hasumi
CL: Ueno Zoological Gardens

A visitor guide map and pictograms designed for the signage system of the Ueno Zoo.
上野動物園のサインシステムを表した来園者用のガイドマップとピクトグラム。

The Netherlands 1998
CD, AD, D: Paul Vermijs
AD, D, I: Eugène Heijblom
I: Maikel Van Wijk
DF: Tel Design
CL: Town of Zoetermeer

Part of the town of Zoetermeer's signing and information system, which is utilized in parks, rural areas, and sport facilities.
ゼタミール市の案内表示システムの一部。公園、田園地帯、スポーツ施設などで使用されている。

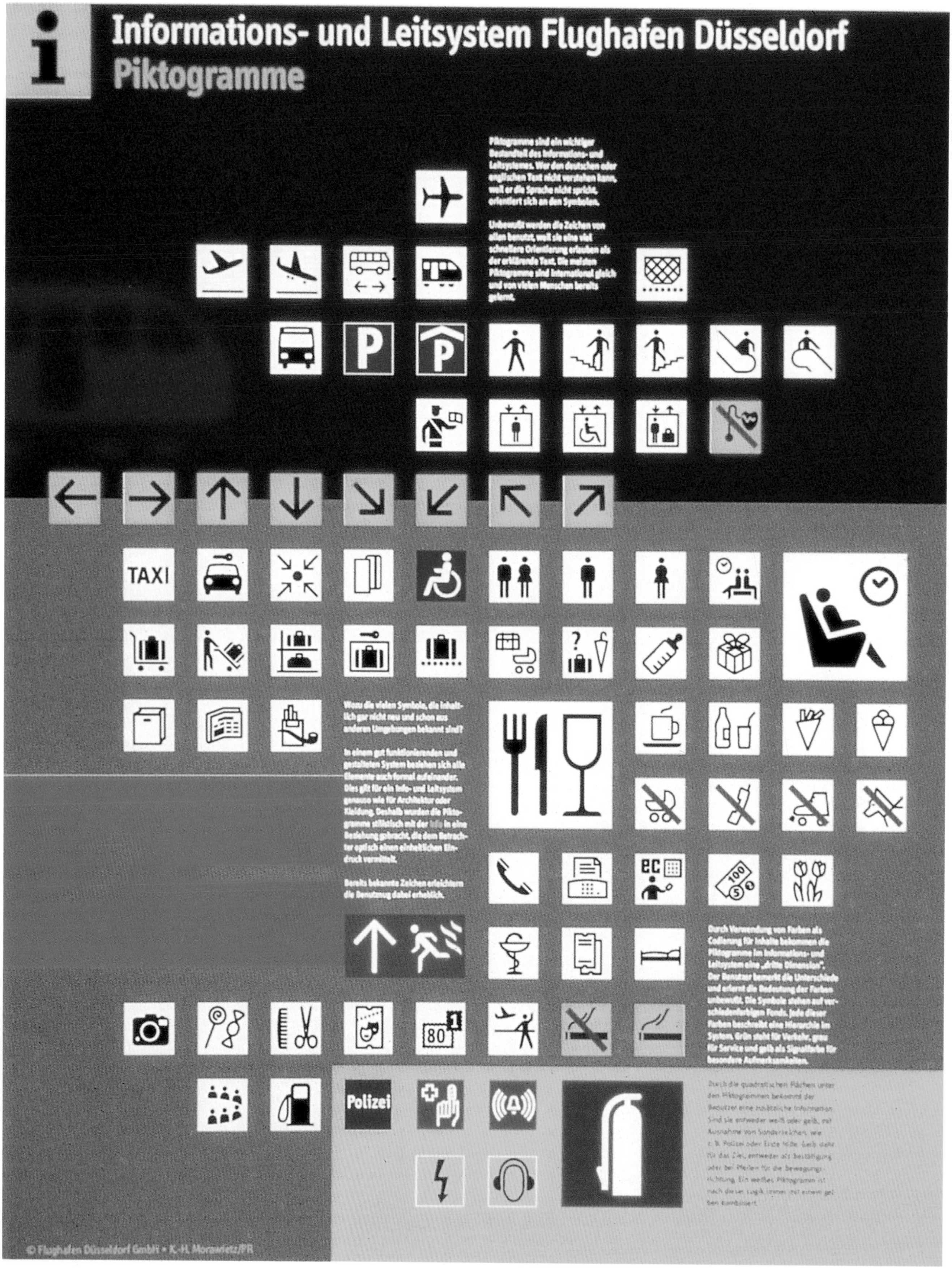

Informations- und Leitsystem Flughafen Düsseldorf
Piktogramme

Germany 1998
CD, AD, D, DF: Meta Design
P: Stefan Schilling
CL: Airport Düsseldorf International

A permanent signage system for the Dusseldorf airport, one that takes passengers from Autobahn to departure lounge by means of a unified visual system. Developed from a temporary signage system implemented after a fire rendered the Airport site unusable.

デュッセルドルフ空港の案内表示システム。アウトバーンから出発ラウンジまで、統一的なビジュアルシステムによって乗客を誘導するもの。

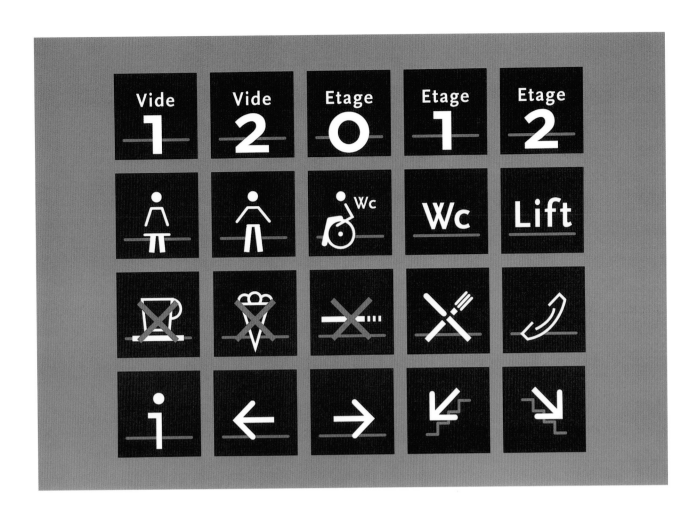

The Netherlands 1999
CD, AD, D: Paul Vermijs
D: Maikel Van Wijk
I: Eugène Heijblom
DF: Tel Design
CL: University Congress Centre Delft

Custom-made routing and signing for one of Delft University's buildings.
デルフト大学の建物のための案内表示。

Basiselemente Schriften
Integral Aspects Typefaces

Piktogrammübersicht / Overview of pictograms

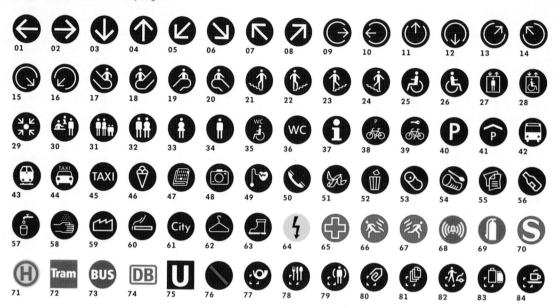

Servicebereiche der Volkswagen Werke
Business units of Volkswagen plants

Grund- und Zeichenfarbe der Piktogramme richten sich nach dem nebenstehenden Farbkonzept. Da heute Piktogramme für Beschilderungen meist aus selbstklebender Folie geschnitten werden, sind die jeweiligen Farbfestlegungen für Folien gleich mitangegeben.

The basic and symbol colours of pictograms are taken from the colour system shown here. As pictograms for signage are today most commonly set on self-adhesive foils, the colour specifications for foils have also been included.

Allgemeine Benutzung
For general use
Volkswagen Blau
C100/M75
O·3M matt 10380
T·3M VT 4183

Einrichtungen für Benachteiligte
Facilities for the disabled
Volkswagen Blau
C100/M75
O·3M matt 10380
T·3M VT 4183

Hochspannungskennzeichnung
Identification of high-voltage area
M5/Y100
RAL 1023 Verkehrsgelb
O·3M 100-15
T·3M 3630-015

Gefahrenbekämpfung
Hazard area
M100/Y100
RAL 3020 Verkehrsrot
O·3M 100-13
T·3M 3630-143

Technische Hinweise
Technical information
C5/K30
RAL 7051 Schiefergrau
O·3M 100-12

Gefahrenschutz
Hazard control
C100/Y85/K5
RAL 6024 Verkehrsgrün
O·3M 100-27
T·3M 3630-146

Germany   1998
DF: Meta Design
CL: Volkswagen Ag

Documentation of typefaces, information charts, and other elements,
to ensure the correct world-wide implementation of the Volkswagen corporate design.
フォルクスワーゲン社のコーポレート・デザインが世界中で正しく使用されるよう、
タイプフェイス、情報のチャート、その他の要素について規定したもの。

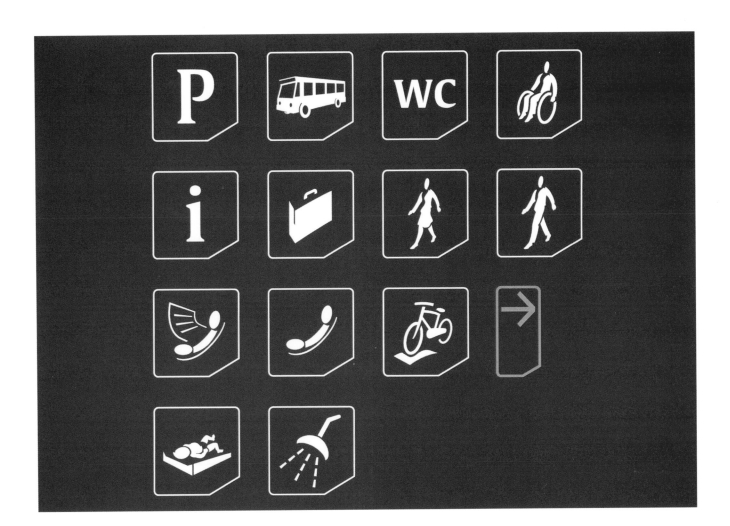

The Netherlands 1997
CD, AD, D: Paul Vermijs
AD: Jaco Emmen
D, I: Eugène Heijblom
DF: Tel Design
CL: The Netherlands Government

Pictograms for use on signs, vehicles, and street furniture, for a project undertaken by the Dutch government. To reduce automobile traffic in city centers, cars are parked in the "Transferium" on the outskirts of the town and the commuter continues by public transport.
オランダ政府のプロジェクトのためにデザインされた、案内標識や、公共車両、道路建造物を表すピクトグラム。

受付 会計 	ナースステーション 	診察1 	処置室1 	理学療法室 
点滴回復室 	デイケア室 	手術室 	救急処置室 	X線CT受付 
CT検査室 	MRI検査室 	X線検査室 	内視鏡室 	検査室 
薬剤室 	D.I.室 	介助浴室 	浴室 	洗濯 
婦長室 	厨房 	談話室 	喫煙所 	トイレ 
トイレ 	トイレ 	トイレ 	関係者以外立入禁止 	Private 
P 	駐輪所 	救急車入口 	車輌入口 	車輌出口 

Japan   1996
CD: Naoki Baba
AD: Shigo Yamaguchi
D: Yoko Yasuno
DF: Shigo Yamaguchi Design Room
CL: Rakuseikai Baba Hospital

Proposed signage for a Meiji Era (1868-1912) hospital, intended to give the hospital a new image.
All pictograms inside the hospital were newly designed.
広島県竹原市に明治時代からある病院の新たなホスピタル・アイデンティティを確立するためのサイン計画。病院内のピクトグラムを一新した。

大回転・回転
滑降・スーパー大回転
クロスカントリースキー
ジャンプ
ノルディック複合
フリースタイルスキー
スノーボード
スピードスケート
フィギュアスケート
ショートトラックスピードスケート
アイスホッケー
ボブスレー
リュージュ
バイアスロン
カーリング

Japan 1998
CD, AD, D, DF: Landor Associates International Ltd.
CL: NAOC

Original pictograms created for the Nagano Winter Olympics.
Each individual event pictogram recalls the motif of the main Olympic emblem, creating a collective event identity.
長野冬季オリンピック競技のためのオリジナルピクトグラム。
イメージは大会エンブルムを踏襲し、大会全体のアイデンティティを形成している。

Japan 1998
AD, D: Tokiyoshi Tsubouchi
CL: Angel Land Fukui

Pictograms representing facilities inside Angel Land Fukui (Fukui Prefectural Children's Science Museum).
エンゼルランドふくい(福井県立児童科学館)内の設備を示すピクトグラム。

Japan 1994
CD: Kengo Kuma & Associates
AD: Masaaki Hiromura
D: Nobuhiko Aizawa
DF: Hiromura Design Office, Inc.
CL: Yoshiumi-cho

Signs at the entrances of restrooms of the Kirosan Panorama Park, Ehime Prefecture.
愛媛県亀老山展望公園のトイレサイン。

©Peter Aaron/Esto

U.S.A. 1997
D: Woody Pirtle/Tracey Cameron/
   Karen Parolek
P: Peter Aaron
Architect: Kenzo Tange
DF: Pentagram Design
CL: Fuji Sankei Communications Group

Restroom signs for the Fuji Television building. The "perforated" strips on either side of the signs recall TV film, as well as referring visually to the structure of the building itself.
フジテレビ社屋のトイレサイン。
両側の穴のあいた補助板が、建物の構造を視覚的に反映させていると同時に、テレビのフィルムを想起させる。

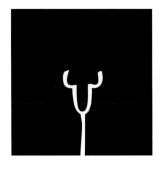 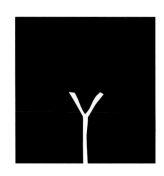

Australia 1998
CD, D: Jeremy Matthews/
   Mia Daminato
P: Sharrin Rees
DF: Matthews Daminato
CL: Staged Developments

Pictograms for the men's and women's restrooms of a cafe/restaurant.
カフェ＆レストランの男性用、
女性用トイレのサイン。

toiletgroup

 monster-room

 copying room

 invalid toilet

 shower

 staircase

 ladies toilet

 wardrobe

 pantry

 gentlemen's toilet

 dressing-room

 big meeting-place

 urinal

 restaurant

 small meeting-place

The Netherlands 1998
DF: Robert Vulkers/Openbaar Gevoel
CL: SVW Housing Corporation

Internal guidance signs developed for a housing corporation in the Netherlands.
オランダの住宅会社の社内案内サイン。

Japan 1998-1999
CD: Tsuyoshi Sugino
AD: Kunihiro Yoshida
AD, D: Toshiyasu Nanbu
P: Yoshio Komatsu
CL: Matsushita Electric Works, Ltd.

A Matsushita Denko calendar picturing interesting homes from around the world.
Pictograms represent styles of homes found in a variety of countries.
世界の面白住宅をテーマに制作した住宅家電メーカー「松下電工」のカレンダー。
世界各地の伝統的な住宅様式をピクトグラムにした。

Explanatory Diagrams

Scientific, Medical, Industrial & Architectural Illustrations

科学、医学、工業、建築イラストレーション

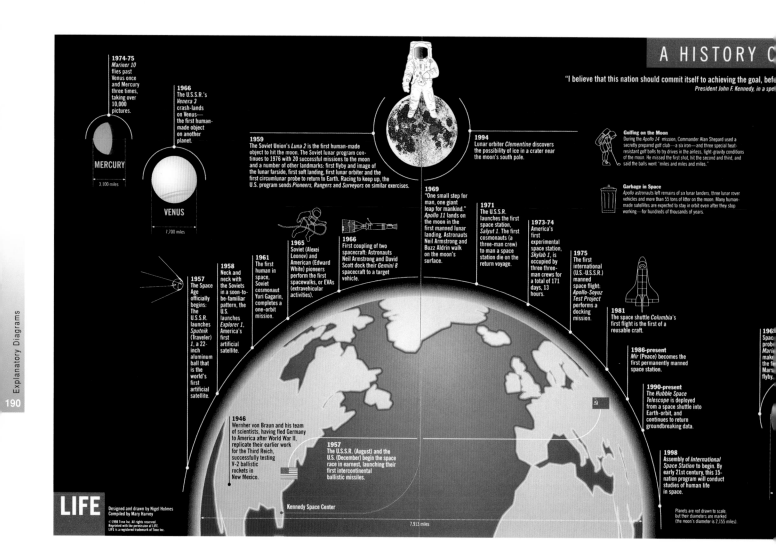

A HISTORY C

"I believe that this nation should commit itself to achieving the goal, befo

President John F. Kennedy, in a spee

1974-75
Mariner 10 flies past Venus once and Mercury three times, taking over 10,000 pictures.

1966
The U.S.S.R.'s *Venera 3* crash-lands on Venus—the first human-made object on another planet.

MERCURY
3,100 miles

VENUS
7,700 miles

1959
The Soviet Union's *Luna 2* is the first human-made object to hit the moon. The Soviet lunar program continues to 1976 with 20 successful missions to the moon and a number of other landmarks: first flyby and image of the lunar farside, first soft landing, first lunar orbiter and the first circumlunar probe to return to Earth. Racing to keep up, the U.S. program sends *Pioneers*, *Rangers* and *Surveyors* on similar exercises.

1994
Lunar orbiter *Clementine* discovers the possibility of ice in a crater near the moon's south pole.

Golfing on the Moon
During the *Apollo 14* mission, Commander Alan Shepard used a secretly prepared golf club—a six iron—and three special heat-resistant golf balls to try drives in the airless, light-gravity conditions of the moon. He missed the first shot, hit the second and third, and said the balls went "miles and miles and miles."

Garbage in Space
Apollo astronauts left remains of six lunar landers, three lunar rover vehicles and more than 55 tons of litter on the moon. Many human-made satelites are expected to stay in orbit even after they stop working—for hundreds of thousands of years.

1969
"One small step for man, one giant leap for mankind." *Apollo 11* lands on the moon in the first manned lunar landing. Astronauts Neil Armstrong and Buzz Aldrin walk on the moon's surface.

1971
The U.S.S.R. launches the first space station, *Salyut 1*. The first cosmonauts (a three-man crew) to man a space station die on the return voyage.

1973-74
America's first experimental space station, *Skylab 1*, is occupied by three three-man crews for a total of 171 days, 13 hours.

1975
The first international (U.S.-U.S.S.R.) manned space flight: *Apollo-Soyuz Test Project* performs a docking mission.

1965
Soviet (Alexei Leonov) and American (Edward White) pioneers perform the first spacewalks, or EVAs (extravehicular activities).

1966
First coupling of two spacecraft: Astronauts Neil Armstrong and David Scott dock their *Gemini 8* spacecraft to a target vehicle.

1961
The first human in space, Soviet cosmonaut Yuri Gagarin, completes a one-orbit mission.

1958
Neck and neck with the Soviets in a soon-to-be-familiar pattern, the U.S. launches *Explorer 1*, America's first artificial satellite.

1957
The Space Age officially begins: The U.S.S.R. launches *Sputnik* (Traveler) *1*, a 22-inch aluminum ball that is the world's first artificial satellite.

1981
The space shuttle *Columbia*'s first flight is the first of a reusable craft.

1986-present
Mir (Peace) becomes the first permanently manned space station.

1990-present
The *Hubble Space Telescope* is deployed from a space shuttle into Earth-orbit, and continues to return groundbreaking data.

1946
Wernher von Braun and his team of scientists, having fled Germany to America after World War II, replicate their earlier work for the Third Reich, successfully testing V-2 ballistic rockets in New Mexico.

1957
The U.S.S.R. (August) and the U.S. (December) begin the space race in earnest, launching their first intercontinental ballistic missiles.

1998
Assembly of *International Space Station* to begin. By early 21st century, this 15-nation program will conduct studies of human life in space.

Kennedy Space Center

7,913 miles

Planets are not drawn to scale, but their diameters are marked (the moon's diameter is 2,155 miles).

U.S.A.   1998
AD: Tom Bentkowski
D, I, DF: Nigel Holmes
CL: Life

Milestones in space exploration, 1957~1998.
1957~98年の宇宙開発の歩み。

...ding a man on the moon and returning him safely to the Earth."
...l Needs," May 25, 1961

1973-present
Probe *Pioneer 10* flies by Jupiter en route to interstellar space beyond the solar system; the first human-made object to leave the solar system (1983), it is now about 6.3 billion miles from home.

1979-present
Voyager 1 explores Jupiter and Saturn, *Voyager 2* goes on to Uranus and Neptune. Both are powered to keep going until 2020.

...97
...s
...finder,
...n a
...otic
...der
... rover,
...ts to
...lore.

JUPITER

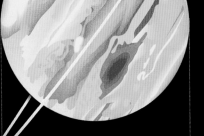

86,700 miles

1979-present
Pioneer 11 is the first craft to explore Saturn; it continues its outward journey.

1997
Cassini, a joint American-European mission, is launched. It will arrive at Saturn in 2004.

SATURN

71,500 miles

URANUS

32,000 miles

NEPTUNE

31,000 miles

PLUTO

4,000 miles

2001
Expected launch of *Pluto Express*, two small spacecraft scheduled to fly by Pluto around 2010

Animal Firsts in Space
Laika, an 11-lb. female dog, was Earth's first living creature in space. She rode aboard the U.S.S.R.'s *Sputnik 2* (1957) and reportedly lived for about a week before the craft's oxygen ran out.

In 1959, female monkeys **Able** and **Baker** flew 300 miles above the earth in a *Jupiter* nose cone—the first animals safely recovered from a space flight.

Space-Age Calamities
1960: Several dozen Russians die in a launchpad explosion.
1967: Three astronauts die in a launchpad fire in *Apollo 1*'s capsule. The deaths of Gus Grissom, Roger Chaffee and Edward White were the first directly attributable to the U.S. space program.
1967: Cosmonaut Vladimir Komarov becomes the first casualty of an actual space flight.
1970: Near disaster occurs when *Apollo 13*, a mission to the moon, has an oxygen tank rupture. The crew must cancel its moon landing and return to Earth.
1971: Three cosmonauts die when their capsule accidentally depressurizes.
1986: Seven crew members, including schoolteacher Christa McAuliffe, die when the *Challenger* space shuttle explodes 73 seconds after takeoff.

Personal Business
Astronauts brush their teeth in space just as on Earth, but without rinsing (the options are spitting into a towel or swallowing edible toothpaste). There are no showers on the space shuttle, so astronauts take sponge baths. The toilets in the shuttle use flowing air instead of water to move waste through the system. Solid wastes are compressed, stored on board and removed after landing. Since there is no gravity to hold the crew down in space, when they sleep they must be lightly strapped into sleeping bags secured to the spacecraft.

 # 1

First human in space and in orbit
Soviet cosmonaut Yuri Gagarin, 1961

First American in space
Astronaut Alan Shepard, 1961

First American in orbit
Astronaut John Glenn, 1962

First woman in space
Cosmonaut Valentina Tereshkova, 1963

First American woman in space
Astronaut Sally Ride, 1983

First black astronaut in space
Astronaut Guion Bluford, 1983

First free-flying (untethered) human in space
Astronaut Bruce McCandless, 1984

Record time in space on a single flight
Cosmonaut Valeri Polyakov (438 days aboard the Russian space station *Mir*), 1994-95

For more information visit www.space.lifemag.com

Explanatory Diagrams

191

2005: Getting rocks from Mars by remote control

In November this year, NASA will begin a series of trips to Mars in preparation for the two-year rock-collecting mission shown here, which would start around 2003.

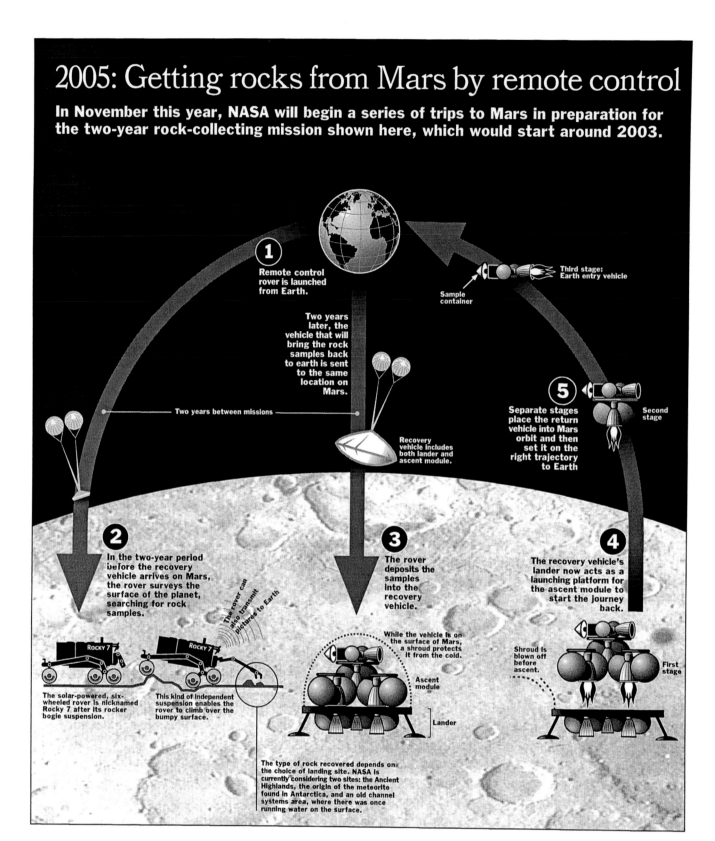

① Remote control rover is launched from Earth.

Two years later, the vehicle that will bring the rock samples back to earth is sent to the same location on Mars.

Third stage: Earth entry vehicle

Sample container

⑤ Separate stages place the return vehicle into Mars orbit and then set it on the right trajectory to Earth

Second stage

──── Two years between missions ────

Recovery vehicle includes both lander and ascent module.

② In the two-year period before the recovery vehicle arrives on Mars, the rover surveys the surface of the planet, searching for rock samples.

The rover can also transmit pictures to Earth

③ The rover deposits the samples into the recovery vehicle.

While the vehicle is on the surface of Mars, a shroud protects it from the cold.

Ascent module

Lander

④ The recovery vehicle's lander now acts as a launching platform for the ascent module to start the journey back.

Shroud is blown off before ascent.

First stage

ROCKY 7

ROCKY 7

The solar-powered, six-wheeled rover is nicknamed Rocky 7 after its rocker bogie suspension.

This kind of independent suspension enables the rover to climb over the bumpy surface.

The type of rock recovered depends on the choice of landing site. NASA is currently considering two sites: the Ancient Highlands, the origin of the meteorite found in Antarctica, and an old channel systems area, where there was once running water on the surface.

U.S.A. 1996
AD: Michael Valenti
D, I, CW, DF: Nigel Holmes
CL: New York Times

Illustration explaining a mission to Mars that will bring rocks back to Earth.
火星から地球に石を持ち帰る方法を図解したもの。

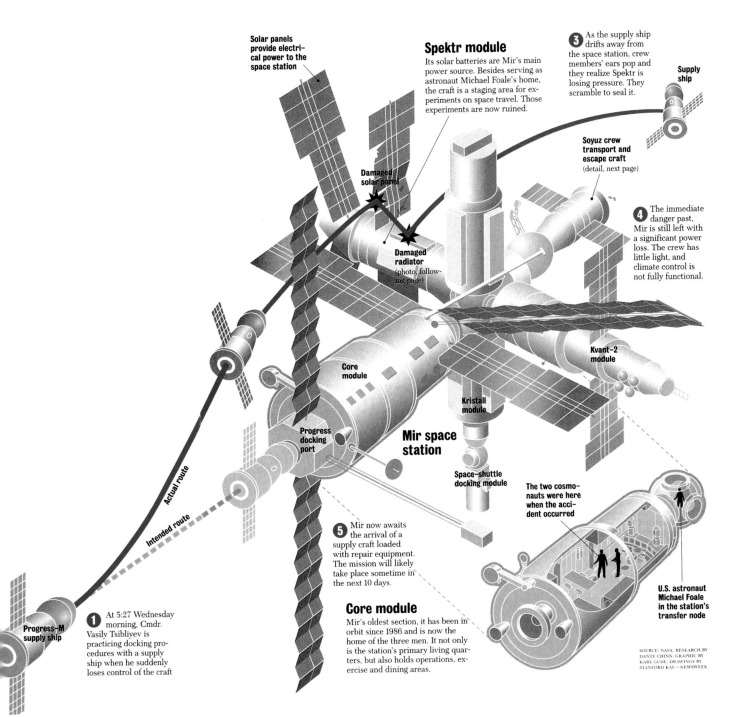

Solar panels provide electrical power to the space station

Spektr module

Its solar batteries are Mir's main power source. Besides serving as astronaut Michael Foale's home, the craft is a staging area for experiments on space travel. Those experiments are now ruined.

3 As the supply ship drifts away from the space station, crew members' ears pop and they realize Spektr is losing pressure. They scramble to seal it.

Supply ship

Damaged solar panel

Soyuz crew transport and escape craft (detail, next page)

4 The immediate danger past, Mir is still left with a significant power loss. The crew has little light, and climate control is not fully functional.

Damaged radiator (photo, following page)

Kvant-2 module

Core module

Mir space station

Kristall module

Progress docking port

Space-shuttle docking module

The two cosmonauts were here when the accident occurred

Actual route

Intended route

5 Mir now awaits the arrival of a supply craft loaded with repair equipment. The mission will likely take place sometime in the next 10 days.

U.S. astronaut Michael Foale in the station's transfer node

1 At 5:27 Wednesday morning, Cmdr. Vasily Tsibliyev is practicing docking procedures with a supply ship when he suddenly loses control of the craft

Progress-M supply ship

Core module

Mir's oldest section, it has been in orbit since 1986 and is now the home of the three men. It not only is the station's primary living quarters, but also holds operations, exercise and dining areas.

SOURCE: NASA. RESEARCH BY DANTE CHINN. GRAPHIC BY KARL GUDE. DRAWINGS BY STANFORD KAY — NEWSWEEK

U.S.A. 1997
Design Director: Lynn Staley
Graphics Director: Bonnie Scranton
D: Karl Gude
I: Stanford Kay
CW: Dante Chinni
CL: Newsweek Magazine

A graphic re-creation of the events related to the damage in space of the Mir Space Station's Spektr module.
ミール宇宙ステーションのスペクトル・モジュールで起きた破損事故について、グラフィックで再現したもの。

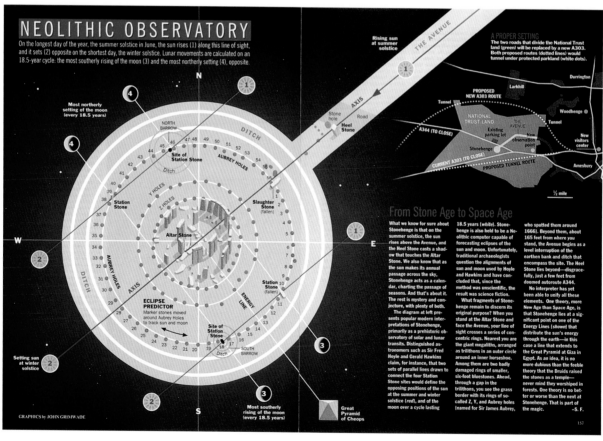

Denmark 1997
D: Ida Trier Dahlkild
I: Henning Dalhoff
CW: Sebastian Relster
CL: Illustreret Videnskab

Illustration accompanying an article about future tourism in space. Presented are some of the possible forms of entertainment that travellers would be offered on a trip to the moon. (1)
未来の宇宙旅行についての記事に使用されたイラスト。
月への旅行者が体験できるエンタテインメントの種類が
いくつか提案されている。(1)

U.S.A. 1995
AD: Diana Laguardia
D: Stephen Orr
I: John Grimwade
CL: Condé Nast Traveler

An explanation of the possible significance of England's Stonehenge. (2)
イギリスのストーンヘンジについて、
考えられる解釈を示したもの。(2)

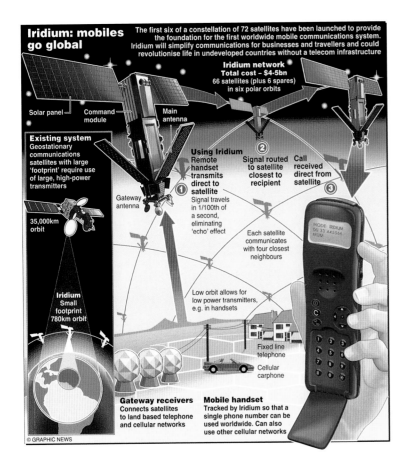

Iridium: mobiles go global

The first six of a constellation of 72 satellites have been launched to provide the foundation for the first worldwide mobile communications system. Iridium will simplify communications for businesses and travellers and could revolutionise life in undeveloped countries without a telecom infrastructure

Iridium network
Total cost – $4-5bn
66 satellites (plus 6 spares)
in six polar orbits

Solar panel
Command module
Main antenna

Existing system
Geostationary communications satellites with large 'footprint' require use of large, high-power transmitters

35,000km orbit

Gateway antenna

Using Iridium
① Remote handset transmits direct to satellite
Signal travels in 1/100th of a second, eliminating 'echo' effect

② Signal routed to satellite closest to recipient

③ Call received direct from satellite

Each satellite communicates with four closest neighbours

Iridium
Small footprint
780km orbit

Low orbit allows for low power transmitters, e.g. in handsets

MODE: IRIDIUM
00 33 445566
MUM

Fixed line telephone
Cellular carphone

Gateway receivers
Connects satellites to land based telephone and cellular networks

Mobile handset
Tracked by Iridium so that a single phone number can be used worldwide. Can also use other cellular networks

© GRAPHIC NEWS

U.K.   1997
AD: Duncan Mil
DF: Graphic News
CL: Subscribing Newspapers

Illustrations detailing the Iridium global mobile telecommunications satellite system.
イリジウム計画（衛星による移動通信システム）を図解したもの。

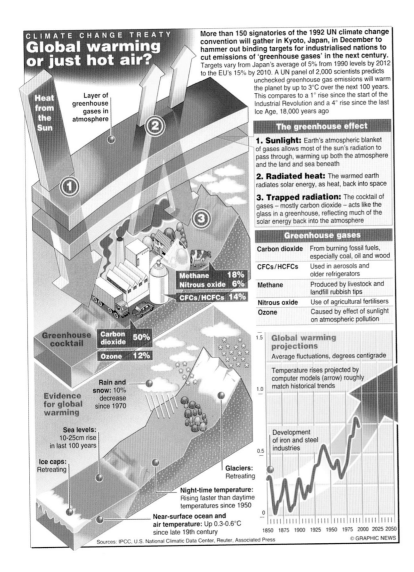

CLIMATE CHANGE TREATY
Global warming or just hot air?

More than 150 signatories of the 1992 UN climate change convention will gather in Kyoto, Japan, in December to hammer out binding targets for industrialised nations to cut emissions of 'greenhouse gases' in the next century. Targets vary from Japan's average of 5% from 1990 levels by 2012 to the EU's 15% by 2010. A UN panel of 2,000 scientists predicts unchecked greenhouse gas emissions will warm the planet by up to 3°C over the next 100 years. This compares to a 1° rise since the start of the Industrial Revolution and a 4° rise since the last Ice Age, 18,000 years ago

Heat from the Sun

Layer of greenhouse gases in atmosphere

The greenhouse effect

1. Sunlight: Earth's atmospheric blanket of gases allows most of the sun's radiation to pass through, warming up both the atmosphere and the land and sea beneath

2. Radiated heat: The warmed earth radiates solar energy, as heat, back into space

3. Trapped radiation: The cocktail of gases – mostly carbon dioxide – acts like the glass in a greenhouse, reflecting much of the solar energy back into the atmosphere

Greenhouse gases

Carbon dioxide	From burning fossil fuels, especially coal, oil and wood
CFCs/HCFCs	Used in aerosols and older refrigerators
Methane	Produced by livestock and landfill rubbish tips
Nitrous oxide	Use of agricultural fertilisers
Ozone	Caused by effect of sunlight on atmospheric pollution

Methane 18%
Nitrous oxide 6%
CFCs/HCFCs 14%

Greenhouse cocktail
Carbon dioxide 50%
Ozone 12%

Global warming projections
Average fluctuations, degrees centigrade

Temperature rises projected by computer models (arrow) roughly match historical trends

Evidence for global warming

Rain and snow: 10% decrease since 1970

Development of iron and steel industries

Sea levels: 10-25cm rise in last 100 years

Ice caps: Retreating

Glaciers: Retreating

Night-time temperature: Rising faster than daytime temperatures since 1950

Near-surface ocean and air temperature: Up 0.3-0.6°C since late 19th century

1850 1875 1900 1925 1950 1975 2000 2025 2050

Sources: IPCC, U.S. National Climatic Data Center, Reuter, Associated Press

© GRAPHIC NEWS

U.K.   1997
AD: Duncan Mil
DF: Graphic News
CL: Subscribing Newspapers

Graphic illustrations of some of the statistics related to the global warming phenomenon.
地球温暖化現象に関する統計。

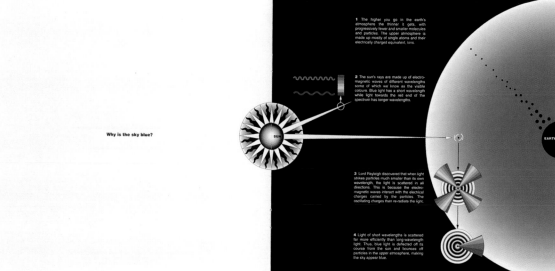

Why is the sky blue?

Why do we grow old?

A theory of aging by Sir Macfarlane Burnet

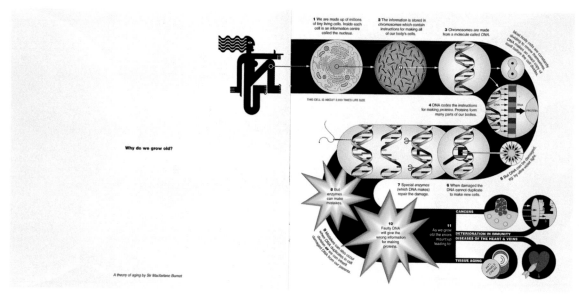

U.K.   1997
CD, AD, D, I, CW: Tilly Northedge
DF: Grundy & Northedge
CL: Tilly Northedge

A booklet of diagams explaining three different science theories.
Intended for self-promotion, it is also a means of learning to use computer programmes.
3つの異なる科学的理論を図解した小冊子。セルフ・プロモーションのために制作したものであり、
コンピューター・プログラムを学習できるようになっている。

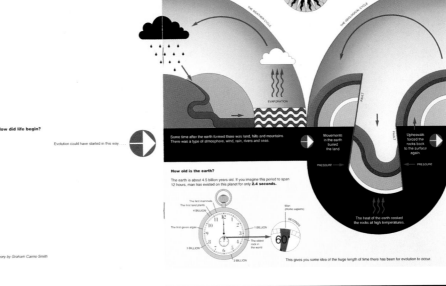
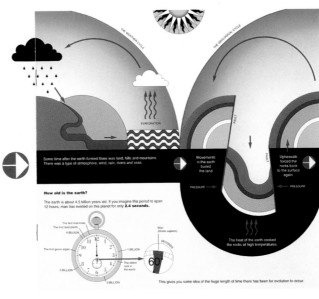
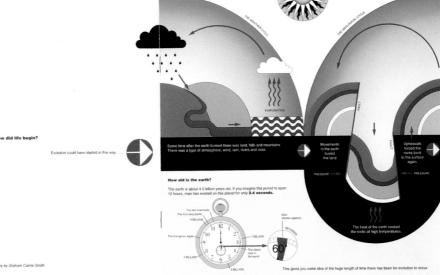

How did life begin?

Evolution could have started in this way . . .

A theory by Graham Cairns-Smith

Some time after the earth formed there was land, hills and mountains. There was a type of atmosphere, wind, rain, rivers and seas.

THE WEATHER CYCLE

THE GEOLOGICAL CYCLE

EVAPORATION

Movements in the earth buried the land

Upheavals forced the rocks back to the surface again.

FAULT

PRESSURE   PRESSURE

The heat of the earth cooked the rocks at high temperatures.

How old is the earth?

The earth is about 4.5 billion years old. If you imagine this period to span 12 hours, man has existed on this planet for only **2.4 seconds**.

The first mammals
The first land plants
4 BILLION

The first green algae

1 BILLION

Man (Homo sapiens)

SECONDS

The oldest rock in the world

3 BILLION

2 BILLION

This gives you some idea of the huge length of time there has been for evolution to occur.

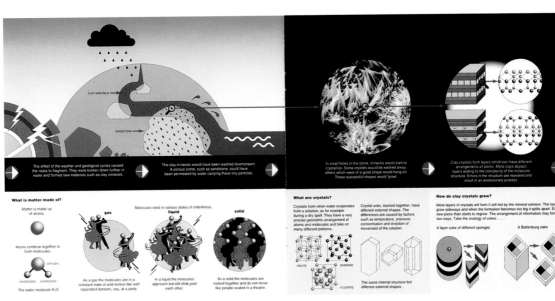

CLAY MINERALS

SANDSTONE

The effect of the weather and geological cycles caused the rocks to fragment. They were broken down further in water and formed new materials such as clay minerals.

The clay minerals would have been washed downstream. A porous stone, such as sandstone, could have been permeated by water carrying these tiny particles.

In small holes in the stone, minerals would start to crystalise. Some crystals would be washed away, others which were of a good shape would hang on. These successful shapes would 'grow'.

Clay crystals form layers which can have different arrangements of atoms. More clays deposit layers adding to the complexity of the molecular structure. Errors in the structure are repeated and result in an evolutionary process.

What is matter made of?

Matter is made up of atoms.

Atoms combine together to form molecules.

HYDROGEN   OXYGEN

The water molecule H_2O

Molecules exist in various states of orderliness.

gas

liquid

solid

As a gas the molecules are in a constant state of wild motion like well separated dancers, say, at a party.

In a liquid the molecules approach but still slide past each other.

As a solid the molecules are locked together and do not move like people sealed in a theatre.

What are crystals?

Crystals form when water evaporates from a solution, as for example during a dry spell. They have a very precise geometric arrangement of atoms and molecules and take on many different patterns.

Crystal units, stacked together, have different external shapes. The differences are caused by factors such as temperature, pressure, concentration and direction of movement of the solution.

HALITE   DIAMOND

FLUORITE

The same internal structure but different external shapes...

How do clay crystals grow?

More layers of crystals will form if still fed by the mineral solution. The layers grow sideways and when the formation becomes too big it splits apart. Each new piece than starts to regrow. The arrangement of information may form in two ways. Take the analogy of cakes . . . .

A layer cake of different sponges

A Battenburg cake

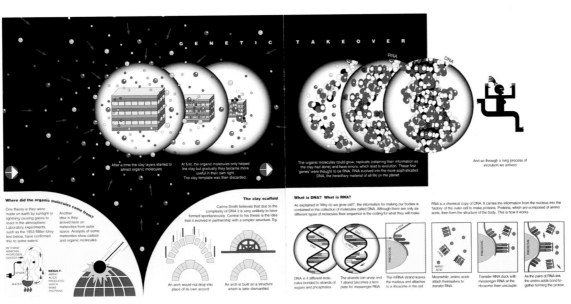

G E N E T I C   T A K E O V E R

RNA

DNA

After a time the clay layers started to attract organic molecules.

At first, the organic molecules only helped the clay but gradually they became more useful in their own right. The clay template was then discarded.

The organic molecules could grow, replicate (retaining their information as the clay had done) and have errors, which lead to evolution. These first 'genes' were thought to be RNA. RNA evolved into the more sophisticated DNA, the hereditary material of all life on the planet.

And so through a long process of evolution we arrived.

Where did the organic molecules come from?

One theory is they were made on earth by sunlight or lightning causing gasses to react in the atmosphere. Laboratory experiments, such as the 1953 Miller-Urey test below, have confirmed this to some extent.

Another idea is they arrived here on meteorites from outer space. Analysis of some meteorites show carbon and organic molecules.

METHANE
AMMONIA
HYDROGEN
GASSES

SPARK

WATER

RESULT:
AMINO
ACIDS
PRODUCED
WHICH
MAKE
PROTEINS

The clay scaffold

Cairns-Smith believes that due to the complexity of DNA it is very unlikely to have formed spontaneously. Central to his thesis is the idea that it evolved in partnership with a simpler structure. Eg:

An arch would not drop into place of its own accord.

An arch is built on a structure which is later dismantled.

What is DNA? What is RNA?

As explained in 'Why do we grow old?', the information for making our bodies is contained in the collection of molecules called DNA. Although there are only six different types of molecules their sequence is the coding for what they will make.

RNA is a chemical copy of DNA. It carries the information from the nucleus into the 'factory' of the outer cell to make proteins. Proteins, which are composed of amino acids, then form the structure of the body. This is how it works.

RIBOSOME

DNA is 4 different molecules bonded to strands of sugars and phosphates.

The strands can unzip and 1 strand becomes a template for messenger RNA.

The mRNA strand leaves the nucleus and attaches to a ribosome in the cell.

Meanwhile, amino acids attach themselves to transfer RNA.

Transfer RNA dock with messenger RNA at the ribosome then uncouple.

As the pairs of RNA link the amino acids bond together forming the protein.

AMINO ACID

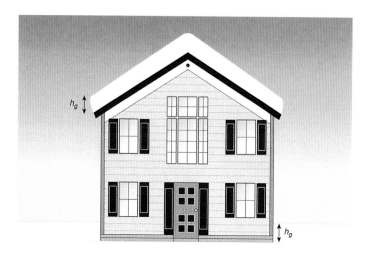

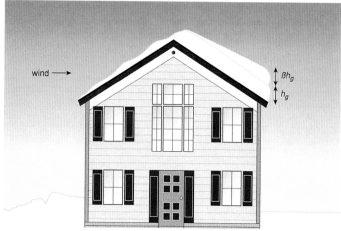

wind →

h_g

βh_g

h_g

1

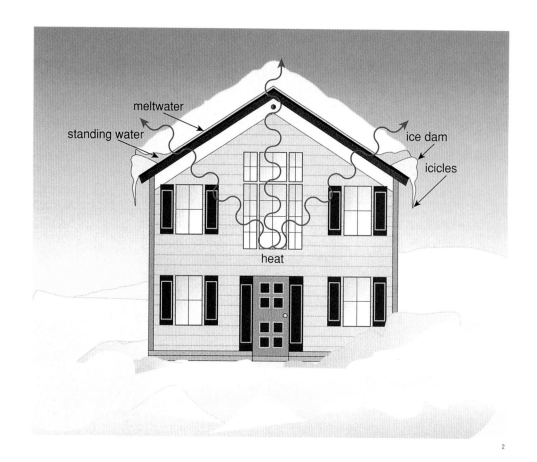

meltwater

standing water

ice dam

icicles

heat

2

U.S.A. 1997
AD: Linda K. Huff
D, I: Edward D. Roberts, III
D: Mike May (2)
CW: Mike May (1)
DF: American Scientist Magazine Art and Design Department
CL: Sigma Xi

*Snow can weigh a roof down to the point of collapse when it forms a drift,
and the wind shifts the snow from its original distribution (left)
into a lopsided arrangement (right).* (1)

積雪量が増え、風によって最初に降りつもった場所から吹き流されると、積もり方に偏りができるため、
屋根を押しつぶすほどの重さになることがあることを表したイラスト。(1)

*Perched snow can give rise to damaging accumulations
of water when heat from a building melts the bottom layer and "ice dams"
in the eaves prevent this moisture from escaping.* (2)

堆積した雪は、水分を蓄積し、建物に悪影響を及ぼすことがある。建物の熱によって最下位の層が溶け、
といの中に「氷のダム」ができ、水分の流出を妨げるということを表したイラスト。(2)

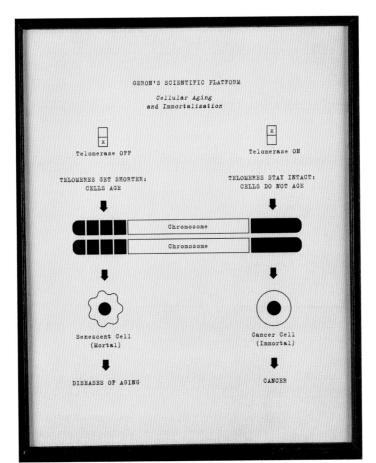

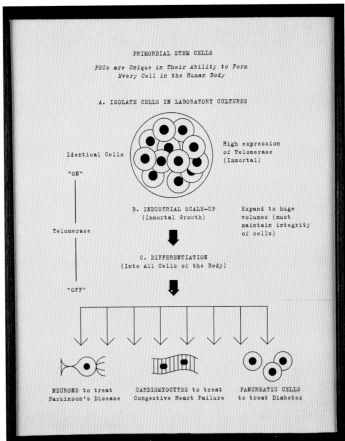

U.S.A. 1998
CD, AD: Bill Cahan
D, I, CW: Bob Dinetz
CW: Carole Melis
DF: Cahan & Associates
CL: Geron

This chart shows how telomerase and telomeres affect the life span of a human cell. (1)
テロメラズとテロミアが人間の細胞の寿命に与える影響について図解したもの。(1)

This chart highlights the importance of the primordial stem cells by illustrating their ability to become any cell in the body. (2)
幹細胞は体内のどんな細胞にも変化できることを図解し、その重要性を強調したチャート。(2)

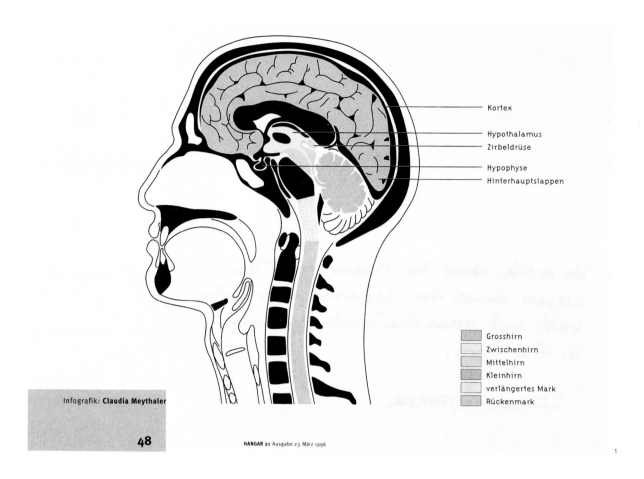

Kortex

Hypothalamus
Zirbeldrüse

Hypophyse
Hinterhauptslappen

Grosshirn
Zwischenhirn
Mittelhirn
Kleinhirn
verlängertes Mark
Rückenmark

Infografik: **Claudia Meythaler**

48

HANGAR 21 Ausgabe 23 März 1996

1

2

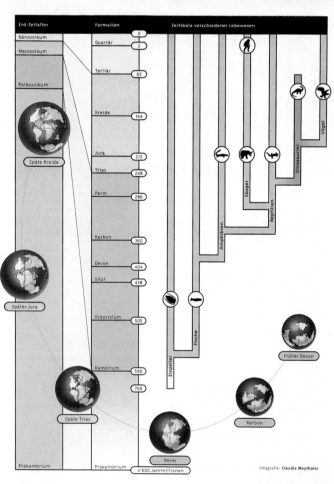

Switzerland   1995 (2)/1996 (1)
D: Claudia Meythaler
DF: 9D Design
CL: Winterthur Versicherungen

*From an article about the human brain.
The diagram shows the different parts
of the brain, and includes terms
discussed in the text.* (1)

人間の脳についての記事より。
脳の構成要素を図解し、
本文で取り上げた用語を説明している。(1)

*From an article about dinosaurs.
The diagram shows the ages
and formations of the earth,
and includes a time scale indicating
when different beings lived.* (2)

恐竜についての記事より。
図は、各時代における地球の形成レベル
およびそれぞれの生物がどのくらいの期間、
生存していたかを示す。(2)

Infografik: **Claudia Meythaler**

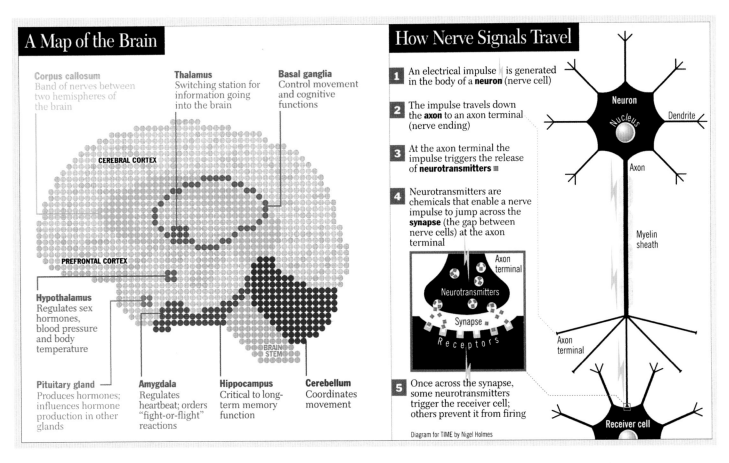

A Map of the Brain

Corpus callosum
Band of nerves between
two hemispheres of
the brain

Thalamus
Switching station for
information going
into the brain

Basal ganglia
Control movement
and cognitive
functions

CEREBRAL CORTEX

PREFRONTAL CORTEX

BRAIN STEM

Hypothalamus
Regulates sex
hormones,
blood pressure
and body
temperature

Pituitary gland
Produces hormones;
influences hormone
production in other
glands

Amygdala
Regulates
heartbeat; orders
"fight-or-flight"
reactions

Hippocampus
Critical to long-
term memory
function

Cerebellum
Coordinates
movement

How Nerve Signals Travel

1 An electrical impulse is generated
in the body of a **neuron** (nerve cell)

2 The impulse travels down
the **axon** to an axon terminal
(nerve ending)

3 At the axon terminal the
impulse triggers the release
of **neurotransmitters** ■

4 Neurotransmitters are
chemicals that enable a nerve
impulse to jump across the
synapse (the gap between
nerve cells) at the axon
terminal

Axon terminal
Neurotransmitters
Synapse
Receptors

5 Once across the synapse,
some neurotransmitters
trigger the receiver cell;
others prevent it from firing

Diagram for TIME by Nigel Holmes

Neuron
Nucleus
Dendrite
Axon
Myelin sheath
Axon terminal
Receiver cell

U.S.A. 1996
CD: Arthur Hochstein
AD: David Barnett
D, I, CW, DF: Nigel Holmes
CL: Time

*Explanation of how nerve
signals travel.*
神経系における伝達経路。

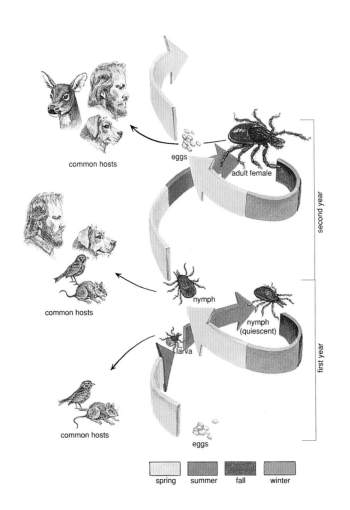

common hosts

eggs

adult female

second year

common hosts

nymph

nymph
(quiescent)

first year

larva

common hosts

eggs

spring   summer   fall   winter

U.S.A. 1997
AD: Linda K. Huff
D: David Schoonmaker/Richard Ostfeld
I: D. W. Miller
DF: American Scientist Magazine Art
    and Design Department
CL: Sigma Xi

*Illustration showing the life cycle
of the black-legged tick in the NE
and North-Central U.S.A.
When people substitute for animal hosts,
they can acquire lyme disease.*
アメリカ東北部および北中部におけるクロアシダニの
ライフサイクルを表した図。動物に代わって
ヒトに寄生するとライム関節炎になることがある。

HOW PAIN TRAVELS IN THE BODY

A pain signal is set off by the stimulation of nerve endings

The nerve endings may be stimulated by pressure, heat or the release of chemicals from a damaged cell

The signal goes to the spinal cord, where it passes instantaneously to a motor nerve ❶ connected to a muscle in the leg. This causes a reflex action that does not involve the brain. But the signal also goes up the spinal cord to the thalamus ❷, where the pain is perceived

Nerve ending

Pain signal

Damaged cell

Spinal — cord

①

Reflex action

②
Thalamus

Pain signal

Spinal cord

Diagram for TIME by Nigel Holmes   Source: American Medical Association *Encyclopedia of Medicine*

1

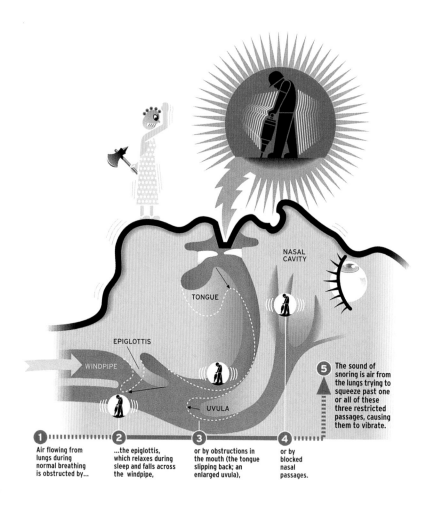

NASAL CAVITY

TONGUE

EPIGLOTTIS

WINDPIPE

UVULA

5 The sound of snoring is air from the lungs trying to squeeze past one or all of these three restricted passages, causing them to vibrate.

1 Air flowing from lungs during normal breathing is obstructed by...

2 ...the epiglottis, which relaxes during sleep and falls across the windpipe,

3 or by obstructions in the mouth (the tongue slipping back; an enlarged uvula),

4 or by blocked nasal passages.

2

U.S.A. 1997
CD: Arthur Hochstein (1)
AD: Linda Bell (1)
AD: Paul Carstensen (2)
D, I, CW, DF: Nigel Holmes
CL: Time (1)/Attaché (2)

How pain travels in the body. (1)
身体における痛みの伝達経路。(1)

Series of diagrams explaining everyday processes: Snoring. (2)
日常的なテーマを取り上げたシリーズ。いびきについて。(2)

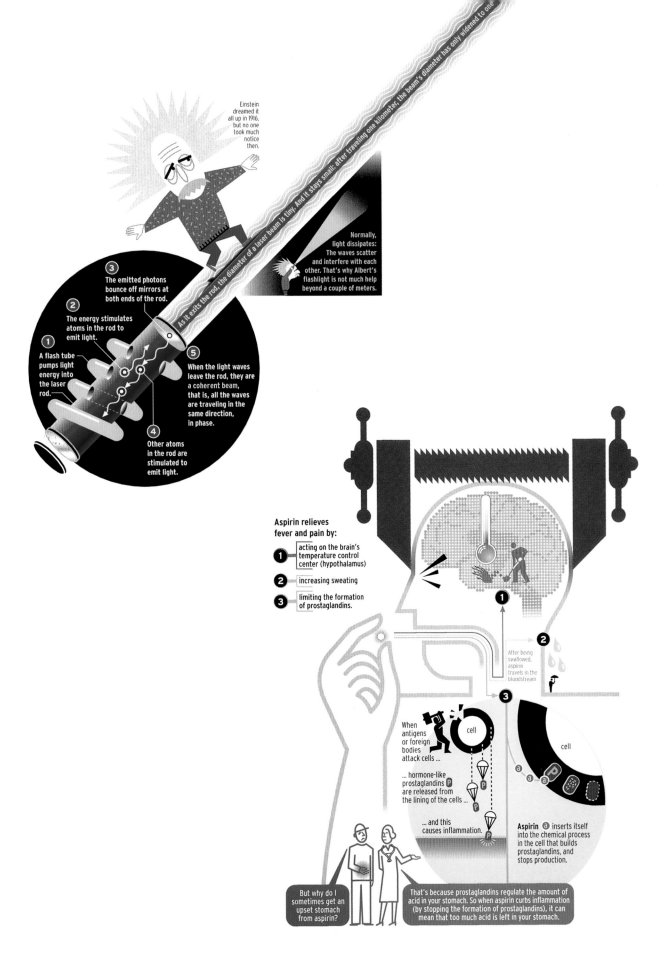

U.S.A. 1998
AD: Paul Carstensen
D, I, DF: Nigel Holmes
CL: Attaché

Series of diagrams explaining everyday processes: Diagram showing how a laser works, and a diagram explaining how aspirin relieves pain.
日常的なテーマを取り上げたシリーズより。レーザー光線の原理を図解したものと、アスピリンがどのように痛みを和らげるかを図解したもの。

a

b

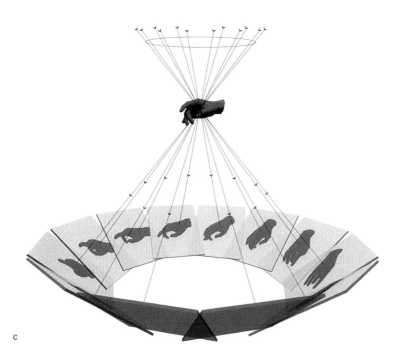

c

1

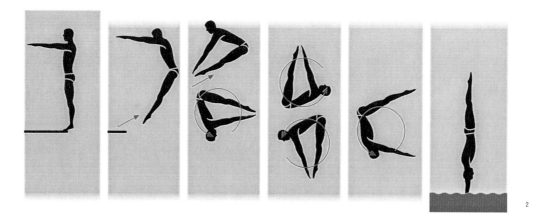

2

U.S.A. 1998
AD, D, I: Linda K. Huff
DF: American Scientist Magazine
    Art and Design Department
CL: Sigma Xi

*Single-particle reconstruction involves
two approaches at different stages of a project.* (1)
素粒子の再構成には、プロジェクトの異なる段階において
２つのアプローチがあることを表している。(1)

U.S.A. 1996
AD: Mirko Ilic
D, I, DF: Nigel Holmes
CL: Rizzoli

*Stages of a 2 1/2-pike dive off
a springboard.* (2)
飛び板からの２回転半飛び込みの図。(2)

How to Keep Your Head in the Game When Your Game's in Hibernation

The ice is still hanging from the gutters, and you've carpet-banged your Christmas balatas around the office until the urge to swing is too much to bear. Here's what to do instead:

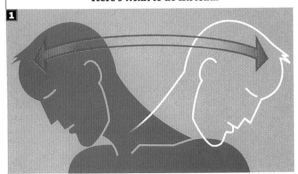

LOOSEN UP. "It's never too early to start loosening up," says Brian Pavlet, who emphasizes flexibility over strength. "The only time I'm not stretching is when I'm swinging the club."

1. By working three muscle groups, you can increase flex within weeks. Work your head and neck by touching your chin to each shoulder in sets of twenty. You can do it furtively at your desk several times a day. Chin tucks and shoulder rolls will contribute to the sense that your body moves fluidly around your spine, as it does in a good golf swing.

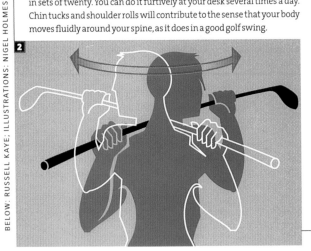

2. Then concentrate on the upper back. Placing a club across your shoulders, perform three to five sets of torso twists, pressing to extend the shoulders a little farther each day, without moving your lower body.

3. Finally, work your hips and thighs. With your back flat against a wall, lower yourself toward a sitting position. Hold for ten to twenty seconds—the longer the better. This will maintain your leg strength and solidify your posture.

The idea is to torque a loose, flexible upper half against a strong, stable lower half. The flexible golfer "gets back" farther, creating a longer swing, and his stable hips pull him back to square, helping him whip through with greater club speed. Ideally, your shoulders should be able to pivot about 90 degrees. One pro estimates that the exceptionally limber Pavlet's shoulders turn at 120 degrees while his hips stay within 10 degrees. The normal golfer maxes out somewhere around 80 degrees in the shoulder, turning his hips a full 20 or more degrees. Do your geometry and consider that Pavlet knocked a ball 435 yards in this year's preliminaries.

GET A GRIP. Do yourself a favor and buy Ben Hogan's book *Five Lessons*. Hide a 7-iron behind the credenza in your office, removing it at key moments to practice the "overlap" grip, which Hogan so eloquently explains. No swinging needed, though you might buy a mirror to get a better look at the grip from below. Hogan recommends gripping and regripping the club for twenty minutes a day.
GET REGRIPPED. Your clubs, that is. Winter's the best time, as the pros have time on their hands. It's cheap ($3 to $7 a club), and the new grips will enable you to hold the club without squeezing down too hard, allowing you to trust the motion and speed of your swing to do the work.

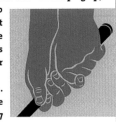

BELOW: RUSSELL KAYE; ILLUSTRATIONS: NIGEL HOLMES

Explanatory Diagrams

205

1

2

U.S.A. 1996 (2)/1998 (1)
CD: Robert Priest (1)/Doris Downes Jewett (2)
AD: Rockwell Harwood (1)
D, I, DF: Nigel Holmes
CW: Sherm Finger (1)
CL: Esquire (1)/Self Magazine (2)

Diagrams showing how to keep fit for playing golf. (1)
ゴルフのために身体を鍛える方法を説明している。(1)

Step-by-step diagrams showing breast cancer tests that can be conducted at home. (2)
家庭で行える乳がん発見法を、ステップごとに図解したもの。(2)

Brazil   1998
AD, P: Alceu Nunes
D: Luiz Iria
CW: Ivonete D. Luci'rio/
    Gabriela Aguerre
DF: Editora Abril
CL: Superinteressante Magazine

*Informational graphics
help to describe the speed
and movement of a rodeo.*
ロデオのスピードや動きを
説明するためのグラフィック。

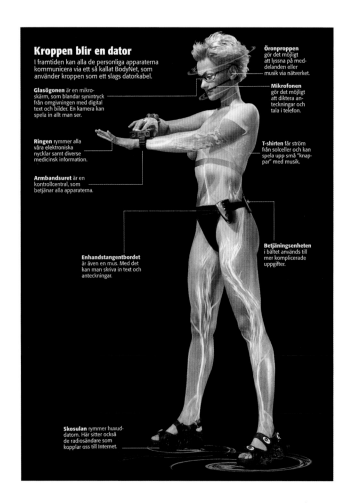

Denmark   1998
D: Ida Trier Dahlkild/Claus Lunau
P: Per Sogaard
I: Claus Lunau
CW: Niels Ole Dam
CL: Illustreret Videnskab

*Visualization of personal
technological equipment of the future,
which will communicate
via a so-called Body Net, using the body
as a form of computer cable.*
未来のパーソナル装置を図解。
人の身体をコンピューター・ケーブルとして使用する
「ボディ・ネット」を経由して動作する。

U.S.A. 1996
AD: Linda K. Huff
I: Tom Dunne
DF: American Scientist Magazine Art and Design Department
CL: Sigma Xi

Drawings showing frequency of laughter: Speakers tend to laugh more often than their audiences,
females more often than males.
笑いの頻度をイラストで表した。話し手は聞き手側よりもよく笑い、女性は男性よりもよく笑う傾向がある。

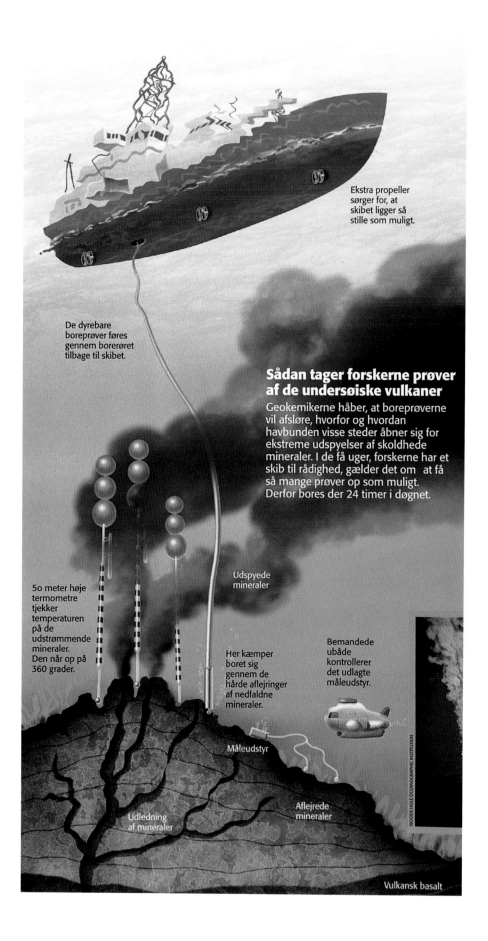

Ekstra propeller
sørger for, at
skibet ligger så
stille som muligt.

De dyrebare
boreprøver føres
gennem borerøret
tilbage til skibet.

Sådan tager forskerne prøver af de undersøiske vulkaner

Geokemikerne håber, at boreprøverne vil afsløre, hvorfor og hvordan havbunden visse steder åbner sig for ekstreme udspyelser af skoldhede mineraler. I de få uger, forskerne har et skib til rådighed, gælder det om at få så mange prøver op som muligt. Derfor bores der 24 timer i døgnet.

50 meter høje termometre tjekker temperaturen på de udstrømmende mineraler. Den når op på 360 grader.

Udspyede mineraler

Her kæmper boret sig gennem de hårde aflejringer af nedfaldne mineraler.

Bemandede ubåde kontrollerer det udlagte måleudstyr.

Måleudstyr

Aflejrede mineraler

Udledning af mineraler

WOODS HOLE OCEANOGRAPHIC INSTITUTION

Vulkansk basalt

Denmark 1998
D: Tine Lund
I: Henning Dalhoff
CW: Brigitte Svennevig
CL: Illustreret Videnskab

Illustration showing drilling of sea bed samples.
Geo-chemists hope that samples will reveal why and how the sea bed in certain places erupts with scalding hot minerals.
海底から土壌サンプルを採取する図。
このサンプルによって、地球化学者はなぜ、どのように海底の特定場所が焼け付くような熱い鉱物を伴って爆発するのかが明らかになると期待している。

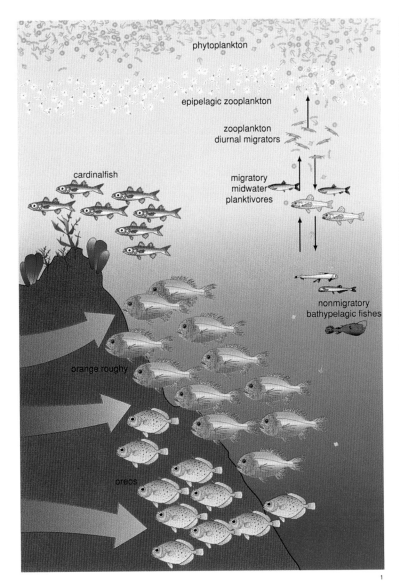

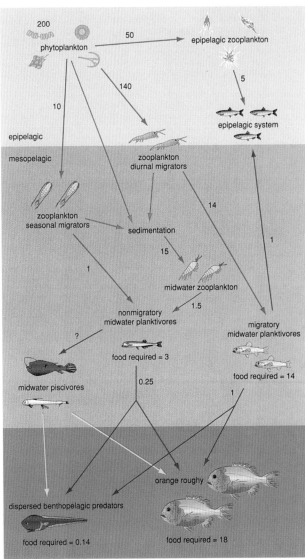

U.S.A. 1997
AD: Linda K. Huff
D: Aaron Cox/Rosalind Reid/Linda K. Huff
I: Aaron Cox/Linda K. Huff
DF: American Scientist Magazine Art
   and Design Department
CL: Sigma Xi

Pelagic life around a Southern Pacific seamount. Seamount aggregators receive food by advection (colored arrows) and via migrations of zooplankton and rain of surface detritus (black arrows). (1)
南大平洋の海床に住む外洋性の生物が、潮流（色矢印）により移動する動物プランクトンと、
海面から沈下する有機堆積物によって食物を摂る様子を表している。(1)

Trophic web linking seamount-aggregating fish to food supply (calculations in annual grams of carbon per square meter). Colors, indicating energy transfer at each trophic level, show orange roughy's food insufficiency. (2)
海床に住む魚の食物摂取と連鎖（1立方メートルごとの炭素量「グラム／年」で計算）。
色は各レベルにおけるエネルギーの移動を表し、オレンジ・ラフィーの食物が不足していることを示している。(2)

INTERNET   EXTRANET   INTRANET

Enterprise
Information
and Applications

Cyberprise
Services

Browser Users

Cyberprise
Host

Cyberprise
Channels

Remote
Worker

Prospect

Job
Applicant

Marketing

Cyberprise
Data

Cyberprise
Tools

Finance

Partner

Operations

Cyberprise
Server

Vendor

Customers

Public
Information

1

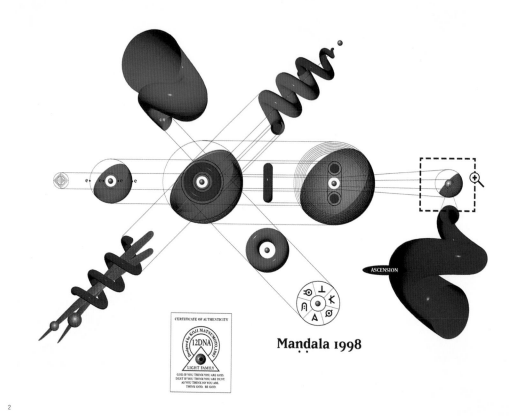

Mandala 1998

CERTIFICATE OF AUTHENTICITY

12DNA

LIGHT FAMILY

GOD IF YOU THINK YOU ARE GOD.
DUST IF YOU THINK YOU ARE DUST.
AS YOU THINK SO YOU ARE.
THINK GOD. BE GOD.

2

U.S.A. 1998
CD, AD: Brian Boram
D: Kevin Henderson/Aki Morino/
   Josh Michels/
   Steve Ahlbom/Chris Spivey
P: Everard Williams
DF: Tim Girvin Design, Inc.
CL: Jeri Goldberg/Wall Data, Inc.

*This diagram illustrates how the various modular
Cyberprise software products work together to
maximize the connectivity between a company's
Internet, intranet and extranet servers.* (1)
Cyberpriseソフトウエア製品のさまざまな
モジュールによって、企業のインターネット、
イントラネット、エクストラネットの各サーバーの
接続性を最大化できることを説明したもの。(1)

Japan 1997
D: Koji Matsumoto

*From "Voice," a magazine
with relaxation as its theme.
This diagram illustrates outer
space as considered
by Eastern philosophy.* (2)
癒しをテーマにした機関誌『VOICE』より。
東洋思想における宇宙のしくみを
図解したダイアグラム。(2)

Environmental impact

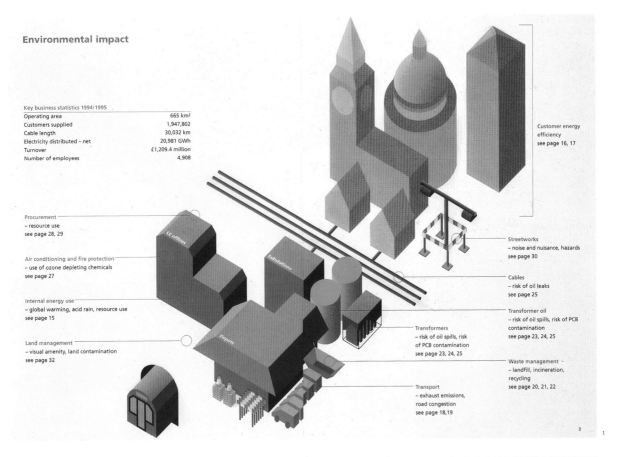

LE offices

Substations

Depots

3

Street works

Continually improving our performance

Seek to minimise the period for
which excavations are open

We undertake in the region of 30,000 street openings a year to
repair or replace underground cables. 90% of excavations and
reinstatement works are carried out by subcontractors working on
our behalf. All are undertaken in accordance with the Road and
Street Works Act 1991. Unfilled holes from street work activities
not only look unsightly, but can be dangerous and encourage
vandalism and litter accumulation.

For all major works a supervisor meets on site with representatives
from the police and the highways authority to agree on what can
be done to minimise disruption. In 1994, we introduced more
rigorous monitoring and inspection of our own and our
subcontractors' street works and our aim is to reduce the level
of complaints.
Where excavations are undertaken near trees, special care is taken
and local authority guidelines followed to avoid potential tree
damage. In the vicinity of roots, hand trowelling is undertaken
and if excavations require the cutting of roots over a certain size,
local authority tree experts are called in. London Electricity
supports the guidelines on excavations near trees recently issued
by the National Joint Utilities Group (NJUG).
We are members of four London Borough considerate street
works initiatives, which seek to achieve higher standards than
those laid down in the Road and Street Works Act. To date
London Electricity and its contractors have received awards for
achievements in carrying out street works.

Noise and nuisance

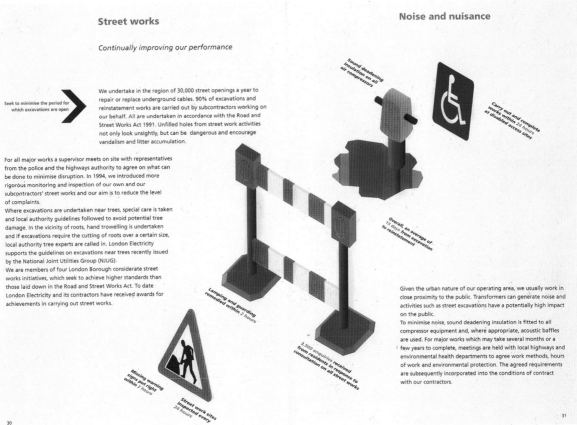

Sound deadening
insulation on all
air compressors

Carry out and complete
works within 24 hours
at disabled access sites

Overall, an average of
15 days from excavation
to reinstatement

Lamping and guarding
remedied within 2 hours

Missing warning
signs put right
within 2 hours

3,500 enquiries received
from residents in response to
consultation on all street works

Street work sites
inspected every
24 hours

Given the urban nature of our operating area, we usually work in
close proximity to the public. Transformers can generate noise and
activities such as street excavations have a potentially high impact
on the public.
To minimise noise, sound deadening insulation is fitted to all
compressor equipment and, where appropriate, acoustic baffles
are used. For major works which may take several months or a
few years to complete, meetings are held with local highways and
environmental health departments to agree work methods, hours
of work and environmental protection. The agreed requirements
are subsequently incorporated into the conditions of contract
with our contractors.

30

31

U.K.   1994 (2)/1995 (1)
CD: Tor Pettersen
AD, D: Craig Johnson
AD: David Brown (1)
D: Cicki Hartmann
I: Julia Wiseman
DF: Tor Pettersen & Partners Ltd.
CL: London Electricity

*Illustrates the key environmental issues and impacts of the electricity supplier,
in the form of a contents spread for the report.* (1)
電力会社の直面する主な環境問題とその影響について、目次を見開きの形で図解したもの。(1)

Illustrates actions taken to minimize effects of streetworks, including noise and nuisance. (2)
騒音や障害物などの道路工事の影響を最低限にするための措置について図解。(2)

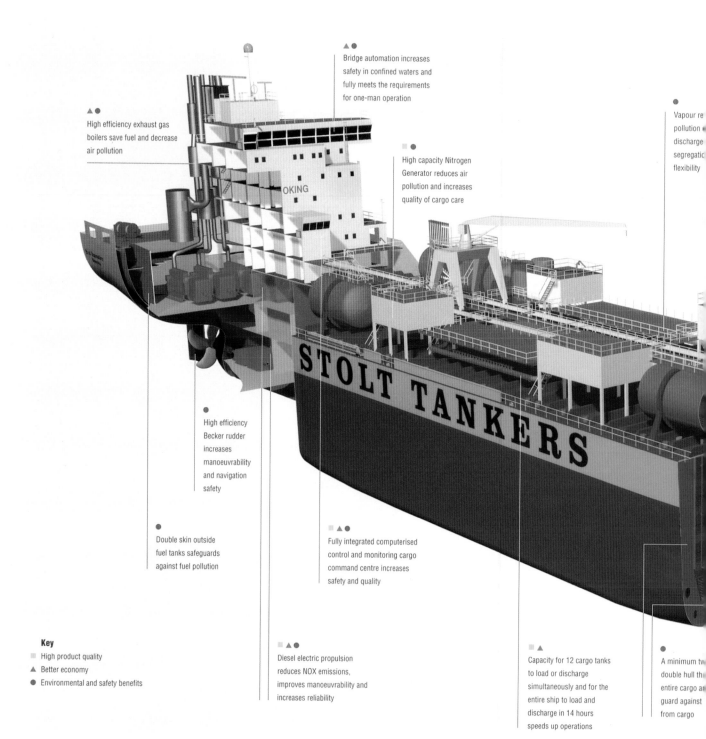

High efficiency exhaust gas
boilers save fuel and decrease
air pollution

Bridge automation increases
safety in confined waters and
fully meets the requirements
for one-man operation

High capacity Nitrogen
Generator reduces air
pollution and increases
quality of cargo care

Vapour re
pollution
discharge
segregatio
flexibility

High efficiency
Becker rudder
increases
manoeuvrability
and navigation
safety

Double skin outside
fuel tanks safeguards
against fuel pollution

Fully integrated computerised
control and monitoring cargo
command centre increases
safety and quality

Key

■ High product quality
▲ Better economy
● Environmental and safety benefits

Diesel electric propulsion
reduces NOX emissions,
improves manoeuvrability and
increases reliability

Capacity for 12 cargo tanks
to load or discharge
simultaneously and for the
entire ship to load and
discharge in 14 hours
speeds up operations

A minimum tw
double hull th
entire cargo a
guard against
from cargo

U.K. 1995
CD: Tor Pettersen
AD, D: Nicholas Kendall
I: Lars Maltha/David Hunter
DF: Tor Pettersen & Partners Ltd.
CL: Stolt-Nielson S.A

*This cut-away diagram, of a new generation of bulk liquid transporting parcel tankers, illustrates technological
and design innovations, safety features, improvements and benefits, in comparison to previous tankers.*
液体の大量輸送用タンカーの断面図。以前のタンカーと比較した技術および設計の新しさ、安全面の特徴、改善点とその恩恵を説明している。

The Stolt Innovation Class
The next generation of parcel tankers

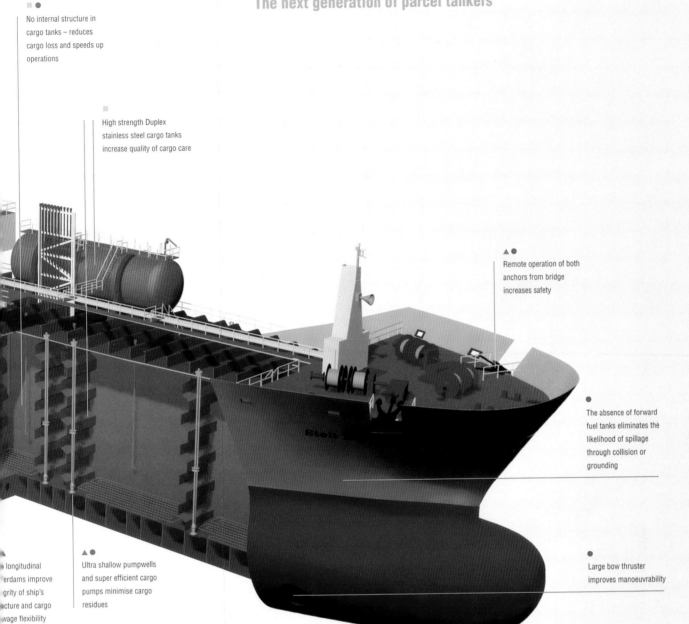

No internal structure in cargo tanks – reduces cargo loss and speeds up operations

High strength Duplex stainless steel cargo tanks increase quality of cargo care

Remote operation of both anchors from bridge increases safety

The absence of forward fuel tanks eliminates the likelihood of spillage through collision or grounding

longitudinal erdams improve grity of ship's cture and cargo wage flexibility

Ultra shallow pumpwells and super efficient cargo pumps minimise cargo residues

Large bow thruster improves manoeuvrability

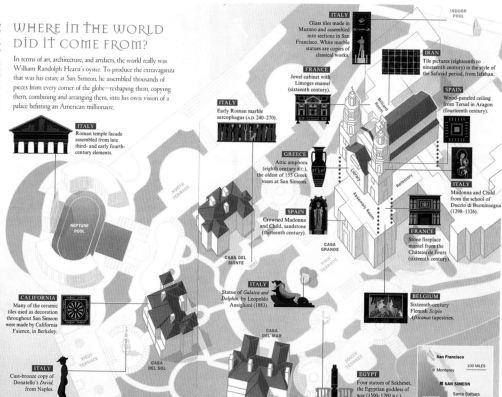

U.S.A. 1996
AD: Robert Best
I: John Grimwade
CL: Condé Nast Traveler

Graphic explanation of the origins of some of the treasures that can be found in San Simeon, California. (1)
カリフォルニア州サンシメオンに収められた所蔵品の起源を図解したもの。(1)

U.K. 1993
CD, AD, D, I: Tilly Northedge
DF: Grundy & Northedge
CL: British Standards Institution

Illustration of a house showing the variety of items which have undergone testing and been awarded certification by the British Standards Institution. (2)
英国基準協会によって検査・認定されたアイテムを家の断面図に表したもの。(2)

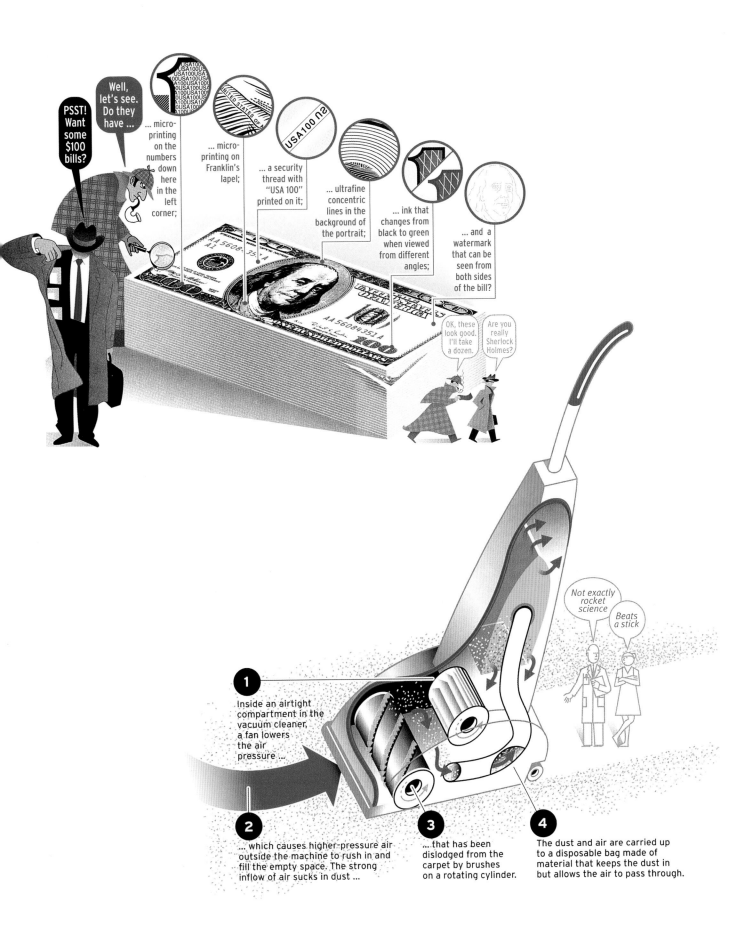

U.S.A. 1997
AD: Paul Carstensen
D, I, CW, DF: Nigel Holmes
CL: Attaché

Series of diagrams explaining everyday processes: New money; a vacuum cleaner.
日常的なテーマを取り上げたシリーズ。新札と掃除機のしくみについて。

ACROSS THE GLOBE, NO PLACE TO HIDE

The International Whaling Commission has agreed that Japan can begin a new research programme to tag and track the world's largest animal, the blue whale.

Japanese satellite whale tracking.
17 December 1995
Phil Green
The Sunday Telegraph
Freehand 3

SONAR TRACKING

SATELITE TRACKING

WEOS
Whale ecology observation satellite

The satellite, weighing 110lbs, is being developed by NEC Corp and Chito Institute of Technology. To be launched into a polar orbit in 1997 by Japan's H2 rocket.

Graphic: Phil Green

① Traditonal methods, sonar tracking and visual sighting are used to find the blue whales. They are then electronically tagged using a non-lethal harpoon to attach a football sized float, which contains a computer, data storage recorder, radio transmitter and a kinetically powered generator.

② Having tagged a whale in a family group, its position is located and tracked by satellite, allowing the whalers to instantly home-in on the whale or group at any time.

POLAR ORBIT

An orbit passing over the North and South Poles allows the satellite to observe every point on the surface of the Earth as it rotates on its axis.

BLUE WHALES
Average length **84ft**
Weight **90-150 tons**
Speed **18.6 mph**

Float generator is powered kinetically by the swimming action

Dive **9,800ft**

Double-decker bus to same scale

③ When the whale surfaces the five-watt Seiko transmitter is triggered by a sensor. Information on the whale's temperature, blood pressure, breathing rate and position are signalled to the satellite.

U.K.   1995
Graphics Editor: Phillip J Green
CL: The Sunday Telegraph

Graphic explaining a system to tag and track blue whales with satellites.
衛星を使ってシロナガスクジラを追跡する方法を説明している。

Index of Submittors⫸

N

O

P

R

S

T

V

W

Y

Index of Submittors

World Diagram Collection
世界のダイアグラムコレクション

Jacket Design	甲谷 一	*Hajime Kabutoya (Happy and Happy)*
Designer	野村恭子	*Kyoko Nomura*
Editor	近藤弘子	*Hiroko Kondo*
Photographer	藤本邦治	*Kuniharu Fujimoto*
Translators	ダグラス・アルソップ	*Douglas Allsopp*
	野口世津子	*Setsuko Noguchi*
Coordinator	桑原利佳	*Rika Kuwahara*
Typesetter	高松悦美	*Yoshimi Takamatsu*
Publisher	三芳伸吾	*Shingo Miyoshi*

2006年10月7日 初版第1刷発行

PIE BOOKS
2-32-4, Minami-Otsuka, Toshima-ku, Tokyo 170-0005 Japan
Tel: +81-3-5395-4811 Fax: +81-3-5395-4812
e-mail: editor@piebooks.com
        sales@piebooks.com

発行所 ピエ・ブックス
〒170-0005 東京都豊島区南大塚2-32-4
編集 Tel: 03-5395-4820 Fax: 03-5395-4821
     e-mail: editor@piebooks.com
営業 Tel: 03-5395-4811 Fax: 03-5395-4812
     e-mail: sales@piebooks.com
     http://www.piebooks.com

印刷・製本 図書印刷株式会社

この本の売上の一部は、出品者の方々のご厚意によりユニセフに寄付されます。
Part of the sales of this book will be donated to UNICEF by courtesy of the submittors.

ご協力のお願い
今回の書籍出版にあたり調査をしましたが、最終的に連絡をとることができなかった出品者の方がいらっしゃいます。
どなたか連絡先をご存じの方がいらっしゃいましたら、お手数ですが小社編集部までご一報下さい。

Please help…
Despite exhaustive investigation in preparing this book, these are still some submittors that we have been unable to contact.
We ask anyone who knows how to contact these people to please notify our editorial staff, and thank you in advance for your assistance.